EDITED BY BORIS SHRAGIN

THE POLITICAL, SOCIAL
AND RELIGIOUS THOUGHT OF RUSSIAN SAMIZDAT
An Anthology, co-edited with M. Meerson-Aksyonov (1977)

LANDMARKS:
*A Collection of Essays on the Russian Intelligentsia, 1909*
co-edited with Albert Todd (1977)

# THE
# CHALLENGE
# OF THE SPIRIT

# BORIS SHRAGIN

# The
# Challenge
# of the Spirit

*Translated from the Russian*
*by P. S. Falla*

ALFRED A. KNOPF

NEW YORK

1978

THIS IS A BORZOI BOOK
PUBLISHED BY ALFRED A. KNOPF, INC.
Translation copyright © 1978 by Alfred A. Knopf, Inc.
All rights reserved under International
and Pan-American Copyright Conventions.
Published in the United States
by Alfred A. Knopf, Inc., New York, and simultaneously
in Canada by Random House of Canada Limited, Toronto.
Distributed by Random House, Inc., New York.
Originally published in Russian as Protivostoyanie Dukha
by Overseas Publications Interchange Ltd., London, England.
Copyright © 1977 by Boris Shragin.
Manufactured in the United States of America
First Edition

Library of Congress Cataloging in Publication Data
Shragin, Boris Iosifovich. (Date)
The challenge of the spirit.
Translation of Protivostoianie dukha.
Includes bibliographical references and index.
1. Russia—Politics and government—1917–
2. Communism—Russia. I. Title.
DK266.3.S5213 1978   947.08   77-15669
ISBN 0-394-40005-4

Grateful acknowledgment is made to Little, Brown and Company
for permission to reprint excerpts from From Under the Rubble
by Alexander Solzhenitsyn, Mikhail Agursky, A.B., Evgeny Barabanov,
Vadim Borisov, F. Korsakov, and Igor Shafarevich.
Translated by A. M. Brock, Milada Haigh, Marita Sapiets, Hilary Sternberg,
and Harry Willetts, under the direction of Michael Scammell.
With an introduction by Max Hayward.
Copyright © 1974 by YMCA-Press, Paris.

*Dedicated to Sergey Kovalyov,*
*a Prisoner and a Heroic Defender*
*of Human Rights*

. . . nothing that is just can die;

evil perishes unless it is, so to speak, objectified,

it cannot live in thought alone; but good,

on the contrary, does not die but lives,

even in a single free idea that is independent

of human authority. . . .

—Letter from the Dekabrist N. I. Turgenyev
to P. Ya. Chaadayev,
March 27, 1820

To the success of our hopeless cause!

—Toast drunk
by Moscow intellectuals

# Contents

# To the Western Reader

I began to write this book in Moscow, where I could see from my apartment window the old church of St. Michael the Archangel at Troparevo, and I finished it on the campus of Amherst College amid the leafy hills of a New England springtime. The period in between included the first, most painful months of life in a strange country.

In Moscow I had to arrange my work so as to be ready for a police raid at any time. As soon as I finished an article or a chapter, it was hurried out of the house and hidden with friends. It was hardly encouraging to know that everything I wrote could become part of my criminal dossier and, if discovered, be hidden forever in the archives of the secret police.

These conditions gave rise to technical difficulties. Often there was no chance to read through a text to cut out repetitions or improve the logical sequence of the argument. The books I needed were rarely available in libraries, and to possess them at home was potentially as incriminating as the work I was myself writing. It was not advisable to copy out extracts and keep them either; so, too often, I had to rely on my memory and accept the fact that there were gaps in it.

Rough drafts were a terrible problem. They piled up in a corner of my room. I couldn't burn them because the place would have filled with smoke and attracted the unwelcome curiosity of neighbors. The only thing to do was to flush the sheets down the toilet. By trial and error I discovered that four pages at a time was the most I could dispose of in this way—a long, tedious procedure.

I agree heartily with Andrey Sinyavsky, who told the KGB that if they wanted to find out what the populace was thinking and at the same time save money on espionage, their best course was to retrieve all the paper from the sewage system. Taught by experience, I realize what freedom of the written word means: it is the situation in which a writer can, without fear of the consequences, throw drafts into the wastebasket. Only one who has been unable to do this can appreciate what a privilege it is.

Because of Moscow conditions, the book contains many literary faults. I am well aware of these, but when it became possible to correct them I felt that there was no call to do so. The reader will, I hope, understand when I say that the book's faults have become dear to me.

The work is written in a personal or, if you will, a lyric vein. It is a distillation of my own experience together with facts that have come to my notice and books that I have read. It is not the work of a mere armchair observer, and I saw no need to polish it into a learned treatise. It would be a fraud to do so, and I have come to distrust statements that are not the fruit of personal suffering. For a long time I was a Marxist, and for a long time after that I was engaged in freeing myself from the false "objectivity" of Marxist method. Today I can understand and sympathize with the contempt that Albert Camus, Gabriel Marcel, and others have expressed at the behavior of philosophers who teach one thing but set a different example in their lives.

Many things in my book are inspired not only by experience in Russia but by my recent life as an émigré. Reading the works written by Russians outside the Soviet Union, I was surprised to discover that their assumptions and conclusions were essentially the opposite of mine. It was a shock to find that Aleksandr Solzhenitsyn, whom I had come to love as did so many Russian intellectuals of my generation, had published works since his arrival in the West in which he arrayed himself with my opponents. All I could do was to try to find a rational explanation for this difference. As a result, my book contains a good deal of polemical matter, both explicitly and in less obvious ways.

The crux of our disagreement will be seen if I quote a passage from Solzhenitsyn's speech at a reception at the Hoover Institute in California, in which he said: ". . . the transition from pre-1917 Russia to the USSR is not a continuation but a mortal fracture of the spine, which almost destroyed Russia as a nation. The Soviet development is not a continuation of the Russian one but a distortion of it in a completely new, unnatural direction, inimical to the Russian people. . . . The terms 'Russian' and 'Soviet,' 'Russia' and 'USSR,' are not only not interchangeable, not equivalent, not part of the same order of ideas: they are irreconcilable opposites, they completely exclude each other, and to confuse them or use them wrongly is a gross error and a mark of slipshod thinking." (Aleksandr Solzhenitsyn, Two Speeches at Stanford. Russian text in *Vestnik RKhD*, Paris / New York / Moscow, No. 118, p. 170).

As the reader will find, my own contention is the exact reverse of this. I do not believe, however, that either point of view can claim to be the only one supported by reason. With even a modicum of knowledge, it is easy to find arguments on either side. One starts with a conviction and then finds reasons for it. Here I agree with the great skeptic David Hume, who said that we must first believe in order to be satisfied by proofs.

It is, of course, not a question of Solzhenitsyn and those who think like him being pro-Russian, and myself anti-Russian. No doubt some will claim that this is the real issue, and will not fail to point out that I am of Jewish parentage. Although this sort of argument is itself "a mark of slipshod thinking," it is pertinent insofar as it raises the issue of an individual's moral stance vis-à-vis his social situation.

The basic principle from which I start is that the historical destiny of a nation depends on the sociopsychological equipment of its people; and I have tried to show that in the case of Russia this national predisposition has led to results that are distasteful equally to Solzhenitsyn and myself. It was not my purpose to denigrate the Russian people but to raise the question of responsibility—in the last resort, the personal responsibility of every individual Russian. Do we in fact feel responsible for what goes on in our country and what our country does? That is the question.

To lay the whole blame on a few wrongdoers who have fractured the nation's backbone—to use Solzhenitsyn's metaphor—is to give a clean bill of health to anyone who identifies with the nation. It is a call to vengeance, not to self-correction. It paves the way for fresh intolerance and a new despotism, instead of liberalism and democracy. On the other hand, to hold the nation responsible for all mistakes, however abundant they may be, is to exonerate oneself without having the right to do so. This seems to be a symptom of irresponsibility no less unfortunate than the old readiness to accept on faith a simplified and stultified Marxism.

The reader may find it easier to understand the sharpness of this dispute if he recalls the spiritual crisis that Germany went through after the defeat of Fascism, which also raised the question of whether and in what sense the whole nation was guilty. But in Russia the problem is still more agonizing because the regime that has committed innumerable crimes is still in power. Although the Russian people recall the Lenin and Stalin terrors and the millions who were oppressed and killed, they have so far avoided forming a judgment as to the causes of these events and have done practically nothing to prevent a recurrence of them.

My conviction as expressed in this book is that the evil lies not in the prevailing ideology or the political system, but in the national tradition in which all participate to some degree. If a national renewal is conceivable at all, it must begin with a spiritual change, an alteration in the attitude toward life of individuals, not of the mass. And this is not only an abstract deduction, but a generalization of the aggregate experience of dissidents in the USSR during their ten-year battle for human rights. The struggle has not been without success, even though the dissidents did not organize themselves into a party, nor did they put forward a uniform political ideology or a program for the destruction of the existing order and its replacement by a new one. Their experience has shown that moral and legal demands are a force in themselves when opposed in specific cases to arbitrary and illegal acts. The basic principle of this struggle is what I have called "opposing good to evil."

I am not inclined to extend this principle beyond the limits of the present situation either in the Soviet Union or in the surrounding world. This principle expresses the spiritual changes that have greatly intensified since the victory over German Fascism. Deriving as it does from these changes and basing itself upon them, the dissident movement in the USSR is part of a worldwide process. It would no doubt be more successful if its guiding principles were better understood both at home and abroad. For this reason, a study of the movement's internal problems may be of interest at the present time from a global point of view as well as in the purely Russian context.

Boris Shragin
New York, May 1977

# THE
# CHALLENGE
# OF THE SPIRIT

# Introduction

The Greek philosopher Diogenes used to go about with a lantern in search of truth and justice—which, he maintained, could not be detected by the ordinary light of day.

The following story of his adventures was told in Moscow in the 1960s.

Diogenes first took his lantern to Britain. "What are you looking for?" they asked. "Honor and respectability," he replied.

"Yes," they said, "we used to have them, but they've disappeared."

Diogenes then journeyed to France, and when they asked him what he was looking for, he replied, "Liberty, equality, and fraternity."

"Yes, we were promised them once, but we never got them."

Everyone advised Diogenes to go to Soviet Russia, by all accounts the new home of goodness, truth, and beauty.

So he went there. He roamed all over the country.

"What are you looking for?" he was asked.

"Well," he replied, "I can't figure out where my lantern's disappeared to."

The recent popularity of this tale epitomizes the despair of thinking people in modern Russia. Perhaps they exaggerate the importance of their own country. Perhaps their loss of hope does not mean that hope is lost for all humankind. But the significant thing is that they believe it does.

The Russian intelligentsia, accustomed to swallowing ideas whole and carrying them to extremes, were at one time captivated by Nietzsche's saying, "God is dead." In compensating for their sense of loss and abandonment, they developed an exalted faith in socialism. Having broken with their native traditions, they rejoiced in the hope that a single leap would carry them into a bright future. Marx had supposedly proved with scientific accuracy that this would be so, and that the ugly features of an alienated world would simply disappear.[1]

Russian intellectuals thought no sacrifice too great for such a noble aim, and spared neither themselves nor others in its pursuit. They believed that one could do away with all forms of barbarity and injustice by simply having a clear idea of what was wrong with society and by presenting a rational plan for perfecting the future.

In the course of the experiment, many people died—so many that they have never been counted, and probably never will be. Those shot, starved, tortured, or worked to death are estimated in millions and tens of millions, but no one ventures an exact figure. We are a long way from the benevolent principle of the infinite spiritual value of a single human being!

The world grew increasingly senseless and cruel, intoxicated with a surfeit of blood that should have choked it. Perhaps "socialism with a human face"[2] is destined to appear elsewhere; maybe fresh crowds, full of hope and faith, will pursue the ideal at some other time. I cannot judge this, I do not know. In different historical soil, the crop may yield a better harvest. But in Russia, in any case, socialism has proven itself bankrupt. Our old ideals have turned out to be a shameful self-deception. The tragicomic effect is like a scene in Charlie Chaplin's *Modern Times* where the hero steps jauntily out of his shanty one morning and dives into what looks like a sparkling stream, only to hit his head on the bottom and find himself ankle-deep in mud.

The Polish writer Jerzy Lec described this transition from revolution to reality in the words, "He beat his head against the wall and broke through to the next cell."

Disappointment, however, has not brought enlightenment. Only for a moment, like men half-awake, did we believe that a fresh morning had dawned and a long, active day lay ahead. In reality, it is still night, and there seems no reason to get up when everyone else is asleep, or to proclaim the bitter truth of the lesson we have learned when no one wants to be aroused. We have learned our lesson not through investigation, nor through skepticism, which is the beginning of wisdom, but through grief and suffering. That is why people do not want to listen, and prefer to bury their heads in the blankets. The prospect it reveals is cold and thankless, and who wants to be told there is no hope?

In fact, our condition is not one of awakening but of an unhealthy, exhausting insomnia. We try in vain to lose consciousness and have nothing to get up for. Our souls are in an almost innate state of fatigue, and we are tempted not to think or react, but to surrender to apathy and inertia and to sink back into unconsciousness like everyone else.* Russia in our day slumbers to the monotonous, senseless lullaby of its "own government." Lies fill the gaps between unfulfilled promises and the present state of hopelessness. The audience's indifference is such that there is no need to care about accuracy. The worse things are, the more they are praised. A life full of highly unpleasant surprises is depicted as prosperous and progressive, to accord with the preordained "Leninist" plan. The blind not only see—they are clairvoyant. Nothing new, unexpected, or disturbing permeates the net of official hypocrisy and platitude.

In reading *Pravda* or *Izvestia* daily, one realizes the spiritual miasma of the country. The empty gibberish that fills their pages is daily food for millions. The systematic exclusion of news and thought, combined with mindless repetitions, produces a soporific effect. The world depicted is an imaginary one. Production rises steadily, harvests improve, the population is more and more content with its lot, while elsewhere, beyond the frontier, poverty

---

*In my opinion the ease of the Soviet government's victory over its own country is due not so much to its lawless and ruthless methods as to this general state of torpor, the refusal to seek a way of escape or to believe that there is one.

A friend of mine in Moscow who was forcibly summoned to an "interview" with the KGB was asked by the official what he thought of the public protests and demonstrations against the injustice and illegality of the KGB's political trials. My friend replied: "I don't approve of them, because they are useless." "Exactly—there you are!" said the official triumphantly, as though he had found a kindred soul. As far as he was concerned, the system and his own job were justified by the very fact that resistance to it was useless.

and crime increase, revolution nears, and all eyes are fixed with love and hope on the Soviet Union. The indoctrination goes on day after day, decade after decade.

Occasionally, when circumstances require it, the pack of lies is shuffled, and some are radically altered; but this arouses little attention. Once the Russians and Chinese were "brothers forever";[3] nowadays the newspapers talk about the "machinations of Peking." But it is unlikely that anyone will write to the editor of *Pravda* and say, "What are you up to; why didn't you tell us this before?" It would be excusable if readers refrained from writing thus out of salutary fear; but, alas, it is out of unconsciousness and indifference.

Count I. I. Vorontsov-Dashkov, a governor in Tsarist times, once replied sarcastically to members of an assembly demanding freedom of speech: "You are perfectly free to say anything you like without fear of the consequences. Long experience has taught me that in Russia, at all levels of society, words are binding neither on those who utter them nor on those to whom they are addressed." Under the socialist regime this prerogative of irresponsibility has been transferred from the people to the ruling party and government, who enjoy it on an extensive scale. It is an attitude that depends on the accepted value system, on what people think is a proper way of spending their lives.

After I had left the Soviet Union for good, a young Italian I met in Rome asked me: "Why didn't you organize, work out a common program, carry on systematic agitation, go to the factories and stir up the workers, demand better conditions, start a wave of strikes?" How could I explain to him the difference in the historical circumstances of our countries? "It's like this," I replied. "We've already had all those things in Russia, and the regime we now have originated in a 'party of a new type' which managed to organize the discontent of the workers and peasants in order to seize power with their help. You can't play the same trick twice—people aren't fish; they won't go for the bait once they've discovered there's a hook inside it. And, to tell you the absolute truth, we ourselves don't want a rising of that sort. Our great poet Pushkin wrote prophetically: 'God save us from seeing a Russian revolt, meaningless and merciless! Those who are plotting impossible violent changes in Russia are either young and do not know our people, or are hardhearted men who do not care about their own lives or about those of other people.'⁴ Our fathers and grandfathers did see a revolt of that kind, and one is enough, thank you."

It is impossible to see a practical solution to modern Russia's problems in socialism, if only because it is socialism that has created them in the first place, and no one has shown us how to get rid of it. Czechoslovakia's modest attempt to give it a "human face" provoked Russian socialism's bestial face to show itself as a lesson to everyone.

Russian society, having undergone the October revolution and its unending consequences, is in a kind of looking-glass situation vis-à-vis other countries and its own former self. What it calls "left" is what it used to call "right," and what is still "right" to the rest of the world. In Soviet terminology, "leftists" are extreme opponents of freedom, worshippers of military discipline, official patriotism, and an autocratic state; "rightists" are liberals who press for democratic freedoms and respect for human dignity. The "left" are Stalinist fossils, thirsting to revive government by the knout, while the "right" are such people as Dubček's followers in Czechoslovakia. The object of the "revolution," so constantly invoked with religious awe, is to preserve the existing order at all costs. Its opponents, concerned with working out humanitarian principles of social life, are tagged "conservatives" and "reactionaries."

The more one looks at this topsy-turvy situation, the more confused one gets between "right" and "left." The national consciousness, awakening but still enfeebled after its trance of half a century, is deprived of a frame of reference that is, throughout the rest of the world, normal and unambiguous.

In our tragic looking-glass existence we cannot tell what is past and what is future. Our Tatar legacy⁵—which, one might have thought, was being gradually eradicated by pre-revolutionary reforms—now appears, thanks to the revolution, to revive itself, for better or for worse.

The twenty years since Stalin's death⁶ have helped link Russia's past and its present. This bridge used to be denied by both partisans and opponents of the revolution. The Stalinist era was viewed in direct opposition to pre-revolutionary Russia, as the new to the old; and it was difficult not to succumb to the hypnotic propaganda of those days. For those few, however, who preserved a critical outlook, the main feature of Stalin's Russia was terror and violence. The regime, in fact, seemed to secure its only foothold by intimidation and lying propaganda. Some, even today, see nothing more serious and discouraging in the Soviet system than lies and violence. If these could be removed, they fancy, the country would automatically return to the "normal" state it was in before the Bolshevik revolution. Such people likewise oppose the "new" Soviet system to the "old" Russian one, but with the reverse emotional connotations to those of Stalinism.

In fact, both those still influenced by official propaganda and those who have shaken free of it (or think they have) fail to understand the link between our country's past and present. A study of our history can demonstrate that lies and violence are deeply rooted in our society. But it has only been in the comparatively quiet times of the past decade, in the absence of all-out terror, that we have begun to discern the historical roots of the present social order and to struggle for civil liberty and individual rights. The indifference of some towards this struggle, and the fury it arouses in others, show how deeply deception and violence remain entrenched in Russian society.

Turning our attention to Russian history is neither uplifting nor reassuring. Modern life provides constant and irrefutable evidence that the past conflicts that caused so much physical and moral suffering to thinking people in Russia are still with us in almost unaltered form today.

Our situation is similar to that of the old woman in Pushkin's fable,[7] who, demanding to be magically transformed into a noblewoman, an empress, and finally Queen of the Seas, is punished for her ambition by ending as she began, a fisherman's wife sitting beside a broken trough. A very Russian story!

Little is new in our reversion to old Russian ways. Minds unhampered by political fanaticism have never lost sight of what is now a matter of everyday experience. As early as 1918, in his essay in the collection *De Profundis,* the philosopher Berdyaev wrote:

At first glance it may seem that Russia has undergone an upheaval of a far more radical character than any before it. But a deeper examination will reveal the revolutionary aspect of old Russia—the specters of revolution that were long ago revealed in the works of our great writers, the demons that have long held possession of the Russian soul. . . . Our old national sicknesses and sins have brought about the revolution and determined its character. The specters of the revolution are Russian specters, though our enemy has used them to our destruction.

As long as the "new god" appeared to be alive, however, he drew everyone's attention to himself. People thought of contemporary Russia, as some still do, as of something completely new and unconnected with the past—the realization of communist theories, and nothing more. Admittedly, it was hard to see a Bolshevik commissar as no more than a special-duty Tsarist official, or a Chekist as a mere gendarme, even though he wore the same blue piping as his predecessor in imperial times. Few people noticed the continuity, while many cherished the hope that the Soviet regime would come to grief and that the nightmare of the "most equitable political system in the world" would be of short duration.

Such illusions are a thing of the past. They are, it may be said, ontologically out of date, since final and complete disillusionment with socialism was bound to embellish, in retrospect, the pre-revolutionary past. As though, because today is unendurable, yesterday must have been better! As though the revolution arose out of nothing, and those who thirsted for change were merely a hard-to-please lot who didn't know when they were well off! The readiness to make every excuse for the Tsarist regime shows how little revulsion there really is against despotism run mad, even among those who cordially detest the present system. The primitive notion that a few malefactors can be responsible for the fate of the biggest country in the world shows how deeply we are imbued with the spirit of social passivity—and this is not an encouraging sign, either.

Russian society today is almost as incomprehensible to itself as it is to the outside world. Deprived of the means of knowing itself—objective science, statistics, information of all kinds, an independent public opinion—since all these have been eradicated by the government, Russian society turns its gaze to the Western world, hoping to receive intellectual support from those who are less oppressed and more knowledgeable than itself. But the Western world judges Russia by its own standards, unable to fathom the specific historical and social background of the Soviet system. It sees the Soviet Union, with all its corruption and stagnation, in terms of Western ideas and problems, ignoring essential differences and laying itself open to cynical deception.

The results can be discouraging, to say the least. Soviet bureaucrats, who ruthlessly destroy all manifestations of life in their own country, are able to take comfort from attacks by American journalists on American .bureaucracy. Angela Davis, the sworn enemy of political and racial oppression, is fêted in Russia by people who are openly out to destroy all opposition to the prevailing system. In Rome, meetings to publicize Solzhenitsyn's *Gulag Archipelago* are held by right-wing parties while the Left keeps silent. The protests of American students against their government's intervention in Vietnam were received with joy by the Soviet propagandists whose task it is to justify Soviet intervention in that country.

It is hard for anyone in the West to understand the perplexity, despair, and pessimism that such phenomena inspire in the few thinking people in Russia. They begin to feel that the world has gone mad, that all values are crumbling, that justice and freedom may be sold at any moment and at the lowest possible price.

It is as though History had decided to perform an experiment on the Russian people by putting into effect the most extreme conclusions of philosophers and confronting us in our daily lives with a situation in which there is no hope, no outlook for the future, and no remedy. How are we to behave, how fill the gap in our existence?

In Russia at the present time such questions are not a matter of social and political speculation but of pressing personal reality. Instead of having to decide between parties and political program, the choice is between two ways of life. One consists of obeying one's own conscience with all the suffering that is bound to ensue; the other, of avoiding anxiety by renouncing one's freedom.

Despite societal constraints, the independent self seems to continue its existence. It resists merging itself in the drabness and anonymity of materialism. Both indoctrination and social pressure tend to dissuade an individual from acting as though he were cleverer or better than his fellows. Obey, conform, follow the crowd—so the message runs—and the system won't do you any harm. But before a man surrenders to the message, he hears a strange inner voice that prompts him otherwise, and, once heard, it will not be silent. It is a disturbing voice, one that found expression a hundred and fifty years ago in lines by the poet and philosopher Khomyakov:

> Arise in the darkness, my sleeping brother! Let your awakened spirit shine and burn like the stars in heaven, like the lamp before the icon![8]

But why, modern man may say, must we arise? What means have we of doing so, what center of gravity prevents our falling again? And where is the fire that will relight our smoldering spirit?

All external support has been removed. The objective laws of historical necessity, in which our fathers blindly trusted, have proved false; and though some still put their faith in Providence at times, it seems in no hurry to come to our aid.

Nonetheless, in this "frontier situation" there is a vision that leaves no room for doubt as to the past, the present, or our own personal lives. Its almost instinctive awareness forms our personal moral core and evolves into an increasingly articulate understanding that leads to action—not in economic or social revolution, but in the assertion of free human beings. The spirit, once awakened, begins to challenge reality and imposes a form on it.

Anyone who cannot perceive the evil of society must be devoid of moral notions. The basic humanist values of truth and goodness are plainly visible, if only because the regime cannot even pretend to embody them in any way. It offers brute force in opposition to human morality.

The clarity of the situation, and the unambiguous choice that it demands, constitutes the basic weakness of the regime and the strength of the opposition. The regime instinctively perceives its spiritual bankruptcy. Its boastful claims are incessantly contradicted by the facts of daily life. To ward off awareness of reality, it clings desperately to outworn formulae. Its leaders are perfectly well aware that any digression from the formulae would cause the official ideological structure to collapse like a house of cards.

The regime's most inveterate and formidable enemy today, and therefore the one it hates the most, is the human conscience. The campaign to stifle it has been going on behind the scenes for years. Its object is the "ideological education" of the intelligentsia. To this end, cowardly persecutions are devised—slander, arrest, confinement, the accusation of "parasitism,"[9] and deportation. Human beings are forced into a repugnant choice between the stick and the carrot. People easily become so accustomed to being harried that they no longer feel pain at their own humiliation. To stand prudently by, or keep silent when conscience bids us to speak out, is an attitude that bears its own punishment. One becomes the accomplice of violence; it corrupts us and corrodes our will. The intellectual is ready with rationalizations: it is the wrong time to act, there's no point to it, best give way for the sake of the cause. . . . And gradually, without noticing it, one turns into the sort of person one would have previously shunned.

This kind of spiritual disintegration, the loss of one's own self and the dishonor of serving iniquity, is more frightening to a conscious human being than bodily suffering or physical annihilation. It is impossible, of course, to explain this to our persecutors, any more than one could explain to a cat why humans don't regard mice as a delicacy. The more we must undergo, the more our disgust increases at those who inflict our subjugation.

This is why there is a great gulf between the regime and its leaders on the one hand and civilization as represented by the intelligentsia on the other. The conflict is not between political doctrines and ideologies, parties and classes: it is another and more fundamental quarrel. It is the conflict between truth and lying on command; between honesty and self-interest; between human sympathy and cruelty; and, finally, between personal dignity and a system in which contempt for the individual is elevated into a rule of life.

The historical issue is being fought out in the arena of personality; the obligatory choice confronts everyone who is mature enough to make it. There is no middle way, no direction in which an honest person can escape. Only by defending ourselves at every moment, keeping the initiative and returning blow for blow, can we preserve ourselves.

Such is the background to the spiritual resistance, the fight for the rights of man in the Soviet Union, the so-called "dissident" movement. The movement is of an unusual character, like the circumstances that produced it. It is rooted in Russian history yet has a message for all humankind. The present work is an attempt to explain that message. Although what I have to say is based on personal experience, I shall not talk about myself but rather about the times—or, more precisely, the times as I have experienced and reacted to them.

# I

# History at a Standstill

H istory stopped in its tracks"—these are the conclud-
ing words of *The Story of a Town,* a satirical novel
about Russia's past by Mikhail Saltykov-Shchedrin (1826–1889).
The phrase refers to Russia's lethargy under the despotic reign of
Nicholas I—a lethargy dispelled only by the shock of military
defeat and the Tsar's death in the middle of the Crimean War. It
*was* dispelled, however, and Russia proceeded to undergo many
more experiences—perhaps too many.

Today, under Brezhnev's rule, it is hard to describe the
situation more succinctly than by saying that "History has
stopped in its tracks."

## The last convulsions

Khrushchev tried to reform the Soviet regime, to bring it into
line with modern demands and remove its more glaring defects.
His object, of course, was not to do away with the existing order
but to preserve it. It could even be said that the regime itself,
when it brought Khrushchev to the top, was trying to find a means
of modernizing itself. But Khrushchev was deposed amid general
ill will or indifference, showing clearly that the regime could not
stand even halfhearted reforms.

As a recent Moscow joke has it, when people are up to their

necks in filth, they say: "Don't make waves." Khrushchev was turned out for doing precisely that.

Personality, even that of the top party leader, is much less important in the present Soviet system than appears at first glance. It is significant that according to official ideology, the only thing wrong with Stalin's government was its "cult of personality."[1] Everyone was oppressed, everyone was equally deprived of rights and guarantees, except for one man exalted above all the rest. This was against the spirit of Soviet development. One-man rule was a necessary symbol of general anonymity, but at the same time it struck a discordant note, bringing with it a sense of insecurity. A single all-powerful leader can dish out anything he likes, and the population has to take it. The "cult of personality" aroused opposition on this account. The Soviet regime needed the "cult of personality" to establish itself, but, once established, the cult no longer served a purpose. The principle of one-man rule was perpetrated to ensure that everyone else was featureless, but it was required only symbolically and to the extent necessary to achieve this goal.

Before this became clear—and it was discovered only empirically, by trial and error, like everything else under "planned leadership"—the regime went through a period of hesitation and instability. People longed for peace and quiet but did not fully understand what they wanted, as they are not used to reflecting on their own desires and the consequences of attaining them. The regime lurched to and fro, like liquid on an uneven surface, until it finally came to rest at the lowest level, which at least provided stability.

The crucial period was that of Khrushchev's rule; had he not presided over the transition, somebody else would have. Khrushchev did not control the system; it was the system which found in him its most convenient instrument in the period of confusion and perplexity after Stalin's death. His dispensability became evident when the system got rid of him, one fine day, effortlessly and without damaging itself.

Stalin left the Soviet Union on the brink of disaster. The peasants, devastated by fierce extortions, were starving. True, there was no resistance and no one thought of rioting, but the country's whole agricultural sector, and therefore the physical subsistence of its people, was in jeopardy. Towns experienced a housing crisis of appalling dimensions, such as cannot be imagined in the West. Stalin piled one problem on top of another, and solutions became increasingly hard to find. Soviet industry remained outside the technical revolution that took place in the West after World War II, and the "Cold War" was kindled to such a degree that it looked as if a real confrontation was imminent. Having acquired the secret of the atomic bomb, Soviet leaders thought that all strategic difficulties could be solved; they were too mentally inept to consider that atomic power cut both ways. Policy was based on "hoping for the best." The situation was precarious and called for caution, moderation, and the avoidance of precipitate action. Khrushchev did not realize this, nor did anyone else in his day. Attempts were made to replace Stalin's "unreasonable" policies with more sensible ones; only later was it understood that the best policy was to do nothing at all except boast of one's own achievements.

Khrushchev came to grief because he wanted to do *something*. He had no coherent plan but merely patched up the more gaping holes when he became aware of them, using picayune methods in a country of two hundred million people. Naturally the results were absurd and catastrophic.

The sudden failure of his policies forced Khrushchev to reverse his course. His innovations threatened to wreck the stability of the system. Feeling the reins slacken from time to time, the population was losing its habit of obedience. The intellectuals had been permitted and even encouraged to criticize "specific deficiencies" of the regime, so as to justify Khrushchev's reforms, but they now exceeded the bounds set for them. The workers got so out of hand that there were even a few strikes. Several serious revolts broke out in the countryside. Members of collective farms slaughtered their cows in protest when Khrushchev raised the tax on their small private plots.[2]

Matters worsened in the "fraternal countries of the socialist camp," where the tradition of implicit obedience to authority had not taken root in the Soviet fashion. The Polish party chose a new leader without consulting Moscow, and allowed collective farms to disband. Hungary rose to arms, and a long, obdurate general strike swept Budapest. More than once, Khrushchev had to use

Soviet troops to maintain order. Events in Hungary so alarmed him that they produced a period of reaction; contacts that had just been resumed with the Yugoslav Communists were abruptly broken off. It was Khrushchev, too, despite his conciliatory intentions, who presided over the rift with the Chinese Communist leaders, an ominous event for the future of the Soviet Union.

In all these matters Khrushchev's policy was hesitant, inconsistent, and halfhearted, taking away with one hand what it gave with the other. Having loosened one or two screws in the state mechanism, he proceeded to panic and tighten them again. His attempted reforms led to no solid result. This was hardly surprising, since the unexpressed aim of the whole exercise was to preserve the status quo. The country was in a state of inarticulate ferment. The fits and starts of Khrushchev's policy caused all the more confusion as each new measure was extolled with all the propaganda resources of the state as the last word in Marxist-Leninist scientific thought. Each time the system came to a jarring halt and reversed itself, the public felt like passengers on a streetcar with faulty brakes and a drunken driver.

Khrushchev's erratic methods were witnessed by the whole world during the Cuban crisis, when Soviet rockets were installed so as to threaten the United States from nearby territory. The reasons are still not clear. Steady American diplomatic pressure forced Khrushchev to withdraw, though he still managed to represent his discomfiture as a triumph of peace-loving policy.

Having spent the decades under Stalin in abject submission and fear, Khrushchev became intoxicated by freedom. The wild ideas that came to him not only were put into instant practice but were extolled as the quintessence of historical wisdom. One of his weaknesses was to be easily taken in by crude flattery. He failed to adapt himself to the social climate that gradually materialized as a result of his own mistakes. He stood for a period of transition and was bound to fall from power once that period was over. He was alone in his fall, for others had been cynically adapting themselves while he was indulging his whims and caprices.

Khrushchev put too much faith in the dead phraseology of official Marxism-Leninism; he took it more seriously than new conditions justified, or at least he flaunted his implicit belief in it.

He lied to his people, as a Soviet leader is expected to do, but he embellished his lies unnecessarily with details that even the laziest could test for themselves. He blurted out things and got entangled in his own mendacity, leaving his audience embarrassed.

Stalin had gone through the school of party in-fighting that placed a high value on the art of disguising one's position in theoretical arguments—preferably invoked against such pundits as Trotsky and Bukharin. Thus Stalin became a past master at justifying his twists of policy with high-sounding reasons and quotations from the Marxist-Leninist classics. Once he had triumphed over his powerful and more educated rivals, however, he made sure that no one else could become established as an interpreter of Marxist wisdom. The few surviving "comrades in arms" who were allowed a tiny share of his autocratic power were left in no doubt as to who was the supreme authority in matters of doctrine, "the great leader of all progressive humanity, the father and teacher of all times and peoples." They took it firmly to heart that "Stalin is the Lenin of our day," and that was that. Anyone who displayed the slightest doubt on this point endangered not only his career—which is no small thing to people of that kind—but also his life.

Khrushchev was one of those who grew up in Stalin's shadow and learned this lesson. He, like others, found that the only way to get ahead was by fawning, sneaking, and plotting, and he showed great skill in mastering these arts. But when he suddenly found himself in Stalin's place, he assumed unthinkingly that it was part of his job to formulate theories, interpret world history, and foretell the future. He adopted the role of a demagogue of the first rank, whereas he was in fact a petty and mediocre one. Stalin, it is true, produced no more than a semiliterate parody of Marxism, but he managed to make his brief, inarticulate utterances sound as if they meant something. Khrushchev was garrulous, and so gave the show away.

Time itself worked remorselessly against Khrushchev. When Lenin seized power, he promised people that world communism was just around the corner. Stalin based his power on the principle that socialism could be built quickly in a single country; later he declared that this had been accomplished and that it was time to go on to the next stage and build a fully communist society. It is hard to say how he would have explained the nonfulfillment of this promise if the war had not come as an excuse for delay.

When Khrushchev came to power, Stalin's promissory note had fallen due. The country was at peace, the aftermath of war had been surmounted after a fashion, and the newspapers, radio, and television were constantly proclaiming unheard-of successes; but communism still failed to dawn, and it became clearer day by day that the capitalist standard of living was an unattainable dream for the "first socialist state in the world." People at large knew no criterion of communism except general welfare, and Khrushchev himself was not too sure on this point; so he felt bound to do something quickly.

He did not realize, however, that to the masses "communism" had become a meaningless term. They had enough trouble in their daily lives without worrying about the millennium. Toiling for mere existence, they were in no state to appreciate the century-old claptrap about "leaping from the realm of necessity to the realm of freedom." They had become more bourgeois than the bourgeoisie, and knew perfectly well that a bird in the hand was better than two in the bush. And it was under Khrushchev's rule, as they obediently applauded every contradiction of his policy, that they hit the depths of protective cynicism. Having learned the simple gamut of slogans and the habit of applying them without hesitation, they concentrated on avoiding responsibility, working no harder than they had to, and stealing back from the Soviet state as much as possible of what it had stolen from them.

Unfortunately, Khrushchev shared the conscientious outlook of party workers in the thirties, who deceived both themselves and the public. He thought it a vital necessity to point to "visible features of communism" there and then. He wanted to make ends meet, in theory and in practice, when it was not only unnecessary but dangerous to try to do so. The only result was to prove that they did not meet and never would.

Khrushchev rashly undertook to "catch up and overtake" the United States in the per capita production of meat and milk. He emphasized Soviet achievements in space as though they were irrefutable proof of the superiority of the Soviet system. He failed to realize that their technological basis was ephemeral and that they too were only temporary. He boasted from the rooftops and had to eat his words the next day.

At the party's Twenty-second Congress in October 1961,[3] Khrushchev surpassed himself by declaring that generations still living would enjoy a life of abundance under full communism. He even committed the ultimate imprudence of naming a date: it would be, he said, in twenty years' time. A suspiciously round figure, evidently chosen so as to be neither so dangerously near as to lead to euphoria nor so far away as to excite no enthusiasm.

At the same Congress, a new party program was approved—a document that was later consigned to rapid oblivion, but which showed the disparity between the romance and the reality of Khrushchev's government. Though it deserves a full analysis, I will quote only a passage from the section entitled "Solution of the Housing Problem and Improvement of Living Conditions." It runs:

> In the course of the first decade an end will be put to the housing shortage in the country. Families that are still housed in overcrowded and substandard dwellings will get new flats. At the end of the second decade every family, including newlyweds, will have a comfortable flat conforming to the requirements of hygiene and cultural living. Peasant houses of the old type will, in the main, give place to new modern dwellings, or—wherever possible—they will be rebuilt and appropriately improved. In the course of the second decade housing will gradually become rent-free for all citizens.[4]

The program is written in the vote-catching style of a Western election manifesto, yet the party had no need to worry about its 97 percent of the poll.[5] The sweeping unreality of its promises stems from a metaphysical necessity rather than a practical one. Party leaders felt the need to compromise between the facts of life and their communist consciences, which they had not yet altogether jettisoned. The ability to shape the future was gradually being replaced by the art of telling lies about it; to make the picture attractive they adopted the set designer's technique of including two or three realistic details in the foreground. They admitted facts which in any other context they would have denounced as slander, e.g., that an unknown number of families were housed in bad, overcrowded conditions, that young married couples had to live in a room or apartment with their parents, and that "peasant houses of the old type"—i.e., huts dating from the age of serfdom—were still so numerous that some would continue to exist under communism, even though they by no means "conform to the requirements of hygiene and cultural living"— that is to say electricity, indoor plumbing, and hot and cold running water. How these "improvements" could be installed in a peasant hut was not divulged by the planners, who had, of course, never given a moment's thought to the matter.

There are many delightful features in the above-quoted passage, such as the reference to "over"-crowded dwellings, as opposed to the plain crowding that is to be the norm under communism, no doubt. In such ways, reality breaks through into a description of the glorious future of humanity—but only so that it can be judiciously mixed with pure invention (such as the statement that everyone will have a decent home, and that within twenty years it will be rent-free).

It is very much as if the program were the joint work of a symposium of some of Gogol's most rascally comic characters: Skvoznik-Dmukhanovsky, Sobakevich, Khlestakov, Manilov . . . Fifteen years have now elapsed since the Twenty-second Congress, so we have only five to go. As Yuly Kim used to sing in Moscow: "If you can't build things on time, how will you keep people satisfied?"

Needless to say, the program was approved unanimously. People don't argue at meetings of that kind, though there may have been plenty present who wished Khrushchev would go to hell.

The whole country, including the aforementioned peasant huts, was plastered with calico banners proclaiming: "The Party solemnly declares that generations now living will experience Communism." The newspapers, radio, and television drew vivid comparisons between the situation of foreign countries today and the welfare state that the Soviet Union was to enjoy in twenty years under full communism; the same lesson was repeated in political reports and lectures that all citizens were required to attend. It was conclusively proven that our standard of living was higher than everybody else's. But in spite of all this optimism, Khrushchev exceeded people's patience, and he was thrown out.

The horrors of Stalin's regime were officially chalked up to the "cult of personality"; the absurdities of the Khrushchev era were ascribed to "voluntarism."[6] These expressions, vague as they are, inadvertently reveal the subconscious attitudes of Soviet leaders. What exactly was it that they did not like and wanted to guard against in the future?

Trumped-up charges, confessions under torture, unjust sentences, the imprisonment of millions in concentration camps, fantastic and exorbitant plans for the "transformation of nature"—in fact, all that Stalin stands for in history books—were not considered by the party elite to be either specially important or particularly repulsive. Khrushchev, a true product of his milieu in this respect, denounced the "cult of personality" at the Twentieth Congress. His protest was not against oppression in general, but only insofar as it was aimed at the ruling class. Despite his rhetoric, he did his best to confine the impartial investigation of the Stalin terror to cases affecting those who had remained orthodox Stalinists to the end.

Khrushchev's successors have been even more zealous in circumscribing the inquiry in this way. Embarrassed by disclosures already made, they mumble something from time to time about the regrettable mistakes of the Stalin period, or assure the public that they are not going to review the decisions of this or that Congress. They have become so spiritually corrupt that they fail to see how self-condemning it is to refer to mass extermination in terms of "mistakes." The murder of a single man by a private person warrants the death penalty, yet when hundreds of thousands are murdered by a state that is supposed to protect their lives and well-being, it is only a "mistake." And we are expected to forgive and forget, after weighing it against its perpetrator's merits and achievements in other areas.

All this does not trouble Russia's leaders. In an emergency they would be quite prepared to repeat the act, like impenitent criminals. Their major concern is to prevent a new chief from rising above the rest of the band and holding them at his mercy, to spare or slaughter as he chooses. That is why the only aspect of three decades of Stalinism that shocks them is the "cult of personality."

In the same way, the word "voluntarism," used to sum up everything that was wrong with Khrushchev's regime, does not in itself connote half-baked, illogical, fantastic projects and actions. As I shall try to show in this book, the privilege of arbitrary rule is the chief "plum" that the Soviet elite hope to enjoy as a reward for usurping control of the country. They abhor any abrupt routine-breaking action. Before doing anything, a party leader should consult with those who put him where he is and make sure he doesn't tread on anyone's corns. Better still, he should do nothing at all, and then there will be no "voluntarism."

When it was first announced that Khrushchev was to retire, officials claimed it was of his own free will and because of age and ill health. Shortly afterwards, vague mumblings about "voluntarism" began to be heard. It was later suggested by way of amplification that state decisions ought to be based on scientific objectivity and not on caprice. But few were taken in by this. Objectivity was never a question of statistics, sociology, cultural anthropology, or political science (which does not exist in the Soviet Union), but merely of Marxism-Leninism, reduced to clichés under Brezhnev. Brezhnev's regime, in fact, has declared war on social science—not, as did Stalin, on grounds of theory (albeit false theory), but simply because it is not amenable to government control. The ability to think scientifically is not a current qualification for office. Look at Brezhnev himself—is he capable of governing scientifically or even pronouncing modern scientific terms, let alone understanding them?

Henri Barbusse, in a book published in the thirties, flattered Stalin by calling him a man with a scholar's face and the hands of a worker, in the uniform of a common soldier. In Brezhnev's case the face is that of a common soldier and the uniform that of a bureaucrat. As to the hands—well, one of Stalin's arms was withered . . .

Rid of the "cult of personality" and "voluntarism," the regime discovered a form appropriate to its own guiding spirit, and became ossified.

# The tragedy and farce of the Soviet state

From an aesthetic viewpoint—which is both easier than economic or sociological analysis, and better suited to a society that has no reliable information about its own government—Khrushchev was a comic character. The shrewd, earthy peasant traits which he could not conceal, and which he complacently exhibited, contrasted sharply with his hieratic role. His bald head and round, potbellied figure, his tipsy speeches to huge open-air audiences, the sentences he began without knowing how he would finish them—all these made him the object of ridicule. He gave away a secret that the public did not want to know, namely, that he was a very ordinary man. He was given nicknames like *"Khrushch"* (cockchafer, an insect injurious to crops; the word also has overtones of slyness) and *"Kukuruznik"* (corn-planter, after one of his economic panaceas; the word also means a low-flying biplane used for observation purposes).

Khrushchev's comic mannerisms were often mistaken for congeniality. He was autocratic and obstinate, like all bureaucrats trained under Stalin. It has become unofficial common knowledge that the victims of fresh political arrests sent to camps under his rule were systematically starved (as they still are), so that in some respects his regime was worse than Stalin's. But all this failed to intimidate people, because they laughed. When Khrushchev falsely declared that there wasn't a single political prisoner left in the Soviet Union, the public believed him: comedy is incompatible with fear and hard to combine with cruelty.

Curiously, people did not enjoy laughing at him. Russians are unaccustomed to being amused at their rulers' expense, and do not like it. Khrushchev's clowning violated the austere decorum of political ritual. If people are to obey they must be cowed by expressionless, inexorable despotism. Laughter incites freedom. By heading the state's mechanism, Khrushchev caused it to falter. Those inclined to assert their freedom, especially some intellectuals, began to do so. From time to time Khrushchev tried to deter them. The story of his rule is one of alternating pressure and détente, the former applied from above and the latter spontaneous.

Intellectuals have pleasant memories of that time, but the mass of "simple Soviet folk" violently disliked Khrushchev. This hatred became a sort of popular cliché. Viewed as a sociopsychological phenomenon, it may explain a great deal both in the present and in the future.

Why, in fact, did simple farmers, workers, and petty officials sustain such a lasting hatred of Khrushchev? Why—especially since such people are not generally given to political passions and usually subscribe to the old Russian proverb "God and the Tsar are a long way off"?

Lenin has taken the place of God in the popular consciousness; Stalin is still a name that evokes admiration as well as terror; Malenkov is totally forgotten; Brezhnev inspires no feelings at all. But Khrushchev is still hated—why?

To ascribe it to Khrushchev's passion for interfering in agriculture, harmful as it was, is insufficient. True prices, under his rule, went up instead of down. Certainly he cheated the population by his financial measures.[7] But, all the same, living standards improved under his rule, both in cities and in the country. There is no comparison with what happened under Stalin!

Why then do people say nostalgically, as "ordinary Soviet folk" almost invariably do, that "Stalin was strict, but he kept order"? Why is it that people forgive Stalin the shootings and labor camps, the collectivization policy that starved the villages, the ferocious drive for industrialization, the reckless sacrifice of soldiers' lives in wartime, and similar "great achievements of communism," when they cannot forgive Khrushchev for his corn-growing schemes, for taxing private plots, or for raising the price of vodka? Under Brezhnev, it may be added, wages are frozen and prices keep going up, but there is no display of popular indignation.

To understand this phenomenon, we must abandon the habit of judging Soviet social development solely by the economic interests of a particular segment of the population. Soviet citizens have grown accustomed to satisfying their economic needs regardless of government policy. Other determinant factors of Soviet history have to be taken into account.

Nor is it much use conjecturing about Kremlin intrigues. Naturally, in a country where the population is deprived of all political initiative, change depends on the personalities and intentions of those in authority. But this is no reason to disregard the lessons of modern historical philosophy and revert to a methodology on the eighteenth-century level.

Khrushchev's general unpopularity signifies that his ouster was not simply the result of a struggle for power within the Kremlin; rather it shows that the outcome of the struggle is, after all, determined by what goes on among the mass of the people outside the Kremlin walls. This is confirmed by the fact that official propaganda since Khrushchev's fall has been devoid of attempts to openly or secretly "unmask" his misdeeds or to patch up Stalin's reputation: both these effects have come about more or less of their own accord, and have not been simply imposed from above.

The role of official propaganda in the Soviet Union should not be exaggerated: it is powerless unless the ground is prepared to receive it. Thus laborers pay little attention to incessant appeals to work harder, whereas the population responds readily to any hint of chauvinism, even in its less obvious forms. In short, contemporary Russian opinion is not like potter's clay, prepared to receive any impression. In the last resort, the country's leaders do what the population wants, or rather they conform to its main desires—for it has many different ones, like any society or human being.

These deep-seated collective desires may be detected to some extent by aesthetic criteria, particularly in a regime like the Soviet Union's, where outward show and ceremony are of primary importance. The government presents itself to the people at all times as a solemn, well-rehearsed, harmonious spectacle. There must be nothing common about the rulers' image; and the public, for its part, must also conform to the rules of scenic presentation. Government and people encounter each other at festive parades and demonstrations or solemn assemblies of a Byzantine character, where everyone keeps strictly to an assigned role. As a result, every citizen becomes a master in the theatrical and ornamental technique that is a requirement of totalitarian society.

Khrushchev's dramatic style, of course, was sharply different from Stalin's. During the Khrushchev era, some liberal intellectuals used to quote Marx's well-known saying: "Hegel remarks somewhere that all facts and personages of great importance in world history occur, as it were, twice. He forgot to add: the first time as tragedy, the second as farce." The farcical nature of Khrushchev's government estranged the public and fostered its sense of being imposed upon. With the best will in the world, it was impossible to overlook the absurdities that were committed. The habit of obedience was undermined by the obvious stupidity of the orders given and the fact that they were reversed almost daily.

Historical situations of this kind lead to radical change and innovation. A system that has turned to farce cries out to be altered; even the blind must see that it has outlived its usefulness. However, the comic spectacle that Khrushchev presented aroused a general feeling of irritation and not of liberation. Only a few individuals grasped at the invitation to choose freely; everyone else heaved a sigh of relief when the buffoon was driven from the stage.

There ensued a fantastic period of a kind not described in the textbooks of aesthetics: neither farce nor tragedy, calculated neither to bring conflicts to a head nor to effect a catharsis. Historical contradictions did not disappear; rather, they were ignored. Society lost interest in harmonizing ends with beginnings; time came to a stop.

# Stagnation

Such is our position in the Brezhnev era. What kind of man he is, is of no importance. His whole concern is not to repeat Khrushchev's mistake. He wants to avoid presenting himself as a human being, a stance which would offend his subjects' pious feelings. Apparently when he was younger he liked women and drink, but now he just acts the old-fashioned part of an ex-*bon vivant,* content to live on memories of twenty or thirty years ago.

He reads his public speeches from a prepared text, as if to show that he is not saying anything on his own account. At first, from force of habit, people laughed at this, but soon they became deathly bored.

There is nothing amusing about Brezhnev, nothing to attract attention or call for a second glance. The only features of any note are his slurred diction and thick eyebrows—but of what importance are these? When people laughed at Khrushchev, it was not on account of his bald head.

Khrushchev's fall from power was a reminder that neither the Soviet constitution nor the regulations governing party life lay down a procedure for changes of leadership. At the Twenty-third Congress in 1966, the party by-laws were amended so as to make it harder to get rid of party bureaucrats of every rank.[8] This best illustrates the true nature of Brezhnev's "new order." The party bosses and the smaller fry, once appointed, hold office for life, or at least for an indefinite period. They must not display human weaknesses, commit mistakes, or succumb to illness. They must personify the unvarying stability of the existing order, and, while mortal, they must feign immortality.[9]

All this is more characteristic of an absolute monarchy than a democratic republic; but the Soviet system differs from a monarchy in making no provision for succession. In a monarchy, the heir to the throne incarnates the nation's future in the people's eyes; he stands for continuity and tradition. The Soviet system takes no account of time. The leader is thought of as an immortal being, although everyone knows this is not so. This is symptomatic of a general aversion and even inability to think about the future. This state of affairs not only does not worry anyone but has so far aroused no one's attention. To raise the question of a successor would be an expression of disloyalty to the present rulers.

This identification of the temporary and transient with the timeless and eternal destroys the whole set of categories whereby people generally contemplate a social system and their place in it. The Soviet regime forfeits all claims to consistency or logic. Appearance is reality, necessity is freedom; the individual is confused with the universal, and mortality with divinity. One might call it an antinomian system, if it did not fiercely reject the notion of antinomy.

These are the norms which it is Brezhnev's lot to embody. The absolute, unlimited power bestowed upon him is confirmed by his impersonality. In this way Russo-Soviet history has shown its opinion of the Khrushchevian farce. Brezhnev personifies Russia's deep desire for a despotism that is not only ruthlessly cruel but also intolerably boring. For the sake of peace and immobility, the country has forced its chosen leader to hide his human features. Those not broken by repression despair at the boredom and mindlessness of their existence.

Brezhnev is sometimes portrayed as a realist compared to the "wishful thinker" Khrushchev. But this is only one more deception, in a world made of them. Brezhnev's so-called realism is simply a complete absence of general ideas. It cannot be called cynical, for even cynicism involves some degree of awareness and responsibility. Brezhnev's policy is to follow the line of least resistance, advancing wherever there are no obstacles. This, however, is not a matter of calculation but of ignorance, of a failure to assess the situation and a disregard for consequences. If an obstacle presents itself the policy is reversed, and not a word is said about the mistake. This method (if it deserves to be called that), continuously adaptable to present circumstances, takes no account of yesterday or tomorrow.

Brezhnev's government began by condemning "voluntarism" and proclaiming the need for scientific methods and "economic reform" based on exact calculations.[10] Credulous people still talk about the regime's conversion to technocracy, but nothing of the kind was envisaged at any time. The "reform" was supposed to confer local initiative on state enterprises while maintaining or strengthening the control of the party bureaucracy over them. In other words, the object was to carry out urgent and necessary changes while leaving everything as before. Whether this was demagogy or a case of high stupidity is not, in the last resort, very important. It was an exercise in squaring the circle, not by any subtle methods but simply by proclaiming that "the impossible was possible."[11] When it became clear that the "reform" had failed, as anyone could have foreseen it would, and that the economy was in a state of chaos, this fact was ignored and the "reform" forgotten, or at least no longer mentioned.

Another example of Brezhnev's tendency to follow the path of least resistance can be seen in the way he dealt with the duality of Soviet government—an essentially autocratic system in which power is theoretically divided between the party, with its own bureaucracy, and the state, representing the "soviets."

Stalin concentrated both party and state power in his own hands, as secretary-general of the party and chairman of the council of ministers. After his death, this was denounced as part of the "personality cult." Consequently, Malenkov, who succeeded Stalin, kept the title of head of government and left the party leadership to Khrushchev. This set the stage for Malenkov's defeat, since as everyone knows (though they do not say so), it is the party apparatus that holds the real power. Khrushchev, however, consolidated his position by following Stalin's example and taking both titles. In so doing, he aroused his colleagues' jealousy and mistrust and conjured up the dangerous phantom of the "personality cult." Fears of his own ambition and growing power aroused rivalry in all members of the leading group.

How did Brezhnev solve this difficulty? He didn't. He revived the title of secretary-general of the party, which had been dropped after Stalin, and assumed the position himself. He realized that it was a rather popular title as long as it remained unthreatening. But then he began to act as head of state as well, although, strictly speaking, this was not his proper job. It was not out of wisdom that he avoided precision but rather that, like his subordinates and the people at large, he saw no need to clarify his position. Why engage in sophistries that wouldn't convince anybody? Brezhnev knew instinctively that there was no need to persuade people or to pay attention to intellectual ideals. It was better to be irresponsible than to spell things out.

When, however, the vagueness of his own political status nevertheless began to cause him embarrassment, or when he resolved to give full play to his love of power (no one has yet managed to divine the true motives of Brezhnev's behavior), he worried no more about external decorum than before. He simply drove his friend Podgorny out of the post of President of the

Union of Soviet Socialist Republics with the same lack of ceremony with which a street hoodlum drives someone weaker from a bench that takes his fancy on a city boulevard. That by acting thus he degraded the government whose prestige he boasts so much of, that after this the longed-for post of President itself begins to look absurd, apparently, did not disturb him. He belongs to that breed of chess players who cannot foresee the development of the pieces beyond the next move. This is the basis for his self-assurance and his satisfaction with his perspicacity.

All that remains of Marxist theory in Brezhnev's time is a few faint abstractions, incapable of serving as a guide to anyone. The generation of party bureaucracy to which he belongs moved upward in the thirties, thanks to the liquidation of Marxist pundits, "half-baked intellectuals," and "Jewish weaklings." These men, who had put their faith in Marxism, were ousted by clods who enjoyed the taste of power unfettered by ideals. The newcomers used Marxist-Leninist ideology only as a stopgap, a bundle of rags to fill up a spiritual vacuum, to keep out new ideas and civilized values that Brezhnev and his like cannot cope with.

Brezhnev's "realism" compels everyone else to be realists in the same way he is. Others must recognize that they have to deal with him, and get used to the fact that he is not going to change or be replaced. In short, he is a realist because he demonstrates to the world the reality and seriousness of a manifest absurdity.

Brezhnev's "realism" recognizes the worth of violence and crude physical force and does not respect words or ideas. He is convinced that all internal difficulties can be dealt with by repression. A former political commissar in the Soviet army, he believes in a discipline that exacts absolute obedience from the rank and file. His ideal is to regiment the whole people, whether intellectuals, schoolchildren, or collective farmers. He devotes all the resources of his huge country to piling up armaments, not to conquer the world with, but to keep it in constant fear of atomic catastrophe and to prove that civilization is powerless before physical force. Inspiring fear and winning concessions by blackmail constitute the essence of "détente" as Brezhnev conceives it.

Brezhnev incarnates the faith of bureaucracy in its own omnipotence and in the passivity of the world upon which it operates. It recognizes no feedback, no reaction, and no obstacle on its chosen course, whether of a logical, moral, or physical nature. The incredible becomes real, because no account is taken of probability. Failures are announced as victories, and by that very fact they become so.

Some skeptics may say: "What then becomes of Marxism, which insists on a reality independent of human consciousness and regards history as a natural process calling for our attentive study? Is it not a confirmation of Marxism that the practical achievement of an aim is only possible when our aim conforms to objective necessity?" Brezhnev certainly learned this theory at one time. But he also "knows" that objective necessity in the modern world coincides with the interests of the working class, and those interests are expressed by communist parties, and he, Brezhnev, is at the head of the international communist movement—from which it follows that objective necessity is what he says it is, or what his own whim declares it to be.

It is not hard to detect the logical flaw in this reasoning, but what is the point of being consistent? Consistency is for people with a human face, but life is much more peaceful without it!

# The endless chain of anniversaries

Ever since Brezhnev came to power, the Soviet Union has celebrated one anniversary after another. In 1965 came the twentieth anniversary of the defeat of Germany; in 1967 the fiftieth anniversary of the October Revolution, and incidentally those of such well-loved institutions as the Red Army, the KGB, the Communist Youth League, and so on; in 1970 the centenary of Lenin's birth; in 1972 the fiftieth anniversary of the foundation of the USSR; and in 1975 the thirtieth anniversary of the defeat of Germany. The years 1968 and 1970 marked the 150th anniversaries of the births of Marx and Engels respectively, but for some reason these dates did not rouse their spiritual heirs to any special display of emotion. Something more patriotic and closer to home politically was necessary to keep popular enthusiasm on the boil.

There is nothing mysterious about the recurrence of round figures in the decimal system, and, while anniversaries mean nothing particular in themselves, it is natural for people to use them to refresh their memories about important past events, as the United States has done in 1976. But in the Soviet Union there has come to be an almost unbroken chain of such celebrations, and each interval is taken up with preparations for the next. The propaganda machine seizes on each successive date as though everything depends on it. If it is a year ahead, preparations go on for a year; if two years, they go on for two. The frenzy of commemoration leaves no time to think of the present. It is as though anniversaries were thought up with the express purpose of filling people's heads with exalted ideas and making them forget about their daily life. This, indeed, is a simple ruse, and little effort is made to conceal it. "The ground gets slippery here, and the less we say about recent times, the better."[12]

The atmosphere of an anniversary discourages people from mentioning shortcomings. As at a funeral, only praise is in order; to talk at such times of everyday, ugly things would be rude. If our minds are filled with memories of the past, they are embellished with every color of the rainbow. Good money is spent on careful, scrupulously detailed reproductions of bygone days, and the spirit is that of the Russian proverb: "He who bears a grudge deserves to lose an eye." In fact, wiping out the blemishes of the past has become one of the major purposes of remembering it. It is not a matter of studying history or drawing useful lessons from it, but of celebrating a solemn ritual, in the course of which true history is shouted down and killed.

An author takes an interesting manuscript to an editor or publisher, who turns it down with a sigh, saying: "It won't do just now, you can see that. There's this anniversary coming on . . ." And, after that anniversary, it's time to get ready for the next. The shelves of bookstores are piled with special literature for the occasion; real, living interests are simply squeezed out—there is no paper on which to print anything not written to order. Writers, journalists, poets, painters, stage directors all strive to execute "social commissions" entrusted to them from above. Using their utmost ingenuity, they must attractively present material that everyone is heartily sick of. As in Stalin's day, this is a period of golden opportunities for all the untalented hacks in the "free" professions. One has only to perform on the anniversary theme to protect oneself from criticism and assure good reviews. To criticize an illiterate "memorial" to Lenin in his jubilee year is as dangerous as to abuse Lenin himself. Even though the execution be wanting, the artist can still be praised for the irreproachable fervor of his civic sentiments. His inventions may have been tantamount to insulting the honored past, but it is not wise to notice this fact either.

In thus celebrating round figures, the regime endeavors to borrow from the past the dignity and authority that it has itself lost. The romance and heroics of war and revolution are intended to cast a veil over the dismal reality of everyday life. Paunchy officials who would sell their mothers for the sake of a trip abroad or a place at an exclusive health resort extol the bravery of those who died on the barricades and in battles long ago.

"Let us meet the —th anniversary worthily! Let us greet the —th anniversary with new victories of labor!" Slogans like these are plastered on every wall, repeated untiringly at meetings of work groups, on radio and television, and in newspapers. The past and future, as it were, change places: the round figure of the anniversary is something definite, while communism is no more than a misty abstraction. The hopeless emptiness of the future is masked by the series of commemorations; the steady advance toward the past distracts attention from the stagnant present. One lives and toils for daily bread in order to encounter what happened decades ago and then get ready for the next meeting of the same kind. In the clamor of verbiage, real human existence abases itself reverentially before bygone deeds and personages that are no longer anything but figures of rhetoric.

The centenary of Lenin's birth in 1970 was especially revealing. Khrushchev in his day extolled Lenin's authority in order to fill the gap left by the denunciation of Stalin's "personality cult." Then rogues and flatterers got onto this bandwagon and used it for all it was worth. Under Brezhnev, they worked themselves and one another up to such a pitch of excitement, for more than a year before the anniversary, that all reasonable bounds were totally forgotten. The same people who had recently denounced the "cult of personality" transformed the original, undersized leader of the revolution into the greatest figure of world history and a surrogate for the Deity. They not only parted company with logic, which, as we have seen, was no trouble to them, but lost all sense of humor as well—not that a sense of humor and Soviet power have ever gotten on very well together.

"The all-knowing, the ever-present!" shrieked a banner headline in *Komsomolskaya Pravda*. Cooler-headed sycophants endowed Lenin with an atheistic version of eternal life: "Lenin's ideas will live forever!"

Years have gone by, and all Lenin's comrades in arms who did not die soon enough were liquidated by his great successor; but Lenin foresaw everything, he knew all that was to come. Years, decades, centuries, and millennia will pass away, our era will become as remote as that of the Pyramids, but Lenin's writings will still be as fresh as they are today, as much needed if humanity is to keep on the right path . . . These, of course, were all lies, and deliberate lies at that, but there was a specific purpose in telling them. Why was Lenin turned into a universal theme of stage and screen, prose and verse, his features reproduced in countless paintings? Why did the authorities extol his modesty and plaster the country with monuments to him? Why did actors, made up to look like Lenin, appear at work meetings and declaim speeches he had made decades ago, taking care to imitate even the way he rolled his *r*'s?

The adulation was so extreme that it almost seemed like mockery, and we can only conjecture the exact reasons for it. By inflating the figure of Lenin, as though it were made of rubber, the present leaders threw a glaring light on their own impersonality and, as it were, justified it by contrast. Compared with such a celestial body, anyone else could be only a satellite. As a defense against a new "personality cult," the ruling group instituted the worship of a figure who eclipsed all others and who had the supreme merit of being safely dead. The cult of Lenin was intended as a guarantee that there would be no more Stalins— Lenin, it was hoped, would become the personality to end all personalities.

Lenin had already expressed all possible ideas in their best form, so that "progressive humanity" had only to repeat them, without trying to be original or clever. Behind this absurd exaggeration it is easy to detect the present leaders' hatred of new ideas and of any suggestion that doctrine should or could be adapted to present needs.

One anniversary slogan was the poet Mayakovsky's phrase—not one of his happiest—that "Lenin is still more alive than anyone else on earth." These words were placarded everywhere—on housefronts, in offices, stores, restaurants, and even public baths, where they struck an apocalyptic note amid the throng of naked bodies.

It is indeed a frightening thought that people today are more dead than corpses, and that incessant anniversary celebrations are held to make sure that they are all aware of the fact.

We must admire the artistic discernment that inspired Aleksandr Tvardovsky, a patriotic enough poet, to write his satire "Terkin in the Other World." He evidently thought at the time that it applied only to the conditions of Stalin's day, but, alas, it is increasingly clear that it also depicts the Soviet present and foreseeable future. The private soldier Terkin, a plain man and a war hero, arrives in the next world and finds it a place where "there are no complaints, as all are satisfied," and nobody is afraid, because there couldn't be a worse place to go to—a very good description of the Brezhnev era. General apathy, the corrosive effect of bureaucracy and red tape, hopelessness and affected optimism, cynical thoughts and the bombastic language of military "orders of the day"—all these crush and stifle every vestige of life in present-day Russia. In the words of Tvardovsky's poem: "Endless corridors stretch out in front—they are the main roads of this world, with traffic-lights overhead. And, in case you should go astray, for half a mile ahead you can see direction indicators, notices, and billboards."

A long time ago, the religious thinker Chaadayev published a "Philosophical Letter" which is still regarded as a slander on Russia and which he dated from "The Necropolis," i.e., Moscow. Anyone looking at Brezhnev's Russia must feel with horror what a prophetic term it was. The letter is dated December 1, 1829—a pity that this does not make a round-figure anniversary!

# The abolition of memory

The jubilees prevent us from correctly understanding either the present or the past. The revolution, whose fiftieth anniversary has come and gone, divides the era of perdition from that of salvation. Particular dates and events, interpreted in a distorted way, are presented so assiduously that one is almost prevented from thinking of anything else.

The gloomy reflections of Chaadayev, who held that Russia's past and present had no meaning, were answered by Pushkin, who declared that Peter the Great was a whole world history in himself. The three-hundredth anniversary of Peter's birth fell on June 9, 1972—and what happened? No one paid the slightest attention except for one or two specialists who, in the strict line of duty, read papers to learned assemblies. The Brezhnev team's passion for anniversaries does not extend far into the past. But actually it is not just a question of the leadership. Even if we make the effort to free ourselves from official ideology, it is not easy to see the present relevance of Peter the Great and others in Russia's past.

Our historical memory has a span of only some five or six decades. Before that, officially, all was black. Some people of independent mind, as opposed to the present regime, believe that everything then was rosy while everything now is dark; but this belief too is unhistorical, and precludes an understanding of important past events. The attitude of these critics emphasizes the gulf between us and the past, and does not show us any bridge. Those who seek to resurrect the past merely return to it.

The narrow Soviet conception of the past leaves no room for historical memory. The purpose of jubilees is to embellish and therefore to falsify. They importune and distract the memory, making us want to stop our ears and get away from all the mindless clamor.

As for current events and declarations officially extolled as "historic," they are forgotten in the space of a week. They are proclaimed and forced on everyone's attention, as if their authors really knew that they mean nothing. The mind fails to take them in, like a noise that is too loud or beyond the compass of the human ear. Since everyone is deaf to the message, it can be altered or manipulated at will.

Even Stalin, who was slavishly adored by whole generations, is virtually forgotten today: his image is blurred and featureless. Who now knows or wants to know what kind of man he really was? Some young people do not even know what he looked like. The portraits that used to hang in every office, and the statues in city squares and other public places, were all removed twenty years ago. The idealization of Stalin among the half-educated is probably due to the fact that practically everything about him has been forgotten.

As for Khrushchev, whose name is linked with a full ten years of the Soviet regime, the latest edition of the official history of the USSR mentions him exactly twice: when he became head of state and when he resigned. This is in a work with 500 pages devoted to the Soviet period; the first volume, containing the whole of history from the Stone Age to 1917, is only half as long.

Millions of people—our own relatives, our friends, and friends of friends—have endured prison and labor camps or been physically destroyed. Almost every Soviet family has suffered some kind of loss, but one rarely hears a word of regret or pity for their fate.

About once a year history is rewritten: some names are erased, others inserted or emphasized. This is done openly and impudently, with complete cynicism, simply because nobody notices it except those who earn their bread by forging the record in this way.

In the popular mind there is no sense of historical continuity. Traditions sustained for ages have suddenly been obliterated. Soviet artists unconsciously bear witness to the truth when they depict Russians amid a group of "brother" peoples, the former in nondescript modern dress whose only distinguishing feature is that it is thirty years out of fashion. Among all the nations of the Soviet Union it is Russia that has led the way in leveling and depersonalization. Russians mistakenly imagine this to be a sign of up-to-dateness—mistakenly, because this trend has no roots in the past and no vitality to preserve it into the future. Its exponents are not people of the modern age, but of no age at all.

In a collection of essays edited by Solzhenitsyn, entitled *From Under the Rubble,* Igor Shafarevich writes:

> Several generations of Russians have been brought up on such a horrendous version of Russian history that all they want to do is to try and forget we ever had a past at all. Russia was the "gendarme of Europe" and the "prison of the peoples"; its history consisted of "one defeat after another" and was always characterized by one and the same phrase: "the accursed past."
>
> Even the broom of new names that has swept away everything linking us with our past has scarcely affected another people more cruelly than the Russian. Let me suggest a simple experiment for those who wish to try it: get on a bus passing through the center of Moscow and listen to the names of the stops as the driver calls them out. It will immediately strike you that streets retaining their old, original names are rare exceptions—it is as if some brush had painted out all reminders of the fact that the Russian people once had a history.[13]

There is much truth in this, but it is possible to look at it from a different angle. I would suggest varying the experiment. Instead of questioning busdrivers, whom Shafarevich mentions because their job requires them to use the new official names, ask ordinary passersby on these streets whether they remember that, say, Metrostroyevskaya used to be called Ostozhenka, or Bogdan Chmelnitsky Street used to be called Maroseyka. Practically none of them do, and this seems to me a more serious matter. For, after all, it is not as if anyone who remembered or used the old names was in danger of being arrested, shot, or even thrown out of his job! In short, officials take care to use the new names, while everyone else couldn't care less. Doesn't this mean that the past is not engraved on people's memories, but is more like chalk on a blackboard? If it were otherwise, how effective would the "broom of new names" have been? And who wields the broom, anyway?

Among the other peoples of the Soviet Union, the broom is plied even more vigorously. The national past is wiped out as part of the process of Russification. Nevertheless the effects are less devastating, because local tradition puts up a stronger resistance.

Shafarevich blames the obliviousness and apathy of the

Russian people on an "all-powerful liberal public opinion" which, from the nineteenth century onward, "declared Russian patriotism to be reactionary, a disgrace to Russians and a menace to everybody." This is an unpleasant and inaccurate way of stating the case, since liberals of old Russia were as patriotic as the chauvinists and reactionaries, but in a different way. To overlook this fact is perhaps even more harmful to the historical consciousness than to forget the old names of streets. In any case, the Russian liberals were by no means as influential in society as Shafarevich makes them out to have been.

Can anyone deny that Russia was the "gendarme of Europe" and a "prison of the peoples," or that the country suffered constant defeat due to backwardness and overweening policies? The British and French beat Russia in the Crimea; she was beaten by the Japanese in 1904-5, and by Germany in World War I.

Shafarevich is wrong, moreover, when he ascribes the loss of an historical sense to the fact that Russia's past has been presented in an unfavorable light: for the days when this was done are also long past and forgotten. No Soviet censor today would let pass the phrase "gendarme of Europe," even with reference to Tsarist Russia—it would be an instructive experiment to test this! For a long time now, Soviet historians have turned the "gendarmes" into civilizers and the "prison" into an earthly paradise. Our generation was not taught at school that old Russia enlarged its empire by fair means or foul, but that other nations begged to be taken under its protection because of the love and confidence they felt toward the Russian people.

The alarming thing is that Russians readily swallow these barefaced lies. This is why they continue to be the gendarmes of Europe and to hold other nationalities captive inside their own frontiers. Oblivion to the past leads to unthinking, irresponsible repetition of former crimes. Once again, as in the time of Nicholas I, Russian troops have shed blood in Budapest and robbed Poland of its hard-won independence, while Germans, Lithuanians, and Jews flee from Russia as though from a prison. And would the Berlin Wall exist for a day longer if it were not defended by Soviet rockets as well as Russian bayonets?

It is both just and logical that Russians themselves are worse off in this jail than anyone else: for servitude inbred as part of a national tradition is stronger and more irrevocable than anything imposed from outside. Moreover, a nation that oppresses others cannot itself be free—this is a true saying, whoever its first author.

However, let us revert to the question of historical memory. Should such a memory be induced to retain only what is good? Leaving the Tsarist past for a moment, let us look at the Stalin era: is there not a tacit agreement to forget anything unpleasant or frightening or unflattering to national pride?

To see selectively and perceive only the good serves to justify inaction and reluctance to change. Ideal conditions belong to the realm of daydreaming, not that of stern historical reality. To forget the bad is to betray the good by blotting out the contrast between them, and this is the true meaning of a lack of historical sense.

I agree with Shafarevich on one point: all our troubles may be due to the sudden decision to do away with "the accursed past" and to start everything anew. To raze everything to its foundations is not the work of historical builders. But does this mean that we should forgive the past all its misdeeds because the present is worse? Irresponsible conservatism is hardly more constructive than happy-go-lucky revolutionism. And should not our renascence begin by understanding the continuity between the evils of the past and those of the present, while at the same time identifying the constructive features on which we can build? If we continue blindly to hate the present and extol the past, we are fated to exchange old "Derzhimordas" (police bullies) for new ones, as history has already shown.

Shafarevich's article is a saddening revelation that the disease of historical insensibility is rooted more deeply than the superficial level of Soviet official claptrap.

Harsh though it is, I would describe our situation by quoting the following passage from Saltykov-Shchedrin. It is on the subject of Mitrofan, the hobbledehoy in Fonvizin's comedy *The Minor* (1782), who is one of the "type" characters in Russian literature:

Mitrofan is no theoretician; he does not analyze or generalize, least of all about himself. If he remembered yesterday clearly it might serve to prick his conscience or at least to make him wiser. But as yesterday has been blotted out by a night of drunken oblivion, there can be no question of this. . . . For Mitrofan there is no such thing as experience or tradition or inference of any kind, as each moment of his life is completely superseded by the next. His impudence is not impudence, his frivolity is not frivolity. He is a new-born human being and a completely empty one; the principle of accountability for one's actions rebounds from him as from a stone wall. His acts might be compared with manifestations of a natural force, but even this is not so, for nature creates and destroys indifferently, while Mitrofan is an unconscious destroyer and nothing more. That is why there has hitherto been nothing like a clear theory of Mitrofanism, justifying the existence of this phenomenon and indicating its future prospects.

It would seem that we have reached the extreme limit of Mitrofanism, if it can be said to have any limits. Of course, from Mitrofan's own point of view this is not so terrible, since he does not choose to contemplate himself. He lives without fear and without taking thought, but for the rest of us there is indeed cause for alarm. Finding ourselves on the brink, we turn around involuntarily and ask how we got there. It is then that we remember the past and understand its connection with the present, and thus, perhaps, attain some glimmer of self-knowledge.

# CHAPTER II

# Nostalgia
# for History

To evolve a "theory of Mitrofanism" would of course require a certain detachment, a process of self-examination and self-analysis; but this is the hardest possible thing to achieve in a period without history. The lack of an historical sense means that all values are conditioned by the present situation. Looking at everything around him from within that situation, a human being identifies justice with his own selfish interests. He believes he is always right. He has the self-assurance of a savage who believes that if he or his tribe rob and murder it is right, while if others rob or murder *them* it is wrong. This belief inspires him to stand up for himself.

A conflict of egoisms makes life extremely insecure. Today's conqueror may be tomorrow's victim, but he is incapable of foreseeing or acting upon this fact. He knows what suffering is and does his best to avoid it, but he does not know the meaning of sympathy or fellow-feeling. He is ready to take part in persecuting the victim of the moment, without reflecting that the latter's situation is the result of mere chance. He does not have the imagination to put himself in the victim's place, and is therefore defenseless when he himself is victimized. Good and bad fortune alternate in a disconnected and inconsistent manner: the alternations are not noticed or remembered, and no conclusions are drawn from them. Experience is neither tragic nor comic, but merely commonplace. Existence in a nonhistorical period is vanity of vanities, nothing more.

# Arbitrariness

The worst of it is that there is nothing essentially new in this situation. It is perhaps only more evident and indisputable at the present time: it has reached the state of classic perfection in which the form of society exactly corresponds to its inner content, thanks to "socialism" and the "expropriation of expropriators."

Saltykov-Shchedrin's remarks about Mitrofanism show that the phenomenon goes back well into the past. Otherwise his words, written about a hundred years ago, would not reflect present-day society so accurately or be so helpful to us in the painful process of coming to know ourselves. There are many other passages, too, in past Russian literature which we would do well to note. Too little use has been made of such literature, precisely because of our lack of understanding of historical continuity.

There is a significant passage about Chaadayev in an essay "The Apology of a Madman," written by the radical critic Chernyshevsky in 1861 and banned by the lenient censorship of that time. But for the Soviet regime's blindness to history, it would probably not have been published in our day either. It runs as follows:

> Our fundamental concept and our most stubborn tradition is to introduce the idea of arbitrariness into everything. Juridical forms and individual efforts seem to us ineffectual and even absurd; we desire and expect everything to be done on a basis of arbitrary decision; we do not expect conscious cooperation from others, and prefer to work without their help; the first condition of success, even when our intentions are just and right, is that others should obey blindly and without opposition.* Each of us is a little Napoleon, or

---

*By "just and right intentions" Chernyshevsky probably meant to convey the idea of "socialism" in such a way that his readers would understand him but the censor would not. It is clear, therefore, that this eminently democratic thinker would not only have disapproved of Lenin's despotic revolution, but that he actually warned against such a revolution taking place as a result of the tradition of arbitrariness.

rather a Khan Batu.[1] But what happens in a society consisting entirely of Batus? Each one will carefully gauge the others' strength, and in every group and every enterprise there will appear an arch-Batu whom the ordinary Batus will obey as implicitly as they themselves are obeyed by the baskaks[2] and the latter by the rank-and-file Tatars, each of whom regards himself as a Batu in relation to some conquered tribe—and, the finest touch of all, that tribe itself believes that this is how things ought to be and that they cannot be otherwise. It is almost as hard for us to shake off this age-old mental habit as for the West to abandon all its traditional ideas and customs. And this is not our only pleasing habit, but we have many others that touchingly resemble it. This whole complex of Asiatic ideas and facts is like a suit of armor, with metal rings strongly linked together: God alone knows how many generations must pass before it begins to rust and to allow civilized feelings to enter our breasts.

Alas, Chernyshevsky was right in his gloomy forebodings, and the future—our present—has turned out worse than he expected. The rings of armor are not made of iron but of human traits and inclinations, which do not rust but are strengthened by tradition.

Lenin's revolution, itself an act of historical arbitrariness, opened up new possibilities of absolute control over men's lives and property; it created innumerable miniature Napoleons—who increasingly acted like Batus. The revolution provided an ostensibly simple and just formula of suppression of a minority by the majority. In practice, every victim figured as an isolated individual and every executioner as a representative of the interests of the masses. The victim felt his own insignificance, and the executioner his power, on every violent occasion. The "insulted and oppressed," as Dostoyevsky called them, were able to become insulters and oppressors, not only with impunity but as the agents of a higher justice. This psychological refinement, rather than Marxist theory, is the key to understanding the revolution and the nightmare of cruelty that it engendered, as well as its final manifestation in the present regime.

In clear contradiction to Marxist theory, the Soviet system from the very outset gave absolute priority to politics over economics. In other words, policies were determined by the leaders' caprices and not by rational aims. Politics was subordinated to an ideology, increasingly obscured and ossified by time. Today, clichés and sterile formulae slip off the tongue effortlessly and without serious thought; history and experience flow around them, leaving them undisturbed.

A core of reality lies within this rigid framework, like a mollusk inside its shell. Rarely mentioned, its existence is common knowledge. On the one hand, the Soviet Union is supposed to be a planned economy; on the other hand, Stalin could arbitrarily double the targets set by economists for the first Five-Year Plan. This is a classic example of irresponsible autocracy. Ignorance disguised as wisdom, impulse masquerading as planning, anarchy in the place of systematic control—in all these ways arbitrariness was raised to the highest pitch of refinement. (It is significant that Soviet bosses, who are guaranteed immunity in carrying out their jobs, are called "responsible workers" in the official jargon.) This essential core of Soviet organization is not referred to in writing or orally, but at best by hints. Yet it is imprinted on the subconscious of anyone who has seen a bit of the world and has lost the wide-eyed innocence of a Boy Scout.[3] For that matter, those who do show such naïveté are still readier victims of an authority that is law unto itself.

This central core, this ultimate mystery, this altar to which only the most faithful are admitted, is the scene of infinite amounts of mockery and humiliation, in both small things and great. It serves no practical purpose; it merely upholds the principle of arbitrariness for its own sake. Currently, the delights of this system are available to almost everyone under the Soviet regime. Few are so low that they cannot find someone else to bully. A female team-leader on a collective farm differs from the secretary of a party district or regional committee only in the number of victims at her disposal. The "people's militia"[4] serves the same purpose. Its youthful members can beat up or humiliate anyone they like, and subsequently can have their victims disciplined for insubordination. The masses are given similar opportunities through "comradely courts,"[5] or through party, Komsomol (Communist Youth League), and factory assemblies with wide powers to try individuals without overstrict attention to law or procedure. In this way almost everyone can be a Batu, if only for a short time.

What is nowadays cautiously called "violation of socialist legality"[6] is not a deviation from the norm; it is the norm itself. If millions of people have fallen victim to such regrettable "violations," it is permissible to ask what this "legality" is and where it resides.

Laws that appear just and democratic, but which leave loopholes for highly flexible interpretation and application, are ideally designed to make lawlessness flagrant. The best way to make a man feel totally deprived of rights is to lure him on by fictitious legal guarantees and then laugh at him and at the law itself. He must be made to see that the law does not benefit him and its protection will cost him dearly—so dearly that he will wish he had never thought of summoning it. "You wanted law and justice—here it is, you swine! Take that, and that!" Oh, what a delight it is to be able to treat a rational, articulate being in this way!

Out-and-out arbitrary rule seems childishly naive compared to such refinement. It would leave no room for a delicate range of feelings on the part of the victim or his tormentor. Open violence crushes and destroys physically, but not morally and spiritually. Lawlessness disguised as scrupulous legality is quite another thing. To imprison or kill a man is not particularly educational in itself, but to do so with all the panoply of bureaucracy, duly observing every vicious little rule and regulation—that really does show the victim his impotence. He knows the law, he clings to it as his final salvation, he allows himself to hope—and then, slowly, hope is taken away from him. To extort absurd confessions from a man and to jot them down solemnly as official record squashes him like a fly, turning him into absolute nothingness, and of course teaches friends who are still at "liberty" a lesson. To make the victim an accomplice against himself—is this not the absolute acme of arbitrary rule? The accused becomes his own executioner. Thus he is given the main role in a devilish performance that ends with his destruction.

His destruction fertilizes the soil for a fresh crop of similar acts. The "just law" and the "democratic freedoms" laid down in the Constitution give aesthetic finality to the whole process. The regime enacted the "most democratic constitution in the world" to destroy innocent victims on an unheard-of scale.[7] Had the victims been even slightly guilty, the arbitrariness of the action would have been less complete.

It was part of the diabolical charm of the system that the hangmen and their victims were liable to change places: today's executioner might be tomorrow's criminal, thus squaring accounts after a fashion. Having had their fill of mocking at others' torments, they received a richly deserved taste of their own medicine.

This enormous state—armed to the teeth, with an apparatus of violence staffed by millions—professes an ideology that violates reason and conscience. It is essentially an arena for countless single acts of petty tyranny, meted out to citizens as their most precious possession. If the practice of petty tyranny were curbed, the whole system would seize up, as if grit were thrown into the machine.

I do not say this to denounce the system once again or inflict a deeper wound on it. It does more to condemn itself than the sharpest critic could; nobody could make its reputation blacker than it is. The smoke screen with which it covers up its proceedings need only be dissipated, and this, it would appear, has started to occur of its own accord.

But the system's vulnerability prompts another dangerous illusion—namely, that it is so morally weak that a single blast will overthrow it. The regime's obvious absurdities arouse outbursts of protest; the exaggerated optimism which may result is bound to end in deep disappointment. We should understand our adversary better. The absurdities summon up our spirit of sober, rational criticism. When confronted by the regime, criticism merely proves the powerlessness of reason. The system, in fact, creates an opposition that becomes part of the system, a buttress instead of a battering ram. The system is self-contained, closed and indestructible. What must be done is to break it open, bring it into the light of day and reveal its secret springs.

The system's wiliness is furthered by inviting methods of analysis and appraisal at variance with its true nature. For instance, the regime is constantly boasting about production, planning, and increased labor achievements; so its critics set about proving that production is poor, plans are not fulfilled, and workers show no enthusiasm whatever. But the critics then have to admit that all these deplorable conditions have not affected the stability of the system, so that "They"[8] are quite unperturbed. The fact that the rulers can make stupid decisions with impunity only emphasizes the absoluteness of their power.

The more easily the system rules over its subjects, the less trouble it has in parrying blows from outside. Sensible people, after listening to equally sensible criticism, say to themselves: "Yes, perfectly true, but what difference has it made?" The victims get the impression that the regime's power is superhuman, and thus it can bully them as much as it likes.

We should therefore avoid applying ordinary concepts and schemas to the situation in Russia. It is a complex of evils bearing more relation to demonology than to sociology. It may not be very new or original, but its solution is not to be found in newfangled sociological constructions.

Everything that has happened and is still happening in the Soviet Union is literally inconceivable. We talk about economics, politics, and government, assuming that they have the same aims and meaning, to some degree, in all states and under all governments and social systems. In all the regimes of the modern Western world—and it is on these that our conceptual framework is based—politics is fairly sharply divided from other spheres. The state and government pursue pragmatic aims dictated by circumstances and designed to satisfy the needs of the whole society or particular groups within it. Having ascertained these aims, we can assess the degree of success or failure, make predictions, and so on: in short, we can perform the proper functions of an expert or observer.

But we lack experience in a situation where politics has stamped out the economic enterprise and intellectual initiative of a whole people, where the state and government are treated as ends in themselves, where they claim absolute authority unfettered by law and dole out scraps of this arbitrary power to individuals. All the rest of society is nothing but an instrument, a means to an end—yet there is no true end. There cannot be one except where the state exists for the benefit of society.

The state arrogates the freedom that belongs to individuals. Society is restrained so that it can be manipulated at will. The arbitrary power thus achieved is to compensate for general enslavement. The right of individuals to use it within certain prescribed bounds is the acme of privilege, along with the right to buy fresh food and enjoy normal medical services. Indeed, all the material privileges conferred by the state are less important in themselves than as symbols of an individual's participation in the luxury of arbitrary power. The logic of the system requires him to covet it above all things.

Thus dominance by arbitrary power acts as a substitute for freedom in a system that excludes freedom. It is like a cancerous growth, the "natural" reaction of an organism to anomalous conditions of development.

We are dealing with a sick society, but its sickness is above all spiritual, not economic or social.

The system cannot be viewed through economic spectacles, because economics plays only a minimal part in it. It has shown more than once that it can remain stable despite economic collapse. It cannot be understood in sociological terms either, for to call it a social entity would be an extreme hyperbole. Economics and sociology both presuppose the limitation of freedom and imply at least a temporary equilibrium between objective possibilities and subjective desires. Arbitrary power, however, is wholly subjective, and its reaction to any kind of objectivity is to leap over it like a runaway horse. Indeed, the very essence of arbitrary power requires its jumping over economic, social, and all the other barriers. Otherwise, it could not exist. As Stalin put it: "There are no fortresses that the Bolsheviks cannot take by storm."

To ascertain whether a system is achieving its object, one compares the result with the proposed goal. But if the aim is arbitrariness for its own sake, with what can the result be compared? The conditions for unlimited tyranny are as flexible and varied as that tyranny itself. Economic and social disasters are unimportant, when there is no shortage of expendable victims; moreover, as a last resort, one can always lie and pretend that a visible loss is actually a gain. Open lying is itself a form of arbitrariness, and one of the most pleasant.

Suppose, however, that the rulers' only aim is to enjoy themselves in the present, without thinking of the future. What if pleasure is delirious irresponsibility, paralyzed conscience, and lack of internal constraints? Who can say whether a drunkard and profligate gains or loses when he spends his last penny on debauchery, not in order to ruin himself, but to indulge his secret passion once more? In other situations he may show skill and perseverance in acquiring money, he may appear a thorough "realist" to the outsider, and yet in the end squander his whole fortune.

No, the solution to our absurdities cannot be found in Marx or Parsons but in Dostoyevsky, who explored all the subtleties and refinements of the taste for arbitrary power. Leaving this rich theme for a more suitable occasion, however, I will only cite a passage from *Notes from the Underground:*

> What about the millions of facts which go to show that only too often man knowingly (that is to say, with a full comprehension of what is his true advantage) puts that advantage aside in favor of some other plan, and betakes himself to a road, to risks, to the unknown, to which no agent nor agency has compelled him, as though, unwilling to follow the appointed path, he preferred to essay a difficult and awkward road along which he must feel his way in darkness? Would it not almost seem as though the directness, the voluntariness of such a course had for him a greater attraction than any advantage? Advantage, indeed? What, after all, *is* advantage? . . . You, gentlemen, take your lists of human interests from averages furnished by statistics and economic formulae. Your lists of interests include only prosperity, riches, freedom, tranquillity, and so forth, and anyone who openly and knowingly disagreed with those lists would, in your opinion (as in mine also, for that matter), be either an obscurantist or a madman. Would he not?

The "man from the underground" who made these remarks was a philosopher, in a way. Consuming self-analysis paralyzed his ability to act and caused him to run away from others. He not only constrained his instincts but also kept a close watch over them, fought them, and was ashamed of them. He was well aware of the impure origins of his thirst for arbitrary power. The novelist who created this fantastic and complicated character endowed it with his own genius.

But if we imagine a "man from the underground" who does not merely think but acts, who emerges from solitude to fulfill his desires, who not only boasts of the motto "Let the heavens fall so long as I can always get a cup of tea," but adopts it as common etiquette—then the position would typify what we are wrestling with in the Soviet Union. This variation on the "underground man" would be simpler but also more dangerous. He would be free of conflict, contradictions, and shame. He would be unable to imagine that different notions of life, different values of pleasure and happiness, existed anywhere. He would be completely unrestrained, since, as Saltykov-Shchedrin put it, "the principle of accountability for one's actions would rebound from him as from a stone wall."

# Despotism and creativity

Those wielding arbitrary power discourage creativity in others, preferring mere executants. Creativity is inseparable from freedom: it presupposes consistent and intelligible acts, unadaptable to arbitrary reversals. It calls for great competence and does not tolerate ignorance. A tyrant who interferes in creative processes merely succeeds in wrecking them.

The public ownership of all means of production, which is called "socialism" in Russia, has made the population indifferent to the results of its labor. This paves the way for "party leadership" of the economy—that is, for arbitrary interference. Since people do not care about the work they perform, they carry out the absurdest orders without protest. This in itself is a kind of arbitrary action, sometimes pleasurable to those who indulge in it. It provides a chance to do damage without responsibility or sacrifice.

In a remote country area, I once met a group of women farm laborers "pulling" flax. This is hard and unpleasant work: one bends over for hours, and the sharp stalks cut into one's hands like knives. I had done it as a schoolboy, and now I decided to show off my skill and demonstrate the "fellowship of the intelligentsia with the common people." To my surprise, I found the flax was unripe. The bolls were still green, and the inside was a spongy green mass; the seeds from which oil is obtained were not yet formed. "What on earth are you doing?" I said, "You're ruining the harvest." "So what?" the women replied, grinning broadly. "We were told to pull the flax, and that's what we're doing." This was their revenge for being made to do heavy work for almost no pay.

Things are somewhat different in the intellectual and artistic fields, but there should be no initiative here either, according to Soviet ideas. Scholars, artists, and writers have to conform to orders as strictly as the rest of the population. They are given assignments and told to carry them out. No personal contribution is expected. Since "socialism" has triumphed in the arts and sciences, there have been whole generations of specialists who meet these requirements perfectly. Artists and writers depict what they are supposed to, conforming to the demands of each new anniversary. Historians adapt their interpretations to the political needs of the moment, and flagrantly contradict today what they said yesterday. Even scientists, who one might think were safe from ignorant interference, carry out crackbrained assignments.

The existence of conforming pseudospecialists affects the general atmosphere of the country. They act as transmitters and executors of arbitrary decisions, producing imitations of art, science, and philosophy without ever understanding any of these; always they exclude any vestige of originality. They are a fairly large group, petty tyrants themselves, with a vested interest in eradicating creative forces in the culture they control.

Nonetheless, things differ in intellectual circles from the world of physical labor. There are always bound to be individual thinkers and artists who take themselves and their work seriously. They love it and are interested in it, and they abhor its profanation. Some of them have worked out a world-view of their own through education. They are concerned with reality and not with mere show, and thus they fail to fit into the strictly controlled social order. The fact that science and art do exist in Russia, and not only their vulgar imitations, is itself a threat to tranquillity.

Petty tyrants seem particularly attracted by philosophy, science, art, and literature. They are either vexed by them or take special pleasure in laying down the law on subjects they know nothing about. At any rate, outside authority has invaded these fields most ignorantly and insolently. In the whole history of the Soviet Union, only two of the earliest ministers or officials responsible for culture, Lunacharsky and Bryusov,[9] had any acquaintance with the activities they were supervising. The others have been totally unknowledgeable. Even the pseudo-artists and pseudowriters, who, as I said, are legion, are not appointed to such powerful positions.

A Soviet intellectual suffers unless he can acquire the habit of servility and implicit obedience. Already noticeable for his aversion for petty tyrants and his inability to be one, he is trained like an animal to conform to the general pattern.

I am not speaking of social questions, in which an intellectual is almost alone in preserving a modicum of historical sense. He seeks such solitary knowledge because he assumes some responsibility for his own decisions. Such a person is capable of reflection and self-awareness, but is forced to act in a manner contrary to his own ideas. He constantly has to express delight at what he finds profoundly repulsive, or conceal his sympathies because it would be fatal to express them openly.

But even in scientific and artistic work, in which he might hope to be his own master—having compromised his conscience time and again to secure the privilege of doing such work—he is still pestered by orders, instructions, and reprimands. However zealously he seeks the truth, his appointed superiors are sure to rebuke him for all sorts of alleged errors, slips, and misjudgments. His creative efforts, his hard-won knowledge and abilities (for the Soviet educational system is designed to stifle criticism and not arouse it, to disinform methodically rather than inform) are useless, because the subjects he is to treat and how he is to treat them are determined before he begins. His finished work, his brainchild, is judged by its conformity to a tedious, featureless stereotype, the inadequacy of which has been obvious to any literate person for decades. Anything that does not fit the bed of Procrustes is lopped off.

This is the first step in mutilating the products of independent thought and genuine art. Some ignoramus—the more ignorant, the more self-assured, imperious, and peremptory—will demolish the writer's work and, without a by-your-leave, embellish it with his own mediocrity and servile deference to his superiors. A writer is constantly being told that this or that passage in his work has been condemned or censored, that an article already set in type has been cut, or that a just-printed edition of a book has been "killed"—that is to say, turned into scrap. Talking over these sad events among a small group of friends in the evening, intellectuals feel like a besieged community depending on their besiegers for food.

With his work and career constantly threatened, the writer accedes to the rules of the game. He tries to elude the vigil of ignorant bosses and of his more intelligent but terrorized colleagues, as well as of reviewers, editors, publishing-house officials, censors, and a whole crew of party despots, each of whom has the right of absolute veto. While placating all these, he tries to say something that will be clearly intelligible to the well-disposed reader. Little by little, he makes concessions in order to save something from the wreck. His first and most sharp-eyed censor is himself. But the game is an unequal one, for if his maneuvers are detected he is hauled over the coals for "sedition" and once more has to begin twisting and turning, lying and cheating.

The result of this endless *via dolorosa* is an occasional work coming off the press capable of arousing the interest of the public or of genuine specialists. The few instances of this are known to every intellectual. The author, and all others who understand the matter, regard it as a rare success, an almost miraculous breach in established custom. Much more often the published work is pitifully distorted and the author explains to his friends that it was planned differently, that some parts were written in on orders and others struck out; and he looks vainly in their faces for some expression of sincere admiration, and finally decides that the book is only fit for scrap, that it is useless if not actually disgraceful.

In any big bookstore in Moscow or Leningrad the shelves are piled high with books that no one will ever open; they are full of resounding emptiness in prose or verse. Anyone who chanced to read them would only plunge into a deeper state of confusion and ignorance. These compilations, with titles as bland as their content, are "collective works" from which all traces of individuality have been carefully removed.[10] Some are misshapen monsters, vitriolic attacks on the enemy of the day; others are stupidly dull, the product of indifference and spurious industry; all are no better than a clumsy simulation of literature, science, or poetry.

Such is the result of cultural supervision by party tyrants. Whereas true culture helps to unite people spiritually, building bridges of sympathy and understanding, the Soviet pseudoculture divides them. There is no true exchange of thoughts and feelings, only a mass production of masks and disguises. Their *raison d'être* is to curry favor with the authorities and improve the authors' standard of living.

Any large bookstore in the Soviet Union perfectly illustrates the stagnation of the country where time has stopped.

People who still think for themselves find the atmosphere intolerable, and are wretched for lack of spiritual nourishment. Their work of self-analysis becomes increasingly hard to perform, and declines into sterility.

From this arises a longing for history, for some kind of change. For the most frightening question of all is, Will it be like this forever? Is this all we have to bequeath to our children?

How can one go on living if conditions are bad and are not expected to improve? It is second nature to us, given our education and long tradition, to accept the primacy of the external over the internal, the power of circumstances over the spirit, the doctrine that it is useless to kick against the traces.

After Stalin's death, there was short-lived hope that the regime would become more humane and liberal. Intellectuals tried reminding new leaders of their promises to observe law and equity. But soon the newcomers fell into the old tyrannical courses, and it became clear that we followed a dead end.

Certainly there is no way out, at least along traditional paths. For a Soviet citizen's first impulse, and in all probability his last, is to conform, subject, and adapt himself, to practice wily and cynical tactics. The enthusiasm of faith has long been dispelled. A cynic adapts more skillfully, since he knows exactly what is expected. One rails at the cowardice of a friend or colleague to ease one's own conscience. One curses those who have deserted or turned tail; but what can be done when everybody is tarred with the same brush?

When Stalin died, over twenty years ago, the country was in a state of economic and spiritual crisis, but very few were aware of this. Primitive distortions of Marxism so held people's minds that they comprehended the life around them, with its poverty, terror, and irresponsibility, as an exceptional case rather than as a single norm. All the trials people experienced did not deepen their political understanding. They were not only miserable, but blind as well; and this blindness helped consolidate the existing order.

Later the government, momentarily losing its assurance and sense of purpose, admitted that all had not been well in the past.[11] At once blinders fell from many peoples' eyes, especially intellectuals'. For a few years, people made immense strides toward comprehending the truth. Submission and passivity gave way to demands for action. I shall never forget an occasion when Dudintsev's novel *Not by Bread Alone* was being discussed in a lecture hall at Moscow University, and an unknown youth mounted the podium to recite Heine's lines: "Strike the drum, be not afraid. . . ."

It would be humiliating to think that all this happened only because it was permitted and even encouraged by the authorities. Certainly a great deal of accumulated discontent found an outlet and a mode of expression. It was amply provoked by the crude postwar Stalinist demagogy with its sudden swing toward chauvinism, anti-Semitism, and imperialism. The ruling party's actions mocked the ideals for which it had originally seized power; this stimulated criticism first of the party's policy and ideology, and then of communist ideals themselves.

In any event, for one reason or another life at that time was suffused with clarity. Light was thrown on the nightmare of Stalin's terror and, soon afterwards, on that of Lenin. Informers and opportunists were publicly shamed. The way a man's "personal file" could blight his career was denounced in a well-known film.[12] The degenerate officeholders of Stalin's day mostly managed to keep their positions, but felt uncomfortable and affected liberal airs. Genuine public opinion emerged—voices not faked to accord with official instructions. Out of the dust and mire of abuse and humiliation, arts and sciences appeared: modern philosophy, sociology, the theory of relativity, cybernetics, genetics, structural analysis, the works of Picasso, Kafka, Meyerhold, Babel, Mandelshtam, Pasternak and Akhmatova, Mikhail Bulgakov and Andrey Platonov, Hemingway and Faulkner, painting from the Impressionists to the Surrealists—the list of subjects is as endless as the artists and thinkers who emerged or were revived during those years.[13] How many poems, novels, films, plays—real, live, exciting ones—were snatched from the dead hand of "socialist realism"! Society was in a state of feverish excitement, hurrying to make up for lost time. Still behind the rest of the world in its methods of stating and handling problems, it compensated for these shortcomings by its fresh approach.

And then all this disappeared without a trace. The old masks were resumed. Were those years a dream, or are we dreaming now? The question may well be asked; around us are still the same kind, intelligent people who, in private, have no difficulty in differentiating between good and bad, but if any faceless official pulls a string—presto!—they will gabble speeches and lift their hands to vote as one man. Praising or condemning as Authority requires, their automatic obsequiousness is truly depressing.

If, at a meeting, a current time-server[14] writes off the last twenty years of culture as a period of "ideological diversion" and calls on writers, artists, and scholars to observe "ideological discipline"[15] (clearly having no notion that this phrase was coined by Goebbels), everyone applauds obediently or sits in gloomy silence. Each time, one gains a fresh understanding of life in Stalin's time. Hitherto we were inclined to attribute the barbarism of those days to terror or deceit. But today there is no such terror, and few people, especially among intellectuals, remain ignorant of what is going on. Nevertheless the atmosphere is unmistakably, day by day, getting closer to what it was then.

Disappointment has been the dominant mood of the last few years, affecting not only intellectuals but the whole country. Defeat was snatched out of the jaws of victory. Apparently all that was needed was for the leadership to change course abruptly, and the whole situation collapsed. The majority now live hoping for a change for the better. They seem to expect this to arise from the rulers' assumption of a more liberal attitude. Since the present team isn't being replaced, we scan them anxiously and try to guess whether any of them are willing to effect a change or are even capable of seeing that the situation is abysmal and cannot continue.

History, which seemed to have stirred for a time, is again at a standstill. Nothing of any significance is happening. There is not even any news worth talking about. Everything is the same, exactly the same.

Pushkin once wrote to his brother: "My dearest Lev, I am sick with anger—wherever I look I see the same baseness, vileness, and stupidity. How long can this go on?" Today people ask the same question. The sense that the present is intolerable, a feverish and impotent desire for change—this is what it means to long for history.

# A look at ourselves

However, an even more bitter experience awaits us when we look into ourselves. We discover that the oppressive circumstances molding our lives derive their power not merely from others' inertness, but from our own as well. Our former expectations of beneficent change and our present embitterment find a common origin in our lack of will or power to change ourselves inwardly. During the deceptive "thaw,"[16] the most zealous progressives put too much faith in the rhetoric of the authorities. Our minds are now hopelessly flawed by deception and self-deception. Now that time has come to a stop again, each of us obediently joins in the official chorus. The supreme act of boldness is to move one's lips soundlessly. Each and every one of us is terrified of being alone in raising his hand "against" while the rest, united in "moral and political unity," gaze at him with surprise painted on their bovine, obedient faces.

Unless we are thoroughly scared or driven into a corner, most of us, of course, try to steer clear of the more repulsive statements and actions—we do not sell our honor quite so lightly—but acts of heroism are distinctly rare. As the poet Mikhail Svetlov remarked: "Among us, a decent man is one who plays dirty tricks but doesn't enjoy it." Most of us would rather keep silent all the time than tell the truth out of season.

Let us try to imagine for a moment, just in theory, that our future is governed not by an impersonal society but by individuals—by each one of us, in fact. Let us try to free ourselves from the implications of Marx's doctrine that a man is only an aggregate of social relationships. For it is no accident that the idea of the overwhelming predominance of society over the individual took such root in Russia and fascinated so many of us. As is generally the case with ideas that spread rapidly and widely, Marx's doctrine gave expression to an already existing sentiment. Once it sounded revolutionary, calling for radical change of the whole system of social relationships that was supposedly responsible for all human vice. Now, however, that the old system has been swept away and we are on the other side of the looking-glass, the maxim is no longer a call to revolution but an iron law of conformity. It serves to justify extreme pessimism and despair, for the crushing weight of social factors is opposed to individual initiative.

If we accept history as the result of individual actions, we eliminate the customary distinction between personal and social conduct. It is generally characteristic of "Soviet man" to permit himself to act in a social context in ways that he never would in private. Many people have no objections to telling lies, behaving harshly, condoning cruelties or even committing them, at a public meeting or in the line of duty. This double standard, or "double-think," of which I shall say more later, produces obedience to social evil even when it is universally evident, i.e., when it is clearly at odds with personal values. The illusion is created that my social acts are not committed by me but by an irresistible objective force working through me. It is thus supposed that the moral decline of a whole nation can be explained, and therefore justified, regardless of what happens to the soul of each and every one of its members.

This comforting view of society and individual conscience is supported by the Marxist doctrine of alienation, which, again not by chance, found many adherents among our intelligentsia, including myself, in recent years. This doctrine views social relationships as primarily impersonal, thus negating the basic responsibility of every human being for the totality of his actions. This includes the ideas he expresses and the opinions he maintains. Though the doctrine explains why men are rendered helpless by the ironical alienation of their powers and abilities, it says nothing about the active role these powers and activities can perform. Marx's recipe for eliminating alienation has not worked in Russia. If anything, alienation has increased. Though this, of course, was hardly an orthodox argument, it served to strengthen the case for conformism in a Soviet context.

In fairness it should be admitted that the urge to conform, like other psychological impulses, precedes philosophical attempts to justify it. What is important is not the metaphysical or logical structure of any particular theory but its status and prevalence, its authoritative and authoritarian nature. Thus even Marxism is convenient to conformists only in its claim to be the only true ideology.

The Russian Orthodox Church was formerly used to justify conformism, and is beginning to be so used again. The idea of "Holy Russia" conferred a sort of plenary indulgence on the country, a clean bill of moral health despite the atrocities of its history and all that it did or suffered. By implication, everything evil is the result of extraneous forces or circumstances and not the fault of individual members of the nation. This is a much more primitive, poorly argued justification of personal irresponsibility than the Marxist theory of alienation. Its recent adoption by some opponents of the Soviet regime is not reassuring. For the source of evil is to be found within ourselves—not in pressing external circumstances, the designs of wicked foreigners, or even insidious Marxist ideology, introduced from the West to lead weaker brethren astray. If we overlook or evade this fundamental point, we shall only double our misfortune.

Interestingly, Dostoyevsky, who has rightly been called the prophet of the Russian revolution, foresaw the tendency to unload responsibility, after the event, onto some mysterious non-Russian agency. In Part III, chapter I, of *The Possessed* he wrote:

> In turbulent times of upheaval or transition, low characters always come to the fore everywhere. I am not speaking now of the so-called "advanced" people who are always in a hurry to be in advance of

everyone else (their absorbing anxiety) and who always have some more or less definite, though often very stupid, aim. No, I am speaking only of the riffraff. In every period of transition this riffraff, which exists in every society, rises to the surface, and is not only without any aim, but has not even a symptom of an idea, and merely does its utmost to give expression to uneasiness and impatience. Moreover, this riffraff almost always falls unconsciously under the control of the little group of "advanced people" who do act with a definite aim, and this little group can direct all this rabble as it pleases, if only it does not itself consist of absolute idiots, which, however, is sometimes the case.

Although expressed too strongly in part, this is a remarkably true description of the sociopsychological mechanism of revolution, with its lack of any clear and positive aim. Once the foundations of a social order are shaken and conduct goes unrestrained, the way is open for hustlers and "riffraff" to rise to the top and become petty despots. Before long they are bound to fall under the influence of some demagogue. Then they start asking themselves: how could this have happened to us, and why did we commit such villainies?

The answer given by the characters in *The Possessed,* as they begin to awaken from the evil spell cast upon them, is very like that which the Russian émigré press is constantly repeating. Similar sentiments can even be found in some works written inside Russia. But, as Dostoyevsky said himself:

> It is said among us, now that it is all over, that Pyotr Stepanovitch was directed by the *Internationale,* and Yulia Mihailovna by Pyotr Stepanovitch, while she controlled, under his rule, a rabble of all sorts. The more sober minds amongst us wonder at themselves now, and can't understand how they came to be so foolish at the time. . . . Now all this is attributed, as I have mentioned already, to the *Internationale.* This idea has taken such root that it is given as the explanation to visitors from other parts.

Saltykov-Shchedrin's statement that Mitrofan "does not analyze or generalize, least of all about himself" is thus admirably illustrated by Dostoyevsky, his great literary antagonist. But unless we shut our eyes to the truth, either intentionally or from weakness, it will be clear that the blame rests not with the "Internationale" but with us. The trouble is not that we have been deluded by an imported idea, but that we had no ideas at all. This was so even before Dostoyevsky's time, and it is still true today.

At the beginning of his *Apologia of a Madman* (1837), Chaadayev sarcastically expresses his gratitude to Nicholas I's government for treating him no worse than society at large could have expected:

> The government, after all, has only done its duty; one may even say that the severities at present against us are in no way excessive, since it is certain that they are far from exceeding the expectations of a large section of the public. What should the best-intentioned government do but conform to what it sincerely believes to be the settled wish of the country?

To this day we sustain a deep-seated love for the oppressions and punishments that have rained on us. We have become used to them, and they are a focus of our emotions, ideas, and actions. We believe they are liable to recur at any time, and so are not surprised when they do so. At certain moments of our lives we even expect them, and if they fail to materialize we are perplexed and worried, as if we had somehow neglected something. A far cry from any protest!

In coming across the above-quoted passage by Chaadayev, I was reminded of an especially unpleasant incident—one that Chaadayev's irony illuminates more deeply than I was able to at the time.

On the outskirts of Moscow, I met a literary critic whose decent opinion of himself I had always shared. He asked me for news—a common phenomenon in a society like ours where facts circulate by word of mouth rather than through newspapers. I told him that Andrei Amalrik had been arrested within the past few days. "At last!" he said, in a tone of acute relief.

Why was this? Naturally it did not please him to know that one more person was behind bars. But Amalrik was a peculiar case. An able, sharp-witted writer, he had openly published his books outside the Soviet Union, neither using a pseudonym nor pretending that the manuscripts had been sent abroad without his knowledge. He even demanded the right to receive royalties on them. More shocking still, he showed no intention of agreeing to modify his writings if he were called to account for them. Nor did his work bear any trace of the all-pervading "self-censorship" which, as everyone knows, affects even *samizdat*[17] productions. All this puzzled those in Russia who read Amalrik's truly free outpourings. (Let it be noted that his readers belonged to the intellectual elite, for the writing in question by no means finds its way to everyone.) They could not understand why Amalrik was not arrested at once, and could only suppose that he was a KGB agent—his apparent independence must mean that he was already shamefully dependent. This rumor was totally absurd, but it vexed Amalrik during his last days of freedom.

So, when my acquaintance heard of Amalrik's arrest, he felt that things had returned to normal, to a state of equilibrium. He felt surer than ever that some things should not be done, because they are dangerous; the assurance justified his own pusillanimity, and therefore he exclaimed with relief, "At last!"

Alas, this is a typical reaction rather than an individual one. For similar reasons, there are constant rumors that the KGB is responsible for the *Chronicle of Current Events*,[18] the most authoritative and long-lived periodical defending the cause of human rights in the Soviet Union. These rumors are just as baseless as those concerning Amalrik. Why should the KGB disseminate information about its own illegal acts, which it tries to keep as secret as possible? But people are governed by their feelings and not their minds. They continue to believe that they are powerless and the state is all-powerful; and to fortify this belief they will stoop to inventions that amount to betrayals of one another.

We may assign to the same psychological category the almost open, involuntary joy with which our liberals receive the news that some dissident, under pressure and the threat of punishment, has "confessed his errors" or, still better, agreed to inform against his comrades. A woman of my acquaintance has astutely called this reaction "the Judas instinct."

The extent to which people welcome such reports is shown by the way they inflate and exaggerate them. Even Solzhenitsyn, for example, writes, about the series of petitions concerning political trials in 1968: "Fifty or so of the most audacious people were deprived of work in their professions. A few were expelled from the party, a few from the unions, and eighty or so protest signers were summoned for discussions with their party committee. And they came away from those 'discussions' pale and crestfallen."[19] It must be said that this is inaccurate. Of those "eighty or so" only two or three came away "pale and crestfallen" from the committee discussions. The signatories did not withdraw the charges they had leveled against the government. Many of them lost their jobs and livelihood and will remain pariahs for years, though they could have avoided all this by uttering a few words of pretended recantation. Why should they now be attacked *en bloc* and deprived of the sole right they still enjoy, the right to be respected?

It does not become us to deceive ourselves: we are all to blame for the state of affairs in which "only tyranny can breathe freely." Only a tiny minority are too young to have this stain on their conscience. If terror and persecution have not recurred on an awe-inspiring scale, it is only because the government has become more lenient or does not wish to apply such methods. All of us, whether victims, executioners, or spectators, would accept them as a matter of course, something as natural as the seasons. How actively we took part would depend more on the official position we happened to occupy than on our personal character.

While this state of affairs continues, all we can do is long for our country to have a history.

# The nonhistorical mind

But the problems of life and history are not solved by simple moralistic arguments. To imagine this is to fall under the spell of that "maximalism"[20] which begins in hysterical excitement and ends in confusion or treachery: first the murder of a Tsar by exalted revolutionaries, then the transformation of one of their leaders into a police informer.[21] The recurrence of this pattern is another symptom of a country without history.

The human personality is not built up of moral precepts like a child's blocks. It develops gradually through complex inner struggles and bitter defeats, proceeding from the relative to the absolute and avoiding spiritual death by not identifying with either. A person lives in history. All his abstract, individual good intentions must take into account historical circumstances.

Where there is no history, there are, strictly speaking, no personalities, only willful individuals uncurbed by any law.

An abstract morality, removed from concrete situations, is especially fatal to the full development of personality. It stifles creative initiative in dead clichés. This type of morality can be seen in Soviet schools, where the teacher is all-powerful and the pupils look up to him for good marks. It tacitly presupposes that the individual is nothing and the crowd everything. There is no comradeship, only the *Führer* principle, and it leads from one form of nonhistoricism to another exactly like it.

What we need is not moral exhortation but an understanding of the Russian past, which would save us from bestowing the unmitigated praise or blame that implies history is something outside ourselves. If we realize that the past is *our* past and continues to live in us, with all the good and bad that it contains, the study of it will cease to be an exercise in self-admiration.

The past lives when it is developed and transformed into the active core of a personality that cannot by its nature relapse into complacency. Self-satisfaction, self-praise, the illusion that one's nation is a model for all ages and peoples—these are the causes and symptoms of the necrosis of our society, and our first task is to rid ourselves of them.

The Christian principle of setting high standards for oneself and forgiving others should apply not only to individuals but to social and historical behavior. As we are beginning to learn from our bleeding past and changeless present, this principle could change a great deal in Russia if it were properly understood and put into practice. As the poet Naum Korzhavin says, "It is you, not the times, that are on trial."

In our longing for history and for some change that would, to a small extent at least, bring the conditions of our life into line with our innermost spiritual demands, we have rarely admitted that the present stagnation is our own doing. We continue to hanker after change as something external and not a transformation of ourselves. We are inclined to imagine that under altered circumstances, reality would take on a "human face," and then perhaps we too would become human beings; but the truth is exactly the converse.

We have failed to understand the evolution of the historical process. We are blind to gradual shading, and see only the contrast of black and white. We expect manna to fall from heaven, and therefore remain empty-handed. For nothing happens in history except through generations of labor and patience.

Merezhkovsky, in an address to Western intellectuals prior to 1917, compared the Russian intelligentsia with them:

> Your genius lies in measure, ours in excess. You know how to stop in time; when you come to a wall you turn back or go round it, while we knock our heads against it. . . . You, even in your utmost freedom, are political beings; we, though sunk in slavery, scarcely ever cease to be rebels and secret anarchists. . . . Politics, to you, is a science; to us it is a religion. Our reasoning and feelings often lead us to complete negation and nihilism, but in the depths of our will we are mystics.

This, of course, is not an objective picture but a self-portrait with a touch of complacency and tenderness for one's own vices. It points clearly, however, to the qualities we still lack in Russia: common sense, responsibility, discretion in the weighing of choices, and a dispassionate self-analysis which would reveal our faults and show us the means of gradually correcting them. What the author calls "measure" is the Hegelian harmonization of individual will with universal trends of historical existence. If we could achieve this we would not be slaves or anarchists (two sides of the same coin), but free agents. The absence of the characteristics in question does not mean, as Russians have flattered themselves for centuries, that we possess a moral nature of our own that is different from Western culture but just as valuable. On the contrary, it signifies formlessness, spiritual sloth, a dead-end existence—not mysticism, but an all-destroying mediocrity of the soul.

Today we certainly cannot console ourselves with dreams of mystical perfection unaffected by what we do and how we live. Everything is all too obviously humdrum and wretched. The merit of stagnation is that it allows neither time nor place for self-flattering delusions. This depressing clarity, this crying nakedness, is our only wealth—the bitter bread of truth, the last warning, perhaps, that fate allows us by way of hope for the future.

Our historical impotence is clearly evident today to any objective observer.

What I am saying has been confirmed in the passionate language of A. Veretennikov, an author whom I do not know. In an article entitled "Rumors and Disputes," in a *samizdat* publication on the subject of Solzhenitsyn's *August 1914,* Veretennikov writes as follows:

> The theme of insensibility to history, of "spider-like deafness," takes shape in my mind as a national catastrophe that still threatens us despite our incipient awakening. We shall not escape it unless we become aware of the vital necessity of learning from history, which shows us the appalling possibilities of evil but also the indestructibility of good. If we value the historical existence of Russia, we must understand that we can have a future only if we are able to recollect the past. . . . None of the problems to which we are awakening can be correctly posed, let alone solved, except in the light of our dolorous history. A responsible, sober understanding of the past, clearing away the myths that envelop our minds—this is the draft of living water that I believe we need now above all things. Without it, faith in our historical future is condemned to disappointment.

# The nature of history

Since Hegel's time, history has been theoretically linked with self-knowledge. Objectively speaking, history exists only when society develops through a critical understanding of the past, and when human activity reflects, clearly and responsibly, the interpretation of ideas and aims. In other words, history exists when nations enact it freely, according to their own perception of alternatives. What they achieve may in each case be less ideal than was originally planned, but the historically free consciousness is not afraid to admit this, as it ascribes a real meaning to continuity and tradition. It understands that each stage of development is only a stage, a transition from past to future, and that, having inherited problems from the past and dealt with them to the best of its ability, it is left to future generations to do likewise. From this point of view the subjective understanding of history, its cultivation as a branch of science, is a necessary element in the process of social construction.

In this concrete sense, apart from all lofty hyperbole, there is no history in Russia now and has not been much in the past. Culture and conscience, which are normally the mainsprings of historical development, have always been crushed and neglected, and this is even more the case today. Culture has an ancillary role, not to say a servile one, of justifying and praising everything the government does, while the state takes good care to deprive it of any independent voice in public affairs.

The Russian state is given to proclaiming high-flown idealistic aims which lend themselves to flights of rhetoric but have little to do with practical reality. The goals are in fact quite unattainable, but anyone who treats them with a dose of healthy skepticism is apt to be regarded as a scoundrel. As a result, there is an ever-widening gap between state policy and the true interests of society.

The estrangement between state practice and the philosophy of history reached a peak in the reign of Nicholas I (1825–55). At the time, the Slavophiles and Westernizers were advancing their rival interpretations of Russia's history and destiny.[22] Attempts of succeeding reigns to introduce a more responsible element into public life were squelched by the Bolshevik catastrophe. Today, as if the experience of a hundred and fifty years had been for naught, the sense of history occupies the same place in our social structure as was assigned to it by the ruthless suppressor of the Decembrists.[23]

To illustrate this, we may recall Uvarov's doctrine of "official nationality"[24] as described later in the nineteenth century by the historian Aleksandr N. Pypin, in his *Characteristics of Literary Opinions from the Twenties to the Fifties:*

> In internal affairs the theory signified the unlimited authority of government and its complete control over all aspects of political, national, and social life. . . . This led to a vast extension of the bureaucracy, the only instrument of the central power's administration and control. Society as such was of no importance; public opinion had no influence; the public could do nothing to further its own interests, even the most elementary, and could act only within

narrow limits; the authorities thought and acted for it, and its role was to obey. . . . Things were generally excellent on paper, but nobody compared the paper with the reality.

Then as now, it was considered improper for a citizen to even express approval of the government's doings in a tone that implied any independent judgment.

I foresee that my comparison of the Tsarist past with the Soviet present may arouse objections. Critics will point out that authority in those days was legal and based on popular approval, instead of on usurpation as at present, and that even in the worst times, as under Nicholas I, there was far less violence and terror than under the Soviets. Normally there was no capital punishment under Nicholas I. The Decembrists were first condemned to be quartered, but this was commuted to hanging, and the sentence was carried out on only five of them. All this is true, but I am not making comparisons of scale. I am only pointing out that there was no real freedom under Nicholas I and the other Tsars, and that there is a direct continuity of oppression from the Tsarist to the Soviet regime. Qualitative rather than quantitative indicators are the criteria of historical change; to lose sight of qualitative similarity because of a difference of scale indicates a lack of historical sense. Another indication, and an important one, is to idealize the past in comparison with the present. The nonhistorical mind regards good and bad features, positive and negative, as being "given" *a priori* and independently of each other, instead of being part of an evolutionary struggle, a process enacted by ourselves and for which we bear responsibility.

The Tsarist government claimed to act in the name of God, while the present one invokes "the only true science." The difference is not without importance, but the two principles have in common that they regard truth as something given *a priori* that reposes in the custody of the powers that be. Truth thus sanctified and supported by state authority leaves no room for pluralism and demands total and unanimous obedience. Any intellectual deviation is a deliberate and culpable heresy. From this stem our absolutism and our intolerance.

Our archetypal disposition toward unanimous obedience was clearly seen in the subjugation of the Orthodox church to the state during the period of the Most Holy Synod,[25] a system maintained by successive Tsarist governments, however pious and God-fearing they wished to appear. The autocracy set an example of contempt for the spiritual realm, and the people followed suit. The danger of this state of affairs was long seen but inertia was great, and independent thought had little influence on public affairs. The absolutism with which opinions were received and professed was such that no notice was taken of their internal inconsistency.

In a memorial submitted to Tsar Alexander I in 1811, the historian Karamzin wrote:

> The Russian clergy has been in a state of decline since the time of Peter I. Our patriarchs and metropolitans were obsequious servants of the Tsars, whom they belauded from the pulpit in Biblical language. If it is praise we want, we have poets [*sic*] and courtiers. The clergy's principal duty is to teach the people to be virtuous, and it will do this the more effectively if it is itself respected. . . . The spiritual power should have its own sphere of activity independent of the civil power.

But the emancipation of the clergy, even thus cautiously and deferentially formulated, proved to be a utopian dream. The political system could not tolerate any kind of freedom or public activity that went beyond the government's own immediate aims. In 1917, after the overthrow of the dynasty, an attempt was made to separate the church from the state and restore its rights,[26] but by then it was too late.

Thus, the authority of Christianity was expended on objectives that were alien and even contrary to its spiritual mission. When Soviet atheist propaganda describes the church as an instrument of oppression, this is a simplified but not wholly distorted picture of Russian history. The church has presently entered into a compact with an atheist government and obeys the state as sincerely as possible under such ambiguous circumstances. In so doing, the church illustrates its own secular character and its subservience to past and present governments. The Religious Affairs Committee of the Council of Ministers of the USSR is essentially a carbon copy of the Most Holy Synod.

The corrupting effect of this situation is clear. It breeds mistrust of anything related to religion, and encourages those without the intellectual power or freedom to distinguish principles from accidental circumstances to view all kinds of culture cynically. Such people gain the impression that spiritual values are nothing but a cloak for somebody's interest. The nineteenth-century critic Belinsky, in a celebrated controversy with Gogol, said that "the Russians are by nature a deeply atheistic people— they have plenty of superstition, but not a vestige of religion." There is a grain of truth in this, and it explains the partial success of Soviet atheistic propaganda, which combats superstition under the delusion that by so doing it is "unmasking" religion.

Today's atmosphere is one of pathological insensitivity to the moral and spiritual content of religion, especially Christianity. This can be attributed to the failure of the Romanovs to take the advice of such observers as Karamzin who promoted the idea of separation of church and state. The spirit was overburdened by the flesh and succumbed to it. Is not the reason for the prevalence of the idea that spiritual and intellectual life is determined by material conditions and class interests due to the age-long humiliation of religious faith? The vulgar gospel of Soviet historical materialists is anticipated in the peasant proverb quoted by Belinsky: "If the icon works, pray to it; if not, use it as a saucepan lid."

The state forced not only religion but other forms of mental and spiritual activity to fit an alien mold as much as possible. As we saw, Karamzin, though himself a poet, spoke of poets and courtiers in the same breath as flatterers of the powers that be. In the same way, artists and men of learning were assigned a strictly pragmatic role.

This, however, was not the Western "bourgeois" form of pragmatism, which was generally looked on with contempt in Russia. The purpose of intellectual life was not held officially to consist in throwing light on practical problems or assisting in the attainment of social aims, even on a humble day-to-day level. It was strictly confined to furthering the interests of the small ruling group and ensuring that the government encountered no opposition. Religion, learning, and art were turned into surrogates of themselves, with no other purpose than to bar the way to true religion, knowledge, and artistic creativity, all of which require freedom.

The perniciousness of censorship, moreover, is not measured

only by the censors' despotism. The harm goes deeper, rooted for centuries in a distorted view of the nature and function of the creative intellect, conceived by ignorant authority and foisted on society at large. As our censors are devoid *ex officio* of any critical sense, just as eunuchs are deprived of the power of reproduction, they can judge only in terms of the arbitrary external criteria they are duty bound to observe. Even if they were defending the truth, it would be a dead truth, for the simple reason that it could not stand up for itself. Censorship is a diabolical mechanism for chopping up consciousness into bits and pieces which can appear and disappear without leaving a trace. Stuck between its creaking wheels are rags and tatters of ideas, each fashioned blindly to meet the needs of the moment. Censorship distorts the role of historical self-analysis, as the transient interests of the present, conceived in a crudely pragmatic light, are allowed to eclipse and blur the past. Bygone events become as if they had never been, and to know them becomes an error and a crime.

As censorship reflects the attitude of the state toward art and culture and its specific interest in them, and as the state is, in our system, the only active social force, it follows that control by censorship suffices to deprive us of history and put us into a state of suspended animation. Or, as one of Aleksandr Galich's songs about Soviet historians has it: "Words come and go; one truth succeeds another."

According to directives laid down by the Religious Schools Commission in the reign of Catherine the Great, history teachers were to guard their pupils against "criticalism" on the one hand and "systematism" on the other, i.e., the search for a single interpretation of the past. The purpose of teaching history was to elevate the mind and character by proposing time-honored examples of heroism and patriotic self-sacrifice. Even such a liberal-minded contemporary as Nikolay Novikov declared that "moral education is as useful as theories are useless." This view of the use of history is very close to the present-day mania for keeping anniversaries.

If the historian's main duty is to edify, he is bound to misrepresent the past, suppressing facts that would arouse critical comment and emphasizing those that suit his moralistic aim.

He must, as it were, bowdlerize past events for the benefit of the young. This of course falsifies the whole picture, as human beings lead their lives for their own sake and not, as a rule, for the edification of posterity.

The moralizing historian is not interested in the past as it actually was; in fact, the past does not exist for him at all. The men and women of past ages are dead and defenseless against edifying interpretations of their conduct; they can be pushed around with impunity. The historian chooses events according to his moralizing purpose, and forces characters into whatever pattern best suits the requirements of his own day. He does this, moreover, as if the present day were to last forever. The only lesson he draws from the past is that it is vitally important to adapt to the conditions of one's own time. The whole purpose of his work is to conserve the present; consequently, not only is the sense of history lost, but also the capacity for historical action. This view of the historian's task was expressed with commendable frankness by Nicholas I's court historian, Mikhail Pogodin: "Russian history should be made the protectress and guardian of public order."

The effect of this doctrine is to make the student of history an object of education and not a subject formulating his own judgment. This is especially grotesque when the person thus being "educated" is himself a Soviet historian. Whatever his field may be, he is under instruction till his dying day. The value and purpose of his activity are determined beforehand; the substance of his work is prescribed before he sits down to write; he has no need to dig about in archives or consult sources in order to know what his conclusions are going to be.

Historical facts are stubborn, and remain what they are. But if the historian is a state-appointed educator, he can and must be asked what is the purpose of his teaching.

In the nineteenth and early twentieth centuries, we had in Russia a flourishing school of history which, of course, bore no resemblance to the above description. Our greatest thinkers grappled with historical explanations of the country's destiny. An interest in the meaning of Russian and world history was one of the outstanding features of our culture. But unfortunately this wealth of knowledge, while by no means purely academic in itself, was cut off from any practical application and never became the property of society as a whole.

As for Soviet historical science, it has lost all interest in the approach whereby an investigator studies the past for a solution to his own existential problems. The Soviet historian's outlook must be frigid and detached. A dry, unreadable style has become an indispensable mark of scholarship; the exceptions to the rule can be counted on the fingers of two hands. Historians no longer engage in a dialogue with the past or listen to its living voice. They set themselves up as judges or schoolteachers, awarding praise or blame to historical events and passing irrevocable sentences. Irrevocable, that is, for the time being, but liable to be reversed whenever the political wind changes; meanwhile they are pronounced with absolute assurance. Historical figures have to be divided into sheep and goats (though, as a rule, the goats are called sheep and vice versa). The truth is assumed to have been known in advance, and it is only a question of ascertaining who maliciously deviated from it or who, as Lenin said of Herzen, "came right up to dialectical materialism" and then "halted before it."[27]

It must be admitted that this is partly the fault of Marxist methodology, which inherited the Hegelian claim to enjoy the privileged position of the world-spirit in full self-attainment, thus putting an end to history forever. This methodological error, which is also a sin of pride, is all the more natural in those who, by the tradition of their society, were outside history and did not know how to relate to it. It is because of this that they imagine they can make the past conform to their own schemas, as they lightheartedly claim to be independent of history and even to manipulate it at will.

However, one cannot opt out of history, and by losing the sense of a just and harmonious relation to it they have become not its masters but its victims. While imagining that they could skillfully divert its course, they have in fact been swept away by it and are not always able to stay on their feet. A man who lacks an organic sense of his relation to history is incapable of understanding how his own will helps bring about social results which he himself finds intolerably painful. He is in fact no better off than a blind kitten which does not know if it is going to be nursed into life or flushed down the toilet.

This is the consequence of our present stagnation. Our longing for history is a desire for genuine understanding of events, and for some prospect that they may be determined by our own deliberate acts and not by the whims of despotic rulers.

# "We"

It is time to explain the sense—admittedly not a very precise one—in which I have been using the words "we" and "our." It is neither a clearly defined social group nor a party sharing a common world-view or a sociopolitical program. By "we" I mean those of the educated class who are aware of the injury that life has dealt them. Their sense of pain is no longer a blind instinctive craving for immediate salvation or momentary relief. The eternal Russian preoccupation with the "trifles of life" (in Saltykov-Shchedrin's phrase) has given way to deeper anxieties. "We" can no longer adapt to circumstances, because we more or less consciously feel ourselves to be bound by an absolute moral judgment. The pain is compounded by a sense of historical responsibility. "We" are those who have by some miracle escaped from the earthbound relativism of material interests and have discovered that we need to belong to a world of values—that we cannot live outside these, still less in opposition to them.

"We" are the intelligentsia in a specifically Russian sense of this term—that is to say, people who have matured spiritually to the point where they feel obliged to make sense of their lives, and can no longer submit unthinkingly to the lies and hypocrisy of Soviet life.

A similar thought is expressed in a *samizdat* article by O. Altayev entitled "Pseudo-culture and the Dual Consciousness of the Intelligentsia." Altayev writes:

> We hear nowadays of the "Soviet intelligentsia," the "technical intelligentsia," the "creative intelligentsia," and one book even speaks of a "Byzantine intelligentsia." It has become customary to

use the term to denote the whole educated class without distinction, all those engaged in mental as opposed to manual labor. But this is a distortion of the original meaning of the word, which referred to a specific historical event: the appearance in a certain place, at a certain time, of a unique category of men and women who, besides their intellectual qualities, were possessed by a moral passion to overcome the deep disharmony between them and their own nation and state.

I would only add to this that there is also a fundamental disharmony within the intelligentsia itself. But of that, more later.

The important point is that the true Russian intelligentsia, after being crushed and stifled and to a great extent physically destroyed during the recent decades of terror, has arisen from the ashes and is now manifestly alive again. Thanks to its efforts and sacrifices, our stagnant existence has once more felt a faint breath of history, a touch of something unrehearsed and creative, which has already set bounds to the excesses of despotism.

Indeed, not everyone, accepts the truth of this. Solzhenitsyn, in his angry essay "The Smatterers" (*Obrazovanshchina*) in the collection *From Under the Rubble,* denies that the Russian intelligentsia has been reborn or that it is playing the part attributed to it by Altayev and other *samizdat* writers such as Grigory Pomerants. The term "smatterers" (*obrazovantsy*) was introduced, I believe, by Pomerants himself to distinguish the innumerable class of those on whom the Soviet regime bestowed a specialized education so that they might serve it wholeheartedly, from the comparatively small group who have reawakened to the true, free meaning of knowledge and creativity. Solzhenitsyn does not like this distinction, and he uses the term "smatterers" to denote the whole educated class.* Thus to his way of thinking, education and knowledge are negative qualities and have become synonyms of servility to the regime. The possessor of knowledge is automatically guilty, while the ignorant are automatically innocent. I do not know how far this is a personal bias of Solzhenitsyn's, but in any case it follows from his argument.

Solzhenitsyn puts his case as follows:

---

*The word *obrazovanshchina* consists of the word for "educated" with a pejorative suffix.—Translator's note.

It is all very well to charge the working class at the present time with being excessively law-abiding, uninterested in the spiritual life, immersed in philistinism and totally preoccupied with material concerns—getting an apartment, buying tasteless furniture (the only kind in the shops), playing cards and dominoes, or watching television and getting drunk—but have the smatterers, even in the capital, risen all that much higher? Dearer furniture, higher-quality concerts, and cognac instead of vodka? . . . You cannot excuse the central smatterers, as you could the peasants in former times, by saying that they were scattered about the provinces, knew nothing of events in general, and were suppressed on the local level. Throughout the years of Soviet power the intelligentsia has been well enough informed, has known what was going on in the world, and *could* have known what was going on in its own country, but it looked away and feebly surrendered in every organization and every office, indifferent to the common cause.[28]

This seems to me a highly erroneous estimate, and one due to hatred rather than carelessness. The intelligentsia was *not* well enough informed throughout the years of Soviet power; the regime distrusted it and held it at arm's length. Those who were well informed were the higher officials, members of the party apparatus and the security service, none of whom were conspicuously intellectual. The intelligentsia—the thinking part of society—was cut off from events, not in the same way as the peasantry, but because it was prevented from exchanging ideas and information and was atomized by mutual distrust and terror. If the situation has begun to change since the death of Stalin, it is due to the intelligentsia's own efforts and sacrifices in collecting information and "preparing and disseminating" it, to use the highly relevant language of the Criminal Code.[29] On the other hand, ordinary workers and peasants, while they may have been "suppressed on the local level" (as were the intellectuals), had as much knowledge as the intelligentsia of what was going on in the country, and like the intellectuals they constituted a large quota of both victims and persecutors. For Solzhenitsyn will hardly claim that all secret police investigators, all camp guards, informers, party activists, and nameless executors of death sentences, were recipients of university degrees.

In general, the traditional opposition between the intelligentsia and the people lost its significance under the Soviet regime. The destruction of the old privileged classes and the spread of universal education, in which preference was given to people of working-class and peasant origin, wiped out the old distinction between the intelligentsia and others. The leveling of the standard of life was a contributing factor, as the intelligentsia, now largely composed of people from plebeian families, lived in the same conditions and the same communal flats[30] as everyone else. The process of integration was further assisted by concentration camps and the war with Germany. Finally, today students and other intellectuals are constantly recruited into construction gangs, harvesting teams, etc.[31]

Solzhenitsyn himself wrote penetratingly of this phenomenon in *The First Circle,* where he describes the experience of the character Nerzhin, representing himself:

> Unlike his intellectual forebears of the nineteenth-century nobility, Nerzhin didn't have to put on simple dress and laboriously seek a way to the People—he was thrown down among them in the shabby quilted trousers and jacket of a prisoner and made to do his work quota side by side with them. He thus lived their life not as a social superior who had deigned to come among them, but as an equal not easily distinguished from them.[32]

Once the privileges of education had disappeared and there was no longer any reason to feel a guilt complex toward the People, it also became apparent that there was no need to idealize them.

> He understood that he had reached rock bottom—beyond this there was nothing and nobody—and that the People possessed no advantage, no great homespun wisdom. . . . They were, if anything, more apt to be taken in by informers. They were also more liable to fall for the blatant lies told by the authorities and they naively waited for the amnesty which Stalin never gave them—he would sooner have died. If some brute of a camp officer happened to be in a good mood and smiled at them, they smiled back, and they were much more eager for small material things: for instance the sour millet cake occasionally given as an "extra," or a pair of unsightly prison trousers if they looked a little newer or brighter. Few of them had the sort of beliefs for which they would willingly have sacrificed their lives.

The only solution left, Nerzhin now felt, was simply to be oneself.

Once he had got over this latest delusion (though whether it was his last or not remained to be seen), he felt he had arrived at his own original view of the People. One belonged to the People neither by virtue of speaking the same language as everybody else nor by being among the select few stamped with the hallmark of genius. You were not born into the People, nor did you become part of it through work or education.

It was only character that mattered, and this was something that everybody had to forge for himself, by constant effort over the years.

Only thus could one make oneself into a human being and hence be regarded as a tiny part of one's people.[33]

The destruction of the old illusion that prompted the intelligentsia to "go among the people" in search of moral ideals or political support is a new phenomenon, arising from the history of the Soviet regime. It has affected the spiritual and intellectual life of thinking Russians. The new situation was well described by Solzhenitsyn in *The First Circle* and *Cancer Ward*. Like other dissident writers, Solzhenitsyn came to see that in the last resort the problem of freedom comes down to a personal choice, which depends not on social position or whether or not one has a degree, but on "the sort of belief for which one would willingly sacrifice one's life."

In the Soviet system the barriers between classes have been broken down and the "way upward" lies open to anyone who is prepared to display the right qualities. Whether or not we approve of education, we must admit that it is *not* a requisite. This is abundantly proved by the present rulers, who, far from possessing any special culture or knowledge, cannot even speak Russian grammatically. A high rung on the ladder of officialdom is achieved not by being of the right social origin, or by knowledge and ability, but only by the capacity to behave despotically, to love arbitrary power above all things, to admire one's superior despots and serve them with humility, flattery, and absolute devotion.

It is under such conditions that the true Russian intelligentsia has been reborn, with its old virtues of self-sacrifice and a deep sense of responsibility, but without the old naiveté and oversimplification of issues. Is this really a time, then, to appeal to old prejudices?

Admittedly, the intelligentsia so suddenly reborn, like a new element precipitated by a chemical reaction, has tended to disintegrate no less rapidly. In the first place it is spiritually more fragile and transparent than its pre-revolutionary counterpart. This time the dawning sense of history and longing for it have appeared among people who are supposed to be obedient servants of the state like all other Soviet citizens. Inasmuch as the intelligentsia does participate in government it is united with the people. It is only those who delay or refuse to obey who are automatically expelled from the tightly closed social system. Such dissidents are cut off from the "people" by their act of protest—not by compliance with the system.

On the other hand, the mind of the new intelligentsia is not yet fully formed; it is almost childishly naive and inadequate to the bewildering complexity of its prospective tasks. To chafe at the stagnation that fills our lives is by no means to be assured of victory over it. Spiritual resistance begins here, but as yet it is only a feeble shoot that may grow into a mighty tree or wither away to nothing. Today, it must be sadly admitted that the second alternative looks more probable.

But the fault here lies, of course, not with education but with its misuse. It is hard to see how the "beliefs for which we would willingly sacrifice our lives" can be formed in present conditions except by means of knowledge, synthesizing individual experience with that of society as expressed in books and culture. It is knowledge and education that endow us with memory of the past, an impartial and objective sense of history that can serve as a basis for historical action. Unfortunately our mental habits are very different, as a rule. We are unaccustomed to perceiving cultural values in the way appropriate to a normal historical existence. If we are "educated," these values have been reduced to a trivial process of appraising individual items: we take up an object, turn it over, put it down again, utter a sophisticated judgment and pass on to the next thing, as if this exhausted the importance of the book, picture, or play in question.

This, however, is a shallow form of culture. Today's "new

discovery"—which may, in the Soviet Union, be fifty years old or more—gives place to tomorrow's; rather than inner significance or logical development, there is simply the whim of authorities who suddenly decide to sanction this or that. Each new fashion goes its way, leaving no mark on our personality. The trouble here is not that people are "educated" but that they have no substance as human beings. They have no idea that culture has any purpose other than to provide material for chatter.

Another disquieting factor is that members of the new intelligentsia, realizing the overwhelming strength of the prevail- ing despotism, often divert their mental energy to areas as far removed as possible from the dangerous field of social and moral problems. Many cherish the hope, ruthlessly shattered by every- day experience, that they can build themselves a snug little nest in which to live the life of intellectual sybarites. They still imagine that it is possible to take refuge from the vital and challenging problems of society by following agreeable pursuits of secondary importance, harmless to others and without danger to themselves. This is but a fruitless attempt of creative people to adapt to a despotic state that completely prohibits the exercise of creative minds.

I am not advocating a strictly utilitarian view of culture after the manner of Pisarev,[34] nor do I suggest that all scientific or artistic activity must be judged by its immediate fruits. Knowl- edge and creativity are ends in themselves and must be treated as such. But for this very reason they must spring from the depths of our nature and not degenerate into what Mikhail Gershenzon once called "a sterile gluttony of the mind." Cultural gourmandiz- ing, which has been a fault of educated Russians since the eighteenth century, is not an alternative to Pisarev's philosophy but simply the other side of the coin. It results, like utilitarianism, from the introduction of culture into a country where it is alien and not needed for its own sake, and where it therefore cannot take its place in history and influence human life at all levels.

As Yefim Etkind acutely pointed out, the Soviet period has seen a substantial increase in the output of poetry translations, since poets who cannot write and publish as their own inspiration dictates are obliged to turn their hand to something more neutral and academic. This is understandable, but by no means healthy:

not only because it emasculates our culture and wastes our best poetic talent, but because it deprives us of the supreme benefit of spiritual communication and comprehension of the world in which we live. It would be another matter if the flood of translations were a response to our society's real needs and those of its members, so that for one reason or another we needed the works of foreign poets at the present time more than original products of the Russian genius; but this is not the case at all. Our writers and artists adopt particular forms and subjects as an adaptation to circumstances in which artistic creation is impossible.

A well-known Soviet structuralist, justifying his choice of field, remarked: "It's better to write this sort of thing than denunciations." This highly understandable motive no doubt explains the recent flourishing of formalist, abstract branches of knowledge, whose esoteric jargon protects them as far as possible from the chill winds of Soviet life and the heavy-handed interference of dunces from the "party leadership." But the winds continue to blow, and the denunciations to multiply!

It cannot be denied that this is a modern version of the escapism to which Saltykov-Shchedrin drew our attention in the last century, when he wrote: "Our frankness and boldness increase in proportion as the chosen subject is a safer one to discuss freely." The truth of this today can easily be seen by leafing through any number of *Literaturnaya Gazeta.*

In this way we try to cure our spiritual toothache with painkillers, but the ache remains until our teeth decay and the nerve finally dies.

But, I repeat, this is not the fault of education or of "smatterdom"—only of the improper use to which knowledge is put. In secret sorrow at the profanation of knowledge, in the stifling of creative impulses and the humiliation of talent wasted on trifles, there lies a germ of discontent which may yet stir the Soviet system from its stagnation.

Whatever Solzhenitsyn may say about the cowardice, venality, and selfishness of the "central smatterers," and however much truth there may be in his words, when he urges us to "stop taking part in the lie" it is to the "smatterers" that his appeal is chiefly addressed. For whom else would one call upon, as he does, not to write a single sentence that distorted the truth; not to repeat such sentences as a teacher or on the stage; not to parrot quotations from the "leaders"; and not to represent a single false idea in painting, photography, sculpture, music, or any technical form?

Solzhenitsyn's appeal is in fact belated; intellectuals have already seen that they must refuse to acquiesce in the lie, and they have developed an independent, underground culture which conforms to the truth as far as possible. There is no dearth, too, of courageous acts. Those that have challenged the conventionalities of the regime have come precisely from the ranks of the "smatterers"—writers, artists, scholars, and scientists.

The newborn intelligentsia has shown that it is the only possible agent of spiritual transformation in our own time. It alone expresses the pain that our stagnant condition causes all sensitive souls. It is a beneficent pain, refusing to let us rest or forget. It warns us of present peril and demands that we take action. It unites the different phases and aspects of our disintegrating personality, making us realize that we cannot be healthy while any part of our spiritual life is diseased. It reminds us of our vulnerability and of life's wounds.

Pain, in short, is the mainspring of historical life in us. Our longing for history is a sign that neither the "people," the state, the nation, nor any other fetish can satisfy our ardent desire for change if we ourselves remain passive. It has become clear that history can be realized only through our freedom and our conscious choice.

When we have realized that the failures of history are our own failures, and have analyzed their cause in ourselves, the way will be clear for us to go forward. We shall begin with what is within our control, the true soil of freedom, which must come from ourselves and not from outside. But for this we must not only have a critical understanding of history, but feel it to be truly ours.

There is a history to which we belong, the banner is in our hands—the history of Russian culture and of the intelligentsia which has created it and bears it onward.

# CHAPTER III

# State Serfdom

I looked about me—my heart was troubled by the sufferings of humanity. I turned my eyes inward—I saw that man's woes arise in man himself, and frequently only because he does not look straight at the objects around him. Is it possible, I said to myself, that nature has been so miserly with her children as to hide the truth forever from him who errs innocently? Is it possible that this stern stepmother has brought us into the world that we may know only calamities, but never happiness? My reason trembled at this thought, and my heart thrust it far away. I found a comforter for man in himself.

It has often been remarked that this passage from the dedication to Aleksandr Radishchev's *Journey from Petersburg to Moscow,* published in 1790, marks the beginning of the history of the Russian intelligentsia. As soon as it awoke to consciousness, it saw suffering all around it. It saw the poverty of people who could not comprehend their own lives, and it rebelled not only against the existing order but against the victims' acceptance of that order. From this first aversion arose a set of positive values which the intelligentsia took upon itself to defend. These values, not being derived from the surrounding sociohistorical reality, had to be introduced from outside. The intellectuals had to liberate themselves from their surroundings in order to plant the first seeds of freedom; and they had to look to human nature, or rather to their own, for the "comfort" that was manifestly not present in the world around them.

The intelligentsia arose as a specifically Russian phenomenon in this way, and not by simple enlightenment, knowledge, or education. Education and culture were only a background for critical self-examination. Knowledge provided points of reference and criteria outside the closed circle of regimented everyday existence. It widened the horizon. Intellectuals began to understand that the world they lived in was not the only possible one and that its values were by no means indisputable.

This realization soon led to the formation of a particular moral attitude which became the very heart and soul of the intelligentsia. Since education is morally neutral, it may be considered a necessary attribute of the intellectual but one that does not define him completely. In the time of Peter the Great, Western education was officially introduced not for the purpose of creating a sophisticated native culture but in order to "catch up and overtake" Western countries in military and technical fields. Peter's idea was that trained intellectuals should constitute a new category of state servants, no less obedient than the rest. This aim was achieved remarkably soon; but the spread of education had side effects that were not welcomed by the official "civilizers." Knowledge brought with it a desire for spiritual freedom and self-development, which led individuals to step outside the limits assigned to them. As a result they found themselves in conflict both with the authoritarian system and with the rank and file who obeyed it. Thus the essence of the Russian intelligentsia is not its intellectual status but its existential dilemma.

During its history, the intelligentsia took up various philosophical and sociopolitical positions, but it was consistently opposed to the existing order and sought ways of changing it. These often took a political form, but they were inspired by a deeper moral impulse. Human dignity, freedom, and equality were constant elements in widely divergent political programs. The struggle was not merely for local political and social changes. It was far more fundamental, displaying the sublimity of human nature and sometimes its degradation also: Dostoyevsky's *The Possessed* is part of the story, as well as Pasternak's *Doctor Zhivago*.

Until now, however, transient concerns have kept both the intelligentsia and its critics from perceiving the universal meaning of its activity, the fact that its opposition is the "challenge of the spirit." This has only become fully clear in the present period of stagnation: we can see now what intellectuals from Radishchev onward have really had to contend with. To grasp this properly, however, we must shake off the preconception, still held by many, that Soviet and Tsarist Russia have nothing in common. Otherwise we shall fail to understand not only the present spiritual conflict that has brought the so-called "dissidents" into being, but the whole history of the intelligentsia as well. Indeed, neither of these can be fully understood without the other.

Attempts were made before 1917 to define the essence of the intelligentsia. Intellectuals themselves were foremost in this task, but their theories were so numerous and for the most part so one-sided that they generally aroused skepticism. In 1926, Georgy Fedotov began an article entitled "The Tragedy of the Intelligentsia" by explaining to the reader why he was reverting to this well-worn theme. He wrote:

> We who experienced the revolution have a tremendous advantage which is sometimes a sad one—we can see further and more distinctly than our fathers who lived in too great comfort under the old roof. Pygmies though we are, we have been raised to a giddy height—to the height, perhaps, of the cross on which Russia is crucified. . . . Everything the nineteenth century wrote about Russia will be naive from now on, and our history lies before us like virgin soil awaiting the plow.

Fifty long years have passed, and we are the richer for many even sadder experiences. The present has dispelled many ambiguities, and we feel we can understand the past better. Russia appears to us in a clearer light, and so does the Russian intelligentsia.

# Back to the starting point

It is sad to read Fedotov's reflections after his emigration, which seem today too hasty and unconfirmed by experience:

All the descriptions of the Russian soul which were appropriate in the past no longer apply to the "new man," who is quite a different being from his ancestors. He seems indeed to belong to the cultural type which always used to be regarded as the Russian's antithesis and *bête noire*—the German, the European, the "boy in pants."[1] . . . There is no doubt that there has been a profound and sudden change, and the reason is not far to seek. A revolution on the scale of ours could not fail to reverse the nation's idea of itself. No nation can be the same after a revolutionary catastrophe as it was before. A whole historical era is canceled, with its experience, tradition, and culture. A new page of life is turned.

From our present "lofty" historical viewpoint, or rather from the depths of our present decline, it is clear that what Fedotov took to be an undoubtable prediction has simply not occurred. Of course some incidentals of life have changed. People wear different clothes and have different tastes in home decoration. Technology and a different system of production give an illusion of radical change. It is a far cry from the Oblomovs[2] of the past to the pushy, bustling young engineer of the present. These obvious differences have misled both foreigners and many Russians. But the "boy without pants" has come to the fore again, despite all predictions, after every one of our country's upheavals, and his flabby countenance is unmistakably evident today. The "new page" has been turned, even the spelling system has been changed,[3] but the message is still what it was before. Here is what the "boy without pants" (as portrayed by the Russian satirist Saltykov-Shchedrin) has to say:

In our parts, brother, you can't take a step without some rule to it. You feel bored—there's a rule. You're merry—another rule; you want to sit—a rule; you get up—another rule. You can't think, or say a word, without a rule. With us, my dear fellow, even a pimple must itch before it breaks out. And at the end of every rule you either have a switching or are locked up. . . . With us, brother, it's a barren land, but at least it's amusing. . . . You expect crops, and instead you get weeds. Weeds today, weeds tomorrow, the day after tomorrow locusts, and then you have to pay your redemption money. . . . I've heard, whether it's true or not, that you have invented such a piece of paper that wherever you take it they'll at once give you real money for it. . . . And I've invented a piece of paper which says that the bearer will receive from the bank—a slap on his mug. Do you follow me?[4]

What change did the revolution bring about in all this? The old life with its compulsive bragging, its endless regulations and instructions, its semistarvation and perpetual bad harvests and "backwardness of agriculture," its paper money and shortage of hard currency, and all the rest of it—all this, apart from one or two features peculiar to the twentieth century, has repeated itself in the minutest detail, only on a larger scale.

Some "boys without pants" have accused Saltykov-Shchedrin of being overcritical—or, in Soviet phraseology, of "putting too much shadow in his picture."[5] They did so in the past, and they will no doubt do so again. But the depressing recurrence of the phenomena he describes sufficiently justifies his account. The ancient landmarks of the past are increasingly visible behind the specifically Soviet features of our present stagnation. As we saw, people don't remember the past, but it is all the more remarkable that they repeat it, emphasizing every line of the drawing. It is built into our system, like a computer program. One proof of this is that Griboyedov's *The Misfortune of Being Clever*[6] or Gogol's *The Government Inspector* can barely pass Soviet theatrical censorship, and Saltykov-Shchedrin is read nowadays as an antigovernment writer. Are not today's officials the same incompetent, venal bullies as Gogol's Skvoznik-Dmukhanovsky, Lyapkin-Tyapkin and Derzhimorda?[7] The only effect of the revolution has been to render these figures less grotesque and closer to reality.

One sign of the nonhistorical consciousness is that it clothes itself in ever-changing phraseology while remaining essentially the same.

The Russian people have always been obedient to authority and accepting of the status quo. Before and after the revolution their public life has been marked by a show of inviolable unanimity and uniformity. But behind this façade there is a fierce battle of strictly private material interests, with no genuine collaboration for the common good. The general interest is represented by the autocratic state and by it alone; citizens must not "dare to have their own opinion."[8] The logical effect of this divorce between public and private interests is to leave a clear field for arbitrary officialdom.

The days pass in dreary monotony, while the government drones on about its achievements. From time to time material conditions get worse or better, as chance dictates. Life has no meaning other than a fight for material advantages, which inevitably take the form of privileges conferred by the state. The fight is carried on in only one way, by conformity with the political trend of the moment. One's career and one's physical existence depend on being able to adapt at the right moment. One must be on the watch for changes in the official line, and be ready for instant change when the hour strikes. Yesterday you may have had a portrait of Khrushchev over your desk, but to keep it there today would be suicide. Such is the experience of every Soviet citizen.

Vladimir Korolenko (1853–1921) spent his period of exile (the lot of most Russian intellectuals then as now) in a township on the Volga called Balakhna. There he came across a curious item in the local archives. It dated from 1741, when a palace revolution brought Peter the Great's daughter Elizabeth to the throne and deposed the infant Tsar Ivan VI, son of the Duke of Brunswick. This event in faraway Petersburg had disastrous consequences for a merchant named Stepan Pavlov of Arzamas, who had a government concession to deal in salt. He inadvertently accepted a silver ruble bearing the image of Tsar Ivan from one of his customers, and forwarded it to the imperial treasury. As Korolenko observes:

> It is perfectly certain that not a single one of the magistrates, tax collectors, and other officials who suddenly saw the fateful coin imagined for a moment that Stepan Pavlov had the slightest intention of conspiring to restore the Brunswick dynasty. . . . Although everyone concerned recognized that he was absolutely innocent, they nevertheless looked on him as a man who had got caught up in some "secret affair" and was henceforth subject, as by natural law, to the tender mercies of written decrees, instructions from on high, and questioning under torture. . . . And each of them, no doubt, cursed himself for having recently been in touch with the condemned man and therefore being liable to suffer the same mysterious punishment, mindless and soulless as the elements themselves.

Does not this occurrence of two centuries ago remind us of the fantastic absurdity of Stalin's purges?[9] When we were children in the 1930s we used to black out the pictures of yesterday's leaders and marshals in our textbooks, realizing even then that they were liable to bring on us some absurd, unforeseeable, ferocious retribution.

One is not supposed to think at all. Instead of a soul a man must have an empty space, to be filled by orders from above. He will notice the void only now and then, when he feels a wave of causeless grief that he hastens to drown in drink or some unworthy pleasure.

As Dostoyevsky wrote in *The House of the Dead,* "No human being can live without having an aim and striving to achieve it. If he loses that aim and that hope, he may well turn into a monster." But there cannot be hope when a man has no power to effect what he desires. The destruction of hope, which turns life into a viscous, monotonous stretch of time, is perhaps the chief reason why lack of freedom corrupts the human soul. Any period of a man's life which is not consciously related to historical time or devoted to the pursuit of social interests, however humdrum, is psychologically void: days merge into weeks, weeks into years, years into decades. Existence turns into nonexistence, life into death. Moral reactions are blunted, manners become degraded and coarse.

But hope is also empty and deceptive when it becomes obsessed with scrounging small advantages—better living quarters, higher quality food, a less subservient job where one can bully others around. Such hopes provide neither inspiration nor pleasure nor meaning. To achieve such objectives only disheartens us, turns us back on ourselves, and throws us back into redoubled emptiness. By training a man to devote his talents and ingenuity to persecuting others, the system turns him into a monster full of pent-up resentment which sooner or later finds an outlet. (And when this happens to the masses instead of an individual, naive observers who mistake their fantasies for reality call it a revolution.)

People view their neighbors as rivals, if only for an extra corner of the communal kitchen. Instead of cooperating in a businesslike manner, officeworkers form shifting coalitions on a backscratching basis, promoting secrecy rather than fair dealing. Secretiveness is indeed one of the chief characteristics of Soviet man, despite deceptive airs of wearing his heart on his sleeve. Knowing that he himself may be swept away by the whim of a superior at any time, he bears with equanimity the fall of others. Sometimes he may go so far as to rejoice at the opportunity to do himself a good turn by reviling the victim. It is, after all, a kind of consolation to find that others are more wretched and insignificant than oneself—in any case, it may be the only consolation available. "Comrades' courts,"[10] factory and office meetings, and other witch-hunts that fill Soviet life demonstrate the ample supply of those ready to kick an unfortunate victim when he or she is down.

There is, of course, nothing essentially communist in this base, spiritless, corrupting way of life. One may detest communism, without claiming that it necessarily produces social and psychological effects of this kind. The innumerable regulations of Soviet society, including ideological ones, are like a carapace sheltering an amorphous form of life. In the last resort, it makes no difference what ideology a man swears by if it has no real influence on his attitude and inhibits his capacity to make his own decisions. An ideology is useless when nobody can really live by it except the cardboard heroes of hack novelists.[11]

The Croat priest and scholar Juraj Križanić (1618–1683), a forerunner of Panslavism who spent many years in Russia, expressed the opinion that

> the deliberation of the Crown [*kazennaya duma*] is one of the most important institutions for a Slav people. It may be less necessary in other lands, where the people are naturally quick-witted, ingenious, prudent, and industrious. But in the glorious Russian state and in all Slav nations, the deliberations of the Crown are not superfluous but highly necessary and profitable. For our peoples are of a sluggish disposition and do not readily devise anything without orders. . . .
> In this country the Tsar's authority and supreme power can cause anything to be done throughout the land, but in other lands this would not be possible.

This trust in a beneficent state authority is typical of most Russian political theories, including Leninism. The standard-model hypothesis is a state unopposed by individuals or by public opinion, and capable of successfully replacing these on its own initiative. The problem with such theories is that they are mistaken. Implicit obedience conceals an unyielding inertia and enables Russian man to stay the same despite the state's prodding. His outward adaptability is itself an expression of this inertia. As men have found the way to keep temperatures stable in all climates by artificial means, so the Russian has learned the trick of being pliable enough to remain himself—i.e., to survive— despite the regime's indifference to his survival. He has an infinite repertoire of dodges for resisting official pressure. The state is, to him, a ruthless force of nature whose incursions cannot be avoided but must be endured as best as possible.

According to current leaders, who succeed one another by death or palace revolution,[12] various aspects of our social life may change, we may wear different clothes or observe a different etiquette, but moral relationships remain the same. At one time Russians took pride in long and bushy beards, then the beards were pulled and shaved off by the Tsar's order;[13] a century later beards were still regarded as an impropriety,[14] and today there are no words bad enough for those who wear long hair.[15] How much true progress is there in all this? What difference does it make to our hopes, what joy does it bring us?

Our whole existence is preempted by "the trifles of life"—we spend all our time and energy conforming to petty orders and prohibitions (or more likely evading them, as no one could possibly conform to all of them), as an all-wise authority decides what arbitrary restrictions to impose in each particular case. The government responds to what it dislikes by drumming up a regulation backed by a fine or, better still, a substantial prison sentence. If this is not effective (which it never is), the penalty is stiffened. Relaxations introduced from time to time are treated as so much expendable capital, to be withdrawn by way of punishment. The "deliberation" which Křizanić so much admired offers only sanctions, physical or otherwise. The population, of course, is allowed its own arena of arbitrary authority, but this is equalized and held in check by centralized despotism.

Every now and then some event occurs which, in our innocence, deluded by analogies with other countries, we take to be a genuine historical development. But the depths of our social being remain as cold and dark as the cellars of the buildings that proudly cover our land.

Russia was supposed to have been radically Europeanized by Peter the Great's reforms. But three years after his death, the Saxon envoy Lefort compared the country to a ship drifting before the wind and threatened by storms, with a captain and crew either drunk or hung over. "It is amazing," he wrote,

> how this enormous machine can function without effort or direction. Everyone is concerned only with avoiding burdens, no one wants the slightest responsibility, everybody dodges to one side. . . . The huge vessel is allowed to drift at random; no one gives a thought to the future; the crew's only idea, it would seem, is to wait for a hurricane so that they can divide the cargo when the ship is wrecked.

Two and a half centuries later, after a revolution greater than Peter's, these words could have been written yesterday. Lefort's description brings out very clearly the puzzle which Russian "socialism" presents to the world today—namely, why does the system not collapse?

There is indeed an old force which keeps the whole rickety mechanism in balance.

# Three episodes

In July 1618, the Orthodox patriarch Iona called a council to compare amendments made to the Russian canonical texts with the Greek originals. The alterations were made by the monk Arseni Glukhoy and the archpriest Ivan Nasedka. Dionisy, the abbot of the monastery of the Trinity and St. Sergius near Moscow and a national hero in his own right, approved the corrections. The two revisers were perhaps the first people in Russia to teach themselves Greek out of devotion, in order to imbibe Scripture from the fountainhead. Their corrections rectified the manifest errors that had crept into the texts over centuries of copying by scribes who did not understand them properly.

However, the revisers had to contend with the ambitious and

semiliterate Loggin Korova, who had been responsible for the Slavonic texts for forty years and whose ignorance was shown up by the new ones. The council meeting turned into a trial of the revisers, with the result a foregone conclusion: their arguments were ignored and they were deprived of the right to exercise priestly functions. What mattered was not the true meaning of the Greek texts but the revisers' presumption, not in tampering with them but in offending Loggin Korova. Arseni Glukhoy and Ivan Nasedka were thrown into jail, disgraced until a new patriarch was appointed.

Dionisy received what the council considered to be his due for approving the corrections. The fact that he had saved Moscow while acting as the garrison commander and defending his monastery against a six-month-long Polish siege failed to impress the council. He was sentenced to be flogged for forty days and to prostrate himself one thousand times as public penance.

The nineteenth-century poet and essayist Ogarev, writing in *The Contemporary* in 1847, tells a story of the persecution by villagers of one of their number, an honest, sensible, hardworking old man named Panteley. The *mir* (peasant commune)[16] instructed him to take legal action against a local squire's widow over a disputed piece of land. To win the case, it was necessary to bribe some court officials, but Panteley, confident in the justice of his case, refused to do this. He lost. His angry neighbors, acting through the *mir,* exiled him and his family to Siberia. The local police supported, if they did not actually inspire, this "initiative from below,"[17] as they too were indignant at Panteley's refusal to offer bribes. Ogarev continues:

> I asked some of the peasants what they had against Panteley—he wasn't a thief, a drunkard, or a bully! One man replied that he saw no harm in him, but if the *mir* decided on exile that was that. "How can I defy the *mir?"* he said. "If they want to exile him, it's not for me to say anything different. He may be a good man, but I can't go against the *mir.*"

The third episode is taken from issue No. 26 of the *Chronicle of Current Events.* Elena Alekseyevna Kosterina, the daughter of

Aleksey Kosterin (a writer and an Old Communist, who spent many years in Stalin's labor camps), was expelled from the party for "supporting anti-Soviet elements." The *Chronicle,* reporting Elena's expulsion, quoted some statements made by her party colleagues and superiors:

> The chairman of the senior party committee: "Our courts know what they are doing, and you have been defending anti-Soviet people. . . . You mentioned your father, who was sentenced in 1937. Well, he must have deserved it." The secretary of the party bureau: "I haven't read the letters signed by Kosterina, but they defend people who aren't in the clear with the higher organs." A party bureau member: "Solzhenitsyn wrote slanders in *A Day in the Life of Ivan Trofimovich* [sic]. . . . I don't know about Bukovsky, but if he was sentenced it must have been for good reason."
>
> After the meeting at which Kosterina was expelled, people who had been present said: "We don't really know what she was expelled for. She signed some letters or other, but they didn't show them or read them to us. But as the party bureau took the decision, there must have been something fishy about her."

In the three cases above, the accused were obviously innocent, and in all three they were condemned by a collective body: the church, the peasants, or the party. In all three, the collective was surrounded by such an aura of respect and authority that no one dared object to its findings. But in fact these bodies decided nothing for themselves: they only guessed, with unerring accuracy, what their superiors wanted them to do. The collective is a blind instrument of the authorities for bringing pressure to bear on the individual who is impudent enough to display any independence.

In Soviet ideology and official morality, this is called the primacy of the collective over the individual. As we have seen, it is not a recent invention. Under the Soviet regime, however, it has become more blatant and therefore more absurd.

The three episodes I have noted remind us of innumerable sessions of "comrades' courts," party and Komsomol discussions of somebody's "personal record,"[18] and factory meetings at which the person singled out for criticism is invariably condemned unanimously. Stalin called this a system of "criticism and self-criticism,"[19] corresponding to the "politico-moral unity of

Soviet society,"[20] another Stalinist term that is still put to frequent use. Without this historical precedent, the present scale of injustice and denial of human rights in the Soviet Union would be unthinkable.

A man may be in the right, and everyone may know that he had good intentions (or no intentions at all), but once he has been publicly accused and the desire to punish him has been hinted at, he is invariably found guilty. Experience should tell him that it is no use trying to prove he was right or innocent—God forbid! This would be regarded as a sign of arrogance, conceit, and disrespect for the collective, and the punishment would be doubled accordingly. "You think you know best, do you? Just wait—we'll show you!"

The victim's friends, who secretly sympathize with him, will say nothing and will avoid his eyes when they meet. A few of the more decent ones will express their sympathy in private, taking care that no one hears them. Even so, their main concern will be to warn him not to be awkward, to take his punishment humbly and not answer back, or, better still, to thank his comrades for their criticism and to invent additional charges against himself. Meanwhile, his friends will invent crimes to demonstrate their loyalty to the collective and to higher authority by denouncing him. Afterwards, they are free to mumble a few words about "extenuating circumstances."

I remember the case of a fellow student of mine, a young philosopher, who was teaching dialectical and historical materialism at Vladivostok in the early fifties. He was a Latvian whose father, like many of his nationality, had supported the Bolsheviks with arms in the early days. My friend was a party member and was convinced, as many then were, of the absolute validity of Stalin's theory and practice. One day a lecture of his was routinely checked by a censor from the party's district committee, who smelled a rat when he came to a section advising students to read some antireligious satires by Holbach. The censor, evidently a man of little education, thought the name suspiciously Jewish, and concluded—by a strange form of logic, quite typical in an official watchdog of party ideology—that this young lecturer was propagating the views of a "modern Western reactionary philosopher" and an "advocate of imperialism." My friend called the censor an ignorant dolt, which was perfectly true, but, as he did so at a meeting of the district committee, he was ordered to apologize and confess that he had made a grave "ideological error." The committee turned a deaf ear to his explanation that Holbach was an eighteenth-century French writer, an atheist, materialist, and forerunner of the revolution and had, moreover, been praised by the founding fathers of Marxism. My friend, being young, hotheaded, and impeccably honest, stuck to his guns and, as a result, was expelled from the party and dismissed from his job. Protests, complaints, *démarches,* and absurd interviews with overbearing officials undermined his health; he suffered a paralytic stroke, lost the power of speech, and died soon afterwards at the age of twenty-three.

The question arises, what earthly point can there be to these fantastic occurrences? Whose interests do they serve? They cannot be explained by the need to preserve the purity of some orthodox line (the nature of which is pretty nebulous anyway), since many of the victims are as orthodox as can be. They cannot be written off as unfortunate accidents, since the trials and purges of the 1930s are, after all, part of the same phenomenon.

In the twenties, when discussions were still permitted within the ruling party, the rank and file of upstarts and careerists from the lower levels of society showed a complete inability to understand the notion of agreeing to differ. Whichever side was outvoted was expected to do penance at once for its "mistakes." Not only in trifling questions but also on main issues of policy, people who had fervently maintained one viewpoint were obliged, the next day, to think and speak the complete opposite. It was as though no one could or should have an opinion different from that of the majority. This was considered a self-evident moral principle.

Absurdity of this kind has a logic of its own, and may serve a truly practical purpose. Strange, almost ritual procedures are employed to emphasize what Dostoyevsky called "the disgrace of having a mind of one's own." To agree with something obviously just and right is a matter of conviction and nothing to be ashamed of, and it is, of course, only honest to admit one's real errors. But to make people confess absurdities in order to ruin themselves or their friends is a refined educational technique, demonstrating the overwhelming strength of general unanimity and the insignificance of the individual.

The above incidents, and many thousands like them, reflect a distinctive attitude which has been recognized in the past by some as dangerous and, by others, regarded as the outstanding moral feature of Russian civilization. This is the celebrated distinction between "truth" and "justice," both of which are traditionally covered by the Russian word *pravda*. The exaltation of fairness and righteousness over strict pedantic accuracy and practicality was supposed to be a sign of Russian openness, sincerity, and breadth of character. Russia's guilt-stricken intelligentsia felt it was these qualities that made the common people far superior to themselves, infected as they were by Western pride and individualism. This notion was given free play in the Soviet period; it became one of the moral foundations of "socialism." It was so totally accepted and assimilated that its connection with the disagreeable features of Soviet society was not noticed at first.

Today's intelligentsia has emerged as a reaction to these unpleasant features. By the same token, it has come to perceive its genetic link with the old intelligentsia, which was crushed by the same monolithic weight of the "collective," the "masses," the "people."

The destructive aspect of the Russian idea of "justice" was articulated in 1970 by Andrei Amalrik in his brilliant book *Will the Soviet Union Survive Until 1984?,* in which he said (pp. 32–33):

> The Russian people, as can be seen from both their past and present history, have at any rate one idea that appears positive: the idea of *justice.* The government that thinks and acts for us in everything must be not only strong but also just. All must live justly and act justly.
>
> It is worth being burnt at the stake [or burning one's neighbor— B.S.] for that idea, but not for the right to "do as you wish." For despite the apparent attractiveness of the idea of justice, if one examines it closely one realizes that it represents the most destructive aspect of Russian psychology. In practice, "justice" involves the idea that "nobody should live better than I do." . . . This idea of justice is motivated by hatred of everything that is outstanding,

which we make no effort to imitate but, on the contrary, try to bring down to our level, by hatred of any sense of initiative, of any higher or more dynamic way of life than the life we live ourselves. This psychology is, of course, most typical of the peasantry and least typical of the "middle class." However, peasants and those of peasant origin constitute the overwhelming majority in our country.

This leveling-down principle of justice is also the reason why people are ashamed, in Dostoyevsky's phrase, to have minds of their own. A man who thinks and behaves differently from others is *ipso facto* guilty. His attitude is regarded as a sign of arrogance and contempt for others. Usually, such a man knows this, and tries to lose himself in the anonymous mass, which only accepts his repentance and self-negation. Harmony is thus restored, the customary values resume their power, and the cause of anxiety and doubt is removed. But as strong as the leveling principle is, it needs to be constantly corroborated, as it has no inner justification of its own. Repression of those who step out of line animates it, inciting the masses with an urge to destroy out of all proportion to the power of the individual whose freedom is at stake.

The fear of having a mind of one's own is not due to terror and cruelty, but rather creates a climate in which these flourish: it is ontologically prior to them. This is at last clear in Russia now that mass terror is at an end; people are no longer frightened, but are still ready to crush and trample anyone who stands out from the rest. Anyone who lives among ordinary people in the Soviet Union can feel this atmosphere of secret, pent-up rage. Nationalism and xenophobia are not, as some suppose,[21] tokens of spiritual emancipation, but reflect the levelers' hatred of everything that is strange and "different" and that therefore ought not to be. The constant quarrels and fights that break out among neighbors, in families, on the street, at work, in stores, among people of all kinds, drunk and sober, are not symptoms of latent discontent with the existing order, but simply express each person's determination that no one shall be better off than he.

Such is the root of the "meaningless and merciless revolts" of which Pushkin spoke.[22] Such, too, was the origin of our so-called revolution, and of the whole Soviet regime. The Bolshevik revolution, radical and destructive as it appeared, reflected the deeply conservative instincts of the masses, who rebelled in order to stifle the incipient process of capitalist development only to re-enslave the Russian people.

In the social sphere, the spiritual phenomenon of "justice" or "fairness" means the abolition of freedom and the withdrawal of all human rights, starting with the right to move about freely.

# The case of Petr Narkizych

Over a century ago, the brothers Meshkov, two serfs of the squire Petr Narkizych Vonlyarlyansky, gave a cello-and-violin duet in St. Petersburg under the patronage of Schubert. A laudatory critique of the concert appeared in the Paris *Journal des Débats,* noting that the squire had been offered 3,000 silver rubles for the serfs' freedom. The squire was much more impressed by the market value of his property than by the musical talents his serfs might offer the world. He denied that anyone had offered him 3,000 rubles and also stated that he wouldn't have sold the serfs even if such an offer had been made. The reason: he had two daughters who needed to be taught music.

This incident, a curious one for a period as recent as that of Alexander II, was recorded for posterity in Herzen's *The Bell.*[23] Today it seems newly relevant.

Since the Brezhnev regime has been forced to allow greater contact with the West, it has become more widely recognized that Soviet citizens are not free to move about as they wish. Reports that one or another Soviet citizen who was officially allowed out of the country for a limited time has decided to seek political asylum and remain abroad as a "defector" continue to appear in the Western press (not in the Soviet Union, of course). The right to emigrate from the Soviet Union is claimed by Jews, Germans, Armenians, and other national minorities, as well as by some religious sects. Other would-be émigrés resort to hunger strikes, demonstrations, public statements, and the renunciation of Soviet citizenship. None of these methods have as yet made any impression on the government, which is evidently determined to prove that Soviet citizenship is a matter of compulsion and not of choice.

It is remarkable that Soviet authorities think themselves

entitled to keep would-be emigrants at home by force—much like serf-owning landlords. There is little difference, for example, between Petr Narkizych's treatment of his musical serfs and that meted out to the ballet dancers Valery and Galina Panov.[24]

When the diplomats of the first socialist state in the world wrangled with the Americans about the right of Soviet citizens to emigrate, the whole world realized that the USSR was one gigantic, reeking slave market—that serfdom had merely been transferred from a private to a national footing, and that human beings, like all other commodities, were subject to the state control of foreign trade enacted by Lenin in 1918.

Restraints on freedom of movement have also been applied by countries in the Soviet sphere of influence. The establishment of "socialism" in East Germany was marked by the building of the Berlin Wall, which turned several German provinces into a corral for human beings. The frontiers of other "socialist" countries have been closed to their own citizens to a greater or lesser degree. But in these countries the policy is often an imported one. In Czechoslovakia, for instance, this peculiar manner of showing the value placed by the government on its subjects was introduced by invading Soviet tanks.

As children in the Soviet Union, we were taught that "Our frontier is locked and barred." This meant, on the face of it, that we were safe from invasion; but the few who tried to cross the frontier found it barred against them as well. Barbed wire fences, plowed-up zones a kilometer wide for detecting footprints, surveillance assisted by all possible technical methods, guards and guard dogs trained to spring at a human quarry—all this was for fellow countrymen, not for foreigners. To cross the frontier without leave or to refuse to return from a trip abroad is regarded as treason and is generally punished by ten years in a strict-regime camp.

An army of an unknown number of uniformed and plain-clothes policemen keeps a sharp watch over the loyalty of people allowed out of the country, and accompanies them wherever they go. The state demands a firm guarantee that they will return, and, to be on the safe side, it prefers to keep their wives, children, and parents inside the USSR as hostages.

One may well ask by what right all this is done. In any case it indicates that a Soviet citizen's talents, knowledge, and experience—and even his bare physical strength—no more belong to him than do the country's other natural resources. From this viewpoint, the state is defrauded whenever it is prevented from exploiting a man's labor, for which he receives little compensation. Citizens, in short, are nothing more nor less than state property, and we have here nothing more than the old Russian institution of serfdom.[25]

The squires of the old regime are with us no more, and we had imagined that serfdom was abolished and branded as accursed. But the modern counterparts of Petr Narkizych—men from the ranks of the people, direct heirs of the Bolsheviks—are no less convinced of their absolute right to treat people as chattels than was the most hardbitten nineteenth-century squire or nobleman.

Those who do succeed in emigrating are subjected to monstrous levies. An artist is made to pay the full estimated value of his paintings, including those the state would never have bought or allowed him to exhibit. Emigrants may not take with them any of their own papers presumed to have literary or scientific value. Zealous officials compel those leaving the country to redeem their own possessions from the state, if they have any special value or exceed the bare necessities of life. It is as though everything earned or created by citizens of our country is theirs on trust or in a purely symbolic sense. Its real owner is the state, which therefore demands full compensation whenever it loses control over citizens' property or forfeits the opportunity to strip them to the bone.

The robber's maxim "What's mine is mine, and what's yours is mine" is rounded off by the doctrine "And *you* are mine too." The ownership of human beings is the tacit basis of ownership of the work of their hands and brains.

In the same way, Petr Narkizych's musicians belonged to him because they were born serfs of his, on his land. It was gracious of him to let them study the violin and cello instead of plowing fields or waiting at table. If he put up with their sawing and scraping it was probably not from love of art but to improve his daughters' chances in the marriage market, and who could blame him for this parental solicitude? If he had taken the 3,000 rubles it would have been no more than his due, but he was entitled to calculate whether or not it was more in his interest to keep the men in his service.

Today's Petr Narkizyches, it is true, are in a somewhat different position, for it is the state and not they who own the serfs. Art, we are told, "belongs to the people,"[26] but only in the sense that artists themselves are public property, lock, stock, and barrel. Not only artists but scholars, doctors, engineers, and every Soviet man, woman, and child are socialist-owned. As Stalin said: "Our most treasured capital consists of people."

But does not this simply mean that the serf-owning system has become public instead of private? Is so-called "socialism" anything but serfdom in the name of the state? And is it better or more humane for "souls" to be owned by the state instead of by private individuals? Very probably it is worse. First, landowners under the old regime were not themselves serfs, and we must admit, whether we like it or not, that if there had not been a privileged landowning class we would not have had Pushkin, Lermontov, Tolstoy, or Dostoyevsky. The whole country would have been a single, ignorant, downtrodden mass, held in subjection by corporal punishment, and Russian culture would not have developed.

But this is not all. In former times there was usually a patriarchal and personal relationship between the squire and his human property. At the very least he had a material interest in seeing that his serfs remained healthy and industrious, that they did not starve or drink themselves to death or turn his land into a wilderness. If a landowner abused his power, the state could intervene. Today, when everyone is equally deprived of rights and freedom, people are wholly dependent on a bureaucracy as slavish and irresponsible as themselves. While the state, in the abstract, still has a vested interest in the production of its subjects, individual bureaucrats do not; so even the personal, patriarchal ties of feudal times rarely develop.

# State serfdom in Russian history

State serfdom preceded serf-owning by the gentry as a Russian institution. From the creation of the Muscovite state in the fourteenth century, the Grand Duke, Tsar, or Emperor directly owned all the State's territory, natural resources, and population. It was only later that he began bestowing parts of this wealth on the nobility. Properly speaking, the system had little in common with Western feudalism. The landowners' right over the peasants was consolidated only in the eighteenth century, at the very time that feudalism was declining in the West. Russia was and remained the Tsar's "patrimony." It was not mere Oriental rhetoric when his subjects—peasants, townsfolk, craftsmen, and merchants, even boyars—described themselves as the Tsar's "bondsmen."

Alessandro Guagnini, an Italian in the Polish service who spent some time in Russia during the reign of Ivan the Terrible (1533–84), gives a foreigner's view of the salient aspects of Russian medieval society:

> The whole nobility, lords and commanders, boyars and officials, consider themselves bondsmen, that is wretched and humble servants of the grand duke, and acknowledge that all their personal property, movable and immovable, is in fact not theirs but his.

The nineteenth-century historian Sergey Solovyov comments as follows on pre-Petrine Russia:

> In a state of vast extent, but empty and poor in resources, it becomes the government's chief preoccupation to ensure a supply of manpower, of manual and industrial labor. Men must be pursued if necessary and attached to the soil so that they may work, earn a living, and pay taxes. It is easy to see the result of this situation. While the government hunted down the common people and did its best to tie them to one place so that they would pay dues and perform heavy services without reward, the oppressed worker was dominated by the desire to escape taxation and compulsory service at all costs.

The system of private serf-ownership evolved in Russia because the government was incapable of making laborers stay in one place and pay required dues and services. For centuries the government's main function was war: all its strength and resources were spent first in warding off surrounding enemies and later in steady territorial expansion. Little was left for administration, which was always a weak point of the Russian system.

Placing peasants under landowners' control was a way of coping with the centuries-long arms race.

Meanwhile, a senseless miserliness became an established trait of the national character. The state's consuming military interests led it to ignore the vital needs of an enslaved populace, leaving people with a sense that they did not control their own affairs. Life was precarious and provisional, and active and enterprising citizens felt an urge to go off "into the blue." These fugitives from government control sought the outlying territories of the state. It was chiefly in these desolate areas, exposed to marauding nomads, that the first Cossack border settlements were established.

State debtors who concealed their revenue were beaten until they disgorged; provincial governors who embezzled tax revenues were dismissed from their posts, flogged with the knout, and sometimes beheaded. But even such ferocious measures had little effect. The society's poverty was reflected in the weakness of the state, which fell further and further behind the thriving nations of Western Europe.

In due course, therefore, the government resolved to create a privileged class that would live off poor peasants, governing and despoiling them as it chose. The privileged class would be responsible to the Crown for the payment of dues and services. Originally the members of this class were granted lands and serfs for their lifetime only, in return for "services" which the state had no other means of obtaining. But as the system grew, as the Crown's possessions increased and conditions became more complex, the reigning sovereign granted land and serfs according to his or her own predilection, while the privileged class was freed from any obligation to serve the Crown. In the eighteenth century the nobility was also granted exemption from corporal punishment.

Another effective means of enslavement, moral rather than physical, was the onus of "group responsibility." Peasants, townsfolk, and merchants were classified for tax purposes into groups of several individuals or households, and each group was collectively responsible for the payment of dues and services to the state. If a member of the group evaded his obligation by fraud or by running away, the additional burden fell on his neighbors.

Thus arose the typically Russian idea of the "commune," in which the group answers for the individual and vice versa. To evade one's proper "load" was unfair not only to the state but also to one's peers. It became a high moral duty to see to it that no member of the group stole, ran away, or otherwise shirked his duty.

This sense of communal solidarity led to the specific concept of "justice" described by Amalrik, and is linked with both good and bad features of the Russian character. It discouraged cupidity and selfishness, but it made a virtue of tattletaling: a man who informed was performing a public duty, helping to defend the interests of the collective and of the state.

The result has been the precise reverse of democracy. For the purpose of "initiative from below" is not to defend the individual's interests but those of the state against him. Without Russia's historic predisposition to informing, it would be hard to account for the success of the Soviet system today.

The historian P. Milyukov described the situation in former days as follows:

> An individual is outside the government's power until it succeeds in placing him in "firm hands"; it can have no serious relations with him except as a member of a group. The system of collective responsibility is used whenever the individual is to be bound by some obligation toward the state. Even when the government wishes to lay some special obligation on the whole people, it can find no better way than to exact a collective guarantee from the people's representatives composing the national assembly. That is why these representatives are not delighted with their task, and look on it as a heavy obligation rather than a right.

The heavy shackles of serfdom would have been thrown off sooner were it not for the moral attitude on which the system rested. Dues and obligations were moral duties, endurance the greatest virtue; evasion was considered a low trick, even by the evaders themselves. The crude simplicity of basing taxation on the number of "souls" was allied to a sentimentality that prompted victims to kiss the rod. The Tsar's power or that of the landowner, like Soviet power today, was thought of as paternalistic rather than as self-serving. Land-bound serfs leading regulated lives were expected to bear their cross without murmuring and to work hard for their country's good. Submissiveness put up with cruelty; anxiety excluded sympathy; justice was considered the equal distribution of inhuman conditions.

This is the background of the peculiar Russian attitude toward those who flee the country. At all times liable to severe punishment by the state, they are also morally condemned by their fellow countrymen.

Prince Kurbsky, who fled from Ivan the Terrible, wrote to the Tsar in 1578: "You shut up the kingdom of Russia—in other words, free human nature—as in a fortress of hell; and whoever . . . goes from your land to strange countries . . . you call a traitor; and if he is caught on the frontier, you punish him with various forms of death."[27] Kurbsky may perhaps be called the first Russian political émigré. In any event, his letter could have appropriately been addressed to Brezhnev four hundred years later; only the archaic Russian would have to be modernized.

From earliest times, serfs and noblemen alike were forbidden to emigrate. The very desire to go abroad was a sign of "corrupting" Western influence.[28] In the reign of Aleksey Mikhailovich (1645–76), the omnipotent minister Ordyn-Nashchokin had a son who refused to return from his studies in Poland; the minister was so ashamed that he immediately offered his resignation. The Tsar refused to accept it, which is more than Brezhnev would have done; but the story illustrates the general Russian opinion of "defectors," then as now.

Later, in the nineteenth century, complicated formalities and strict government control inhibited foreign travel. Pushkin himself was unable to obtain permission to visit Europe.

The prohibition or severe restriction of foreign travel is based on the same philosophy as serfdom. It is also a way of attaching people to the soil—not to a particular scrap of territory, but to the "motherland" itself. This is the prime manifestation of state serfdom, applied to Russian nationals of all classes and circumstances. Legislative measures on this subject are based on a supreme moral principle requiring devotion to the state and absolute willingness to bear its burdens.

The nineteenth century witnessed the struggle against landowning serfdom, regarded as the root cause of Russian despotism and slavery. The gross inequality which gave some men complete control over the lives of others was regarded as the nation's chief disease by thinking people from Radishchev onward. Even after Alexander II emancipated the serfs in 1861, the reactionary waves that erupted from time to time, the repression of personality and freedom, the government's inability or unwillingness to rule by law, were all attributed to the fact that emancipation had been incomplete. People forgot that the right of landowners to possess serfs was only one consequence of an older Russian tradition of state serfdom. The liberation itself was legally possible only because of the Tsar's unlimited power over landowners and serfs alike.

State serfdom was taken so much for granted that it was scarcely criticized even by the most radical thinkers. In opposition to Western egoism and individualism, traditional bugbears of Russian thought, the Slavophiles advanced the principle of *sobornost'* (a word with religious overtones meaning "community" or "collectivity"), while the Westernizers put their faith in the village commune (the *mir* or *obshchina*) as a harbinger of socialism. Neither side realized that both these typically Russian concepts involved a latent danger to freedom. The revolutionaries hoped for a rapid transition to socialism, bypassing capitalism, bolstered by surviving communal traditions. They did not foresee that this socialism would only be a new and all-embracing form of state serfdom. They hoped to use the coercive power of the state to eradicate oppression once and for all, not realizing that oppression had been the work of the Russian state from time immemorial.

It is true that in the decades after 1861 Russia experienced an increase in private ownership which should have made the individual more independent of the state and furthered respect for the rights of man. But this trend ran counter to deep-rooted moral ideas and aroused mistrust on both the extreme right and the extreme left. On Russian soil, property relationships easily resulted in persecution, by such characters as Saltykov-Shchedrin's Razuvayev and Kolupayev, of the weak and needy. The fat-bellied merchants who were yesterday's serfs still had a slave mentality and took delight in overreaching others. The power of property atomized Russian society and loosened it from its moorings. One symptom of this was the behavior of manufacturers and contractors who supplied the army with shoddy uniforms, tainted provisions, and defective weapons. A Russian who made money and who felt control slackening proceeded immediately to rob the state, as he had been accustomed to do throughout the years of serfdom.

Attempts at constitutional reform during this period were also halfhearted. The idea of a plurality of parties, with competition of interests regulated by law, was alien to the traditional feeling that there was only one "justice" and that it was guaranteed by the leveling influence of an autocracy. The notion of trial by jury also felt foreign. Court pleadings by opposing parties were generally ridiculed[29] and were regarded as a weakness of government and of the judiciary. Many thought then, as they do now, that it is better to thrash a suspect than handle him with kid gloves and encourage him to further mischief. The government's timid steps toward liberalization resulted in outbursts of dangerous anarchy. Constitutional reform was immediately followed by a "meaningless revolt" (to use Pushkin's words again). The efforts of the constitutionalists were doomed to failure. They were condemned as foreign eccentrics, and their reforms collapsed.

What Russia unconsciously longed for was not popular initiative, democratic freedoms, constitutional principles, and the rights of man, but a strong authoritarian government which would firmly grip everything and everyone, as it had under strong autocracy. The Romanov dynasty fell, not because it ruled harshly but because Nicholas II did not have sufficient force to inspire terror. Without realizing it, Russia was looking for a form of national organization in which a modernized state system would enlarge the scope of serfdom and ensure that its burdens rested equally on all citizens.

# "Justice" in action

It is not hard to see that, in practice, the October revolution reversed every single tenet and prophecy of Marxism. The last thing it can be blamed for is dogmatism. For instance, it boldly asserted the primacy of politics over economics, subjecting the whole life of the country to the maintenance of Bolshevik power. Its heirs today are naively convinced that the "masses," whom they continue to flatter in Marxist style with the title of "makers of history," are influenced by opinions, and that these opinions are formed by skillful propaganda. At any rate they have been unable to find a more scientific explanation of what happened in Czechoslovakia in 1968 or Hungary in 1956. The scientific-objective rhetoric of Marxism has been battered by the storms of history. There is little left of it but prolix, empty phraseology preserved, in simplified form, only because no one is clever enough to revise it.

But the heaviest blow to the Marxist philosophy of history stems from the fact that the Russian revolution was inspired by formulae and slogans that failed to express the actual sociopsychological circumstances and traditions of Russia. The Russian consciousness, or rather the archetypes of its subconscious, proved much more decisive than economic factors, relationships of production, and so on. The latter turn out to be expendable considerations.

Despite its internationalist claims, the Russian revolution is a purely national affair. Even in foreign affairs it soon adopted the imperialist aims of Tsarism and became a military threat to Europe once again. The claim to the Straits, it appears, has been dropped for the time being;[30] but Poland has been subjugated once again, together with half of Germany and a large part of the Balkans which the Tsars had never successfully obtained. As Berdyaev remarked, the dream of the "Third Rome"[31] has taken on modern shape in the Third International, the idea of Russia as the fatherland of workers everywhere.

Russian "socialism" is so specifically Russian that it is hardly exportable to other countries without the aid of tanks: the "Prague spring" is convincing proof of this.

It is true that in China, Cuba, and Vietnam there have been spontaneous developments resembling the Russian variety of "socialism." But, in the first place, even in these countries there was a measure of Soviet support, and, in the second, we may suppose that the Russian variety is attractive to backward countries that have never known democracy. This idea has been developed by Grigory Pomerants in an interesting *samizdat* article entitled "The Modernization of Nonwestern Countries."

In any case, the last few decades of Russian history seem to have shown that no single historical pattern applies to all societies, as Marx supposed. It has also become clear that as long as a nation's consciousness and social psychology remain stable, the objective parameters of its communal existence will be stable also. Historical circumstances may upset a nation's psychology, but it will always reassert itself, like a weighted doll returning to the vertical. The nation's fate is rooted in its consciousness, its character and spiritual substance. People arrange their lives to suit themselves, and from the way they live one can judge what they are.

This would have been unquestionable were it not for the hypocritical use of communist slogans. Their true meaning has been lost. But this humbug is possible only because of Russia's tradition of indifference to politics and political principles. They are regarded as concerns of higher authority, and if we are ordered to parrot a set of slogans with tears of rapturous sincerity, we will do so; but life will go on in the old customary way.

I know that these remarks will displease not only the paid ideologists of the Soviet regime, but also many of its opponents. I may even be accused of slandering the Russian people, or, at best, taking a fanciful and pessimistic view. But a writer should not write according to what he imagines his readers' reaction will be. Moreover, the idea of national repentance, currently popular, cannot bear fruit without a clear notion of what the Russian people are to blame for. Certainly it would be futile to start by flattering their national vanity. The blame is in fact enormous, and there are no other shoulders to shift it onto. Both in the past and at present, Russia and the Russians have committed plenty of disgraceful acts, and in the future they may commit many more. Rather than whitewash our country's faults, we should do our best to understand them fully. In all honesty I see no way out, and certainly no room for optimism, except through repentance based on critical self-analysis.

The more superficial kind of Sovietology emphasizes the conscious villainy and deceitfulness of the leaders of the October revolution. But it must be acknowledged that they were more followers than leaders, agents and interpreters of the deep-seated desires latent in the national subconscious. They did not swim against the tide of national feeling, but rather enabled it to display its full potential. Their chief aim was to create and maintain an all-powerful, irresponsible, terrorist system of authority, without which the country would probably have fallen into anarchy and chaos. Such slogans as "All land to the peasants" or "Rob those who have stolen from you" were of course demagogy; but demagogy expresses the instincts of the masses and gives them an outlet.

In the early days of the Soviet regime, an intelligent opponent of it, Vasily Shulgin, realized that its victories and power were due to the Bolsheviks' flexibility and their success in putting White ideals into practice better than the Whites themselves could. In his book *The Year 1920* Shulgin wrote:

> They [the Reds] understood that the army had to be an army without committees, without "spontaneous discipline"—in short, an army on "White" lines. . . . And they re-created the army. . . . That was the first thing. . . .
>
> We [the Whites] had a single important slogan, the unity of Russia. . . . And who understood its importance, who raised the banner aloft? Outlandish as it may seem, it was the Bolsheviks. They didn't say so openly, of course, and they don't now. Lenin and Trotsky keep on ranting about the International, and the communist army is supposed to have been fighting to establish "Soviet republics." But that is all for show. . . . In actual fact their armies fought the Poles because they were Poles and had invaded Russian territory. And the third thing the Reds took from us was the principle of one-man rule. At the big Moscow conference in August 1917 they talked about the dictatorship of the proletariat and we said: "Rubbish—you can't govern by committees at a time of war and revolution." And, sure enough, it has come out our way.

Soviet power has in fact achieved what the Tsars tried and failed to do. Peasant risings have been crushed; strikes have been dealt with so firmly that no one dreams of trying them anymore. And all this is so that national resources can be concentrated on piling up armaments. As in former times, the main purpose of the

Russian state is foreign conquest: external successes console the masses for all their suffering and sacrifice. As Shulgin also observes:

> The International has become an instrument of Moscow's territorial expansion to the utmost limit, that is to the point where it encounters real resistance from other state organisms of sufficient strength. Such will be the natural frontiers of Russian power.

In a blind, groping, unconscious manner, without any theoretical formulation, we have reached the point where Russia consists only of the authorities on the one hand and obedient millions on the other. Internal policy is founded on the "pursuit of manpower"; all human activity is reduced to serving the state; no classes have any rights, for "no one is indispensable," as Stalin said. This is the acme of state servitude, and the essence of stagnation à la Brezhnev.

It cannot be proven logically that Russian communism is the only variety possible, or that any country aspiring to socialism must follow the Russian path. Some anti-Soviet Russian writers are inclined at present to blame everything on communism and on Marx, the German Jew, but this is only another instance of the "Mitrofanism" that shrinks from self-examination.

To tell the truth, however, this argument applies to the details of Marx's philosophy of history rather than its essence. The fact that the Russian experiment took a strictly national form does not speak in favor of communist theory. Its Russian peculiarities are invoked to save the honor of a bloodstained Marxist banner. The Russian experience moreover has demonstrated the danger of playing about with history in the name of rationalism and revolution. Precisely when the Marxist-Leninists thought they saw clearly what they had done and why, they were swept away in a completely different direction.

Ideas, according to Marx, become a material force when they gain possession of the masses. In practice, however, it turns out that the masses take over the ideas and not vice versa. The flood of tradition moves steadily along its own course, sweeping away ingenious plans of social reconstruction. Communism, by destroying private property and with it every source of personal activity and resistance, leaves society defenseless against blind, elemental instincts. The results, inevitably, are far from what communist theory intended: a victory for all the irresponsible forces, hostile to freedom, that have brewed within the dark consciousness of the oppressed Russian masses for centuries.

One of the regime's first measures was to nationalize land and turn it over for the "use of all those who cultivate it." The "survivals" of landlord serfdom were liquidated, as was the landlord class. Their physical extermination ensued. Brought up to believe in their own privileged position, the nobility could not accept the introduction of common lawlessness. Its pretensions to a higher status aroused a popular fury totally out of proportion to the material differences between the classes. The landowners were destroyed in the name of the sovereign principle of universal equality, so as to restore the country to its old, "pure" condition as a patrimony of the state. It may also be noted that the hue and cry in those early days was aimed against the culture of the upper classes—that is to say, to virtually all of Russian culture.

The peasant class, having acquired land, began to prosper and develop a spirit of independence. This meant that it, too, was ripe for bloodletting. The villagers soon found that their right to the land was of a rather symbolic character: they might cultivate it as much as they liked, but without being paid the value of their produce; the true landowner was the state, which had grown strong enough to take what it wanted and give nothing in return. Remarkably, the peasants themselves entered with enthusiasm into the process of "dekulakization" (elimination of the kulaks, the more affluent peasantry): they looted one farm after another, reduced their neighbors to destitution, and made use of the stolen property with no pangs of conscience. If anything, they objected to a prosperous peasant more than to a landowner: "Who does he think he is?" The party fomented jealousy by distinguishing among "kulaks," "middle peasants," and "poor peasants." It became worth one's life to have one sheep more than one's neighbor. Envious peasants could be relied on to underrate their own wealth and exaggerate that of others.

The "liquidation of kulaks as a class" paralleled the creation of collective farms. These were an up-to-date version of the *mir,* complete with enforced taxation and services, and with the inevitable "collective responsibility." Now, as before, peasants had no incentive to till the land properly, and were tempted to run away from the collective and seek their fortune elsewhere. The Bolshevik land reform culminated in tying peasants to the soil. Their passports (without which no Soviet citizen can change his job or place of residence) were confiscated, and they were forced to deliver produce to the state virtually without payment.

The old system of landowners' serfdom was sustained as long as possible, abolished only when it proved unsuited to intensified agriculture. Now the country returned to an even more primitive system, which irreversibly tended to reduce productivity to zero. In former times, low productivity had worried both landowners and the state, but now nobody cared.

The purely Russian character of the collective farms is evidenced by the fact that they have been disbanded by communist rulers in some parts of Eastern Europe. In Russia, "socialism" is unthinkable without collective farms or state farms.

In the towns, the new regime energetically proceeded to eliminate large-scale and then small-scale private property. Using fanciful communist phraseology, it represented all this as a policy designed to produce a universal proletariat. The class which, as we know, has "nothing to lose but its chains," has no property but its own two hands and becomes completely dependent on its employer, in this case the state. In Marx's romantic view, the proletariat would throw off this abject status by means of revolution, rather than reducing the whole of society to it. The worship of proletarianism as such is a long way from Marxist orthodoxy. However, in the Soviet system everyone was successfully proletarianized and stripped of all means of defense against authority. This is what Stalin meant when he said in 1936 that the "building of socialism" in the Soviet Union was at last completed.[32]

According to Stalin's well-known theory, a socialist society is one in which private property has been eliminated and only state property remains. The state is fully protected against internal competition or the growth of independent forces within its borders. It may reward or punish, execute or pardon, give to its subjects or take away from them, with impunity. Rank-and-file citizens are treated like small children, led by the hand; to the end of their days they remain objects of "communist education" by party careerists, and are expected to be grateful for this fatherly care.

For the benefit of those who condemn Marxism because it leads to tyranny—i.e., who take the word of modern tyrants that they are true Marxists—and also for those who ignorantly assume that Marx is an obscure writer, it should be pointed out that Marx himself would have described Soviet-type communism as "crude and thoughtless." He foresaw that communism was liable to take this form in any backward country. The following accurate prediction comes from his *Economic and Philosophical Manuscripts* of 1844:

> This communism, inasmuch as it negates the personality of man in every sphere, is simply the logical expression of the private property which is this negation. Universal envy constituting itself as a power is the hidden form in which greed reasserts itself and satisfies itself, but in another way. The thoughts of every piece of private property as such are at least turned against richer private property in the form of envy and the desire to level everything down; hence these feelings in fact constitute the essence of competition. The crude communist is merely the culmination of this envy and desire to level down on the basis of a preconceived minimum. It has a definite, limited measure. How little this abolition of private property is a true appropriation is shown by the abstract negation of the entire world of culture and civilization, and the return to the unnatural simplicity of the poor, unrefined man who has no needs and who has not even reached the stage of private property, let alone gone beyond it.
>
> [For crude communism] the community is simply a community of labor and equality of wages, which are paid out by the communal capital, the community as universal capitalist. Both sides of the relation are raised to an imaginary universality—labor as the condition in which everyone is placed and capital as the acknowledged universality and power of the community.[33]

Whatever the flaws in Marx's theory, it is an undeserved insult to place him on a level with the present leaders of the Soviet communist party. And those who criticize him without taking the trouble to read and understand him have, alas, too much of the purely Soviet spirit.

The Stalinist liquidation of private property led the whole

Russian populace to become the state's property. To follow up its victory, the state has perfected a system of restricting people to a particular residence and job. This system goes unmentioned in the extensive propaganda and posters that attract credulous foreigners. It is stipulated, for the most part, in secret instructions, for punitive rather than informational purposes; but it strictly regulates the life of every citizen from the cradle to the grave. It lies at the foundation of common law and the Soviet way of life, and is much closer to the nature of our "socialism" than, for instance, the Constitution now in force.[34]

During the decades of "education," it was forcefully established that everyone must work for the state. Forms of activity that fail to bring the state any revenue or other advantage, that are not dictated by it and take place outside its control, are branded as immoral and illegal. All private initiative is banned. Outside observers often do not notice this, and the great uncritical majority regard the absence of private initiative as natural.

To obtain a residence permit anywhere, a citizen must produce a certificate of employment from some firm or institution (all of which are, of course, state-owned). However, a place of residence, registered by the police, is a prerequisite for obtaining a job. Passports are essential to all this; governed by intricate regulations, they control freedom of movement and the right to take a job. Besides a passport, everyone must also hold a "labor booklet" in order to work. It contains a record of all his breaches of labor regulations, and any commendations he may have earned. He may be dismissed from his job as punishment for any transgression. This diminishes his chances of finding another job. The personnel department of every institution is under the direct control of state security organs, which ascertain that management conforms strictly to instructions. In this way, too, the state can victimize any individual secretly. In addition, "cadre policy" is an important part of party organization work, and controls the fate of party members and nonmembers alike. Unions are organized to support repressive measures of the administration. The co-opted unions would be a most unlikely forum for opposing such measures—should anyone conceive of the idea.

Factories and offices function as arenas for supervising the conduct of employees. They are held on a tight rein by the "collective," which is in turn responsible for the good behavior of its members. If its attitude is too lenient, punishment is meted out by higher authority on the refractory members and, if necessary (but it seldom is), on the collective itself and especially on its administrative staff. These administrative "responsible workers" have to answer for what goes wrong. Their careers hang by a thread, and the higher their position, the harder they fall. Everyone is bound hand and foot by "collective responsibility," and all live under the threat of a lockout by the state, an incomparably stronger weapon than is possible under capitalism. Dismissal means the loss of livelihood and of all social rights; the victim becomes a pariah and an outcast, at the mercy of bureaucratic harassment. So a worker shelters himself within the collective. A man's heart beats faster when, though himself a nobody, he partakes in the collective right to instruct, punish, and reward.

The complete absence of liberty is complemented by criminal sanctions for breaching labor discipline. These regulations reached a ferocious peak under Stalin and are now gradually being revived. Pay deductions, dismissal, and finally imprisonment as a penalty for being late or absent or for trying to change jobs—all these are integral parts of the "socialist organization of labor." In the past few years the state has made concerted efforts to prevent what it calls "labor leaks"—attempts by manual and office workers to change their place of employment. Regardless of the lessons of history, fresh attempts are being made to keep the population under a "firm hand." Special regional labor commissions have been established to keep track of individuals' residence status, and deal with them if they persist in trying to evade restriction to a particular job.

The system of state servitude is completed by Soviet prisons, now called "corrective labor institutions," in which the compulsion to work is reinforced by starvation and other physical mistreatment. The mass arrests of Stalin's day were at times indistinguishable from the wholesale conscription of labor. The belief that the state has unlimited authority to compel citizens to work wherever it chooses created a special moral atmosphere in favor of mass repression. Slave labor in concentration camps was condoned by the same peculiar sense of "justice" or "fairness" that has already been considered.

I began to understand this after a chance conversation in a restaurant with a friend and a fat-cheeked elderly man who sat down at our table. My friend and I had been talking about the terror and the Stalinist camps, and continued despite the newcomer's presence. Suddenly he interrupted and told us, sipping his beer the while, that he had been a camp commandant in Siberia. He was now retired on a pension and our talk about the camps was nonsense, he told us. He evidently had the subject much at heart, and, once begun, there was no stopping him. We listened in fascination: up to then we had only known in theory that murderers were living among us, but here was a living specimen. The ex-commandant evinced neither shame nor the slightest pang of conscience. The burden of his song was: "Of course, you understand the times were difficult—war, famine, enemies all around; things were grim, but they were just." To prove this he told one anecdote after another. There was one old painter, for instance—he had forgotten the man's name, but he must have been quite well known in the old days. He knew Chaliapin and people like that. The commandant at first thought the man was putting on an act—prisoners are fond of showing off—but he gave him paints and canvas to try him out and told him to do a portrait of Gorky. Sure enough, he turned out an excellent likeness. The commandant then ordered a portrait of himself and, when this task was completed, transferred the old man to the political section of the camp. There he got extra rations for painting slogans and posters urging the prisoners to work harder. This saved the man's life—outdoor work would have finished him off in no time. Not that outdoor labor was so bad, as long as people fulfilled their work quota. The quotas were stiff, certainly, but it was all for the country's good. But there was no nonsense with shirkers—they went right into the cooler, and that was certain death: an unheated concrete cell, 60 degrees below zero Fahrenheit, no food for two or three days, and no warm clothing. The prisoners didn't complain, though—they knew it was fair, and there weren't any alternatives. And now, this double-dyed murderer blandly informed us, should he chance to meet one of his ex-prisoners on the street, they would fall into his arms as if he were their own father. Maybe he was romanticizing here a bit, I don't know, but what amazed us was his assurance that he deserved their affection because he had treated them fairly. He could look back on a life of honest service, enjoy a generous pension, and dig into his shishkebab with a healthy appetite. As for us two "depraved" intellectuals, the food stuck in our throats. . . .

The same despotic idea of justice underlies Khrushchev's law on "parasites."[35] It was clear to lawmakers that anyone who wouldn't work for the state deserved short shrift—why should some have to work and others not? It isn't enough to pay taxes, the government demands service as well. That a man should venture to work for himself or—as a writer or artist might put it—for eternity was a crime requiring no further testimony. A man is equally blameworthy if he loses his job out of carelessness or because of official harassment. There are no unemployed with us; the government has work for all. "Parasites" are exiled to distant areas and work at jobs that bear no relation to their tastes or abilities. Physical work is ennobling. Artists and scholars will be all the better for mucking out cowsheds. The state, in fact, treats "idlers" exactly as the squire used to treat a good-for-nothing serf—by packing him off (as allowed by law) to a penal settlement.

The double system of regimentation by passport details and labor record has been increasingly used since Stalin's death as a less odious and shocking method of inspiring terror than penal sanctions, but one that is equally effective. It ensures an unremitting watch on every citizen. Fear of losing a job and residence permit explains why Soviet people display an otherwise incredible degree of conformity. The system is taken fatalistically for granted, like the Russian winter, and everyone's energy, initiative, and ingenuity are absorbed by the task of adjusting to it. The resulting network of interlocking arrangements is as complicated as a chess game. Besides opening the way to administrative chicanery, these interpenetrate the rigid framework of daily existence and govern the whole complex of social relationships.

It is hard to explain to a foreigner that a Soviet passport is something more than a kind of visa that one needs for traveling inside the country as well as outside. It is in fact essential as a proof of identity even if one remains in one place. It records all the bearer's past and present jobs and movements. It serves as a basis for privileged treatment; people marry, divorce, go to law, or commit crimes, simply in order to obtain or avoid a particular endorsement on this all-powerful document.

Herzen in *The Bell* was at pains to explain to his Russian critics that "passports are an instrument of politico-military policy, designed to impede communication and not to aid it; the passport requirement . . . is a matter of police supervision, in fact of slavery." This, if anything, is even more true at present.

The means of tracking down any man, of tying him to one spot and making him work for nothing are far more efficient in the Soviet Union than they were in Tsarist times. Even the most elusive cannot hide. Wherever he goes, he is a piece of property to be disposed of as the state sees fit. Whatever his job or place of residence, he has only one master throughout his life.

But who precisely is that master? For whose benefit does the totalitarian system operate? These questions can hardly be answered, as they do not fit the nature of the subject. The governing principle is that everyone should be equally deprived of rights. This bears little relation to the Marxist idea of the state as an instrument of coercion by a ruling class, or even by a "new class" of exploiters, as Milovan Djilas suggested. The originality of the Soviet scheme is that it prevents any ruling class from consolidating itself. True, it enables some people to persecute others; but many of the victims would be happy to persecute others in turn, and sometimes they do. The victims are not really enemies of the system, and the present persecutors are not really its defenders. There is no question of "interests" in a political or social sense. The existing order is taken absolutely for granted, but at the same time nobody cares a rap for it. Human beings are only instruments of oppression, whether they are bureaucrats or not. "The Internationale" declares (in its French and Russian versions) that "he who was nothing shall be everything"; this is indeed always a possibility in the Soviet system.

The autocratic monarchy was based on the unlimited power of a single individual. The absolute freedom of the Grand Duke, Tsar, or Emperor was inversely related to the legal impotence of his subjects. But this situation limited the purity of state absolutism, as long as the symbol of power was embodied in a particular human being rather than in the state itself. Under the Soviet system, this flaw has been remedied. The omnipotence of authority now actually rests on the principle that it does not matter what happens to those who wield power at any particular time. As soon as Stalin died, he was reviled or consigned to oblivion. His rivals, of course, had fared even worse. The state and party purges of the 1930s were not only the result of a conventional power struggle, but served to exemplify Stalin's dictum, "No one is indispensable." The disgrace and execution of the mighty served a moral and aesthetic purpose; it was a sacrifice to equality, a practical demonstration that they were nothing and the state everything. The holocaust of 1937 completed the process begun by the extermination of landowners and merchants. It signified, as Stalin put it, that "Only the people is immortal; everything else is transitory."

The same pattern was repeated when Beria was shot in 1953, or when Khrushchev got rid of the "antiparty group"[36] of Molotov, Malenkov, and others—in fact a majority of the leadership then—in 1957, or again when Khrushchev himself was ousted in 1964. It is no accident that official Soviet history does not even mention the names of past leaders, and we may assume that the present ones will likewise disappear from the record.

Any highly placed person in the Soviet Union is the object of a whole range of servile feelings, especially envy. He has, after all, no special qualifications as a leader, and the more exalted his rank, the greater is the risk of his downfall. He can counter the hatred of his subordinates only by watching them like a hawk and concentrating power in his own hands. Thus the chief object of holding power is to be able to get more. The man at the top is like the driver of a team of runaway horses, controlled by events rather than controlling them. Changes are due to blind, elemental forces and not to the leaders' personalities.

# Chinks in the armor

Socialist serfdom is absolute serfdom, a self-contained system brought to perfection. Like death, it is inescapable and irreversible. No matter how much a man strives, he remains a creature without rights, wholly dependent on a faceless state. He cannot improve or alter his condition. All plans for reform lack foundation: there is only the dismal prospect of stagnation *ad infinitum,* except for new variations of stupidity and cruelty.

Where man is born without rights, freedom cannot dawn. If individuals are molded only by external circumstances, change has nowhere to come from.

This, of course, is true only to the extent that socialist serfdom *is* an absolutely closed system. The causes that may lead to its disintegration are outside its frontiers, but they can operate only when the frontier is permeable. The Iron Curtain is a prerequisite for serfdom, especially the socialist variety; and for this reason, relations with the outside world are a major factor in the Soviet Union's internal problems.

Socialist serfdom naturally strives either to embrace the whole world or to cut itself off from it. The fact that it cannot do either is the source of its instability and must lead to its dissolution.

Against this background we may return to our basic theme, that of the intelligentsia.

The intelligentsia is the last, but the most uncompromising, obstacle to the process of universal leveling which is the essence of Soviet history. The abolition of the classes privileged by birth and wealth only emphasized the privilege of mental superiority. As Hegel once remarked with grim humor, intellectual inequality is something in people's heads and can be abolished only by cutting them off. The Soviet regime, to do it justice, has made a real effort to put this suggestion into practice. It has proved impossible, however, to do without intellectuals altogether. To exterminate them as rigorously as it did the gentry, kulaks, and capitalists would have seemed unduly savage.

The Russian intelligentsia owes its birth to Peter the Great. He saw that if Russia, half Byzantine and half Tatar, was to transform itself into a great European power it would first have to be civilized. Only thus could the military pressure of Western Europe be resisted. However, Peter's policy contained the seeds of future tensions. He was less interested in the intellectual roots of European civilization, of which he understood little, than in its products: its firearms, fortifications, a regular army and navy, the art of navigation, and the efficient organization of the state. But until the arts and sciences, laws and philosophy, were implanted in Russia, the country had to make do with borrowing and imitating foreign achievements. The process proved expensive.

During Peter's reign Russia's population fell by 20 percent, from 16 million to 13 million. Starvation and exhaustion were the price of introducing civilization into a country without laws. The process of attaching peasants to the soil, and workmen and merchants to their factories and enterprises, began at the same time. This throws some light on the purpose of Stalin's concentration camps, at a time when Russia once again had to be industrialized.

During and after Peter's reign the unpolished sons of noblemen were sent abroad to learn arts and sciences. Knowing foreign languages became a sign of good breeding. The limited number of imported foreign books were avidly read. Enlightened minds began to develop independently of the government's objectives, until they reached a point expressed by Radishchev: "I looked about me—my heart was troubled by the sufferings of humanity."

This problem of an independent intelligentsia was one of many inherited by the Soviet regime. Peasant revolts no longer break out, nor do strikes; iron discipline prevails in the army; private property has been liquidated—so what are we to do with the intelligentsia?

Lenin himself had to defend the need for the educated "specialists" he so mistrusted. His advice was to suck them dry and replace them in due course with the children of workers and peasants. This was done, but it did not bring peace for long. The hydra of learning and critical thought grew new heads, and intellectuals continue to plague society. Stalin and Khrushchev made a pretense of learning and uttered silly generalizations about the nature of art. Unlike other, well-behaved citizens, intellectuals refuse to remain in the slots assigned them. Their work, by its nature, involves a creative element. It cannot be precisely controlled; it is constantly overstepping the mark and producing surprises. For their benefit you have to open, to some extent at least, channels of information that the ordinary citizen is quite happy to live without. They know history, art, and foreign languages, and they read books that interfere with ideological purity (and sterility). From time to time they manage to cut across the bureaucratic guidelines that decide who shall be heard and who not. Foreigners get to know their names, and some of them, despite all the government's efforts, become part of the international fellowship of writers, scholars, artists, and musicians.

Physically, of course, they are in bondage like the rest, but their minds are freer. They cause trouble. As under the Tsars, they are a permanent potential source of sedition; by their very existence they challenge serfdom and proclaim the right of human personality.

But, for this very reason, the intelligentsia have always been alien to the Russian people. Although they have never ceased to strive for the people and its liberation from bondage, they have been misunderstood (or not understood at all), condemned, and often hated. The Russian intellectual is a Russian, of course, but he is different from a man of the people never seduced by learning. His pursuits, interests, and way of life seem foolishly eccentric both to the people and to its rulers. Three-quarters of the way through the twentieth century, the authorities and the masses still think that physical labor is the only real kind, that intellectuals consume but do not produce. The intellectual "eats Russian bread" (a figure of speech: it is actually grown in the USA, Canada, or Australia), but he reads foreign books, and talks and writes in a way that ordinary people can't understand. He and his kind are tolerated strictly for practical and utilitarian reasons, which have nothing to do with the essence of the culture that intellectuals willingly and unwittingly diffuse.

This antagonism has been present in a more or less acute form throughout Soviet history. Stalin, with his usual skill in articulating the vague instincts of the common man, used the term "cosmopolitanism"[37] to express his mistrust of intellectuals. An organic link with world culture, implied by this term, is out of harmony with those features of the national temperament that lead Russians to accept serfdom as a moral norm. Stalin aroused the superstitious fear of culture always latent in ignorant minds, and directed it in particular against doctors.[38] The same mentality is expressed in fears concerning sabotage and spies and in the pathological obsession with secrecy and security. Like savages faced with the supernatural, the Russian masses expect from science every kind of aid but also every kind of calamity, and they thoroughly mistrust its practitioners.

The Soviet authorities found an even more expressive and popular label to denote the foreignness of intellectuals, by identifying them with the Jews. This is something even the dullest can understand. There is of course nothing new in this. Intellectuals and "Yids" were synonymous to the brutish Tsarist "Black Hundred" gangs. The fathers and educators of "ordinary Soviet people" were themselves anti-Semites.

Since Stalin's campaign against "cosmopolitanism" there has been a revival of anti-Jewish agitation whenever relations between the state and the intelligentsia have been unusually strained. But this conflict has never been as open as now, when full-fledged state serfdom has been exposed to humanism and progress. The intelligentsia, in any event, has lost its illusions. Since Stalin, the state has prohibited and restricted much intellectual activity, applying the machinery of repression for all it's worth, to keep the intelligentsia, if not in a state of genuine submission, at least prepared to cynically buckle under and serve the oppressors. The authorities have resorted to anti-Semitism, in spite of the disgrace this implies in a post-Hitler world. To find disciples of Marx, Engels, and Lenin following in Hitler's footsteps would indeed be scarcely credible, had they not already shown how little they care for honesty or consistency.

Meanwhile the spiritual atmosphere becomes more and more unbearable. It is increasingly difficult for "qualified specialists"—artists, writers, and scholars—to function. Creativity as such is forbidden and illegal, and this suffices to keep the intelligentsia in a state of permanent discontent. The fruits of intellectual activity are fit for the sole consumption of the state; repression is intensified: manuscripts do not get printed, impressions are broken up, books already on the shelves are withdrawn from sale, authors are dismissed and forbidden to publish. If they go on writing, contrary to orders, and resort to *samizdat,* they are flung into jail, concentration camps, or mental hospitals. This saves the authorities from wearing out their desiccated brains over the empty formalities of judicial procedure.

In this way, our know-nothing rulers have managed to

consolidate their position and scramble back onto the "commanding heights." If only they could govern with the sole assistance of ignoramuses like themselves! But unfortunately they need the intellectuals, pernicious as they are, with their Yid passports or Yid mentality. And so the Brezhnev leadership twists and turns, gyrating like a merry-go-round, alternating fits of anger, lies, hypocrisy, and plain thuggery. It deserves the punishment visited on it in the person of Andrey Dmitrievich Sakharov—the eminent scientist who presented his country with the hydrogen bomb "to impress the neighbors," but who is an incorruptible witness to the regime's abominations. Nor can any repressive measures stop the flow of information to foreign countries about the Soviet Union's attempt to remain an armed stronghold of reaction against the tide of world civilization.

We should notice, moreover, the recent emergence of a persistent emigration movement in the Soviet Union. It is hardly by chance that the apparently trivial question of a Soviet citizen's right to leave his country voluntarily has suddenly become a bone of contention between Russia and the West. The stability of the socialist slave state will be undermined if the frontier which is "locked and barred" can be freely crossed from inside. Apart from the Soviet state's loss of its animate property, and the accompanying material loss, emigration creates a grave moral risk. The situation in Russia is stable only as long as there is no way out. The intelligentsia will be inclined to defy repressive measures if escaping the state's all-seeing eye becomes comparatively easier.

In contrast to Tsarist times, it is impossible to buy one's own freedom from serfdom or redeem another under the present system. For the whole population are serfs without distinction, whether they are prison warders, workers, farmhands, or intellectuals. The state shifts people about from one job to another, and it is a good deal safer to be transferred by the authorities in accordance with their needs than to try to change jobs on one's own initiative.

Permitting free emigration would mean allowing freedom to find its own level, so to speak. It would liberate Soviet citizens both materially and spiritually. The Soviet system is implacably opposed to freedom, preferring to keep people in subjection rather than enjoying the economic benefits of freeing them. Therefore, officials are understandably perturbed by demands that they allow people the basic human right of moving about freely. Instead, they protest that this is interference in Soviet internal affairs. Indeed, what can be a more "internal" and intimate matter than deciding what to do with one's own slaves?

Wishing to flee from a master is the worst sin a slaveowner can imagine. Well-conditioned, "ideologically mature" Soviet citizens should not dare to dream of such a thing. And yet, there are malcontents shouting, demanding, demonstrating. They cannot be dealt with in secret in the good old way. The more rabble-rousing ones have been put in jail, and the two men who contemplated hijacking a plane were for a time sentenced to death, but this has only increased the hullabaloo.

The usual methods of repression are failing. For instance, a regulation intended to discourage emigration stipulated that anyone intending to emigrate must receive certification from his or her place of work. Any prospective "traitor" could then be hauled over the coals by his colleagues at a work meeting and then dismissed from his job with his labor booklet suitably endorsed. The ordinary Soviet citizen would be effectively deterred by this, but those currently emigrating pay no attention. . . .

Under such circumstances, the emigration of tens of thousands becomes extremely important. And the Jews are only one group among them. A breach is forming in the existing order, a disturbance created in the workings of a machine that had seemed perfectly adjusted for all time. There is ground for hope that opening the frontier may shake the country out of its inertia, that freedom of movement may be the Archimedes' lever whereby all other human rights are secured.

Peter the Great opened a "window into Europe," and the time has now come to break down the dungeon wall in which that window was pierced. To do so will save Russia from degradation, and will relieve the outside world of its eternal uncertainty concerning this strange, aggressive civilization.

CHAPTER **IV**

# The Challenge
# of the Spirit

## The kingdom of
## communism is within us

Few Russian intellectuals of the past, even the wisest of them, have correctly understood what took place in the fateful years of the revolution. They did not know Russia as we know it today, and events at that time seemed an abrupt deviation from the country's destiny, rather than a manifestation of certain aspects of the national character. These thinkers still cherished filial illusions, and to them the Bolsheviks suddenly appeared like an evil genius destroying "holy Russia."

Only a few philosophers, venturing an independent analysis, managed to rise above such superstitions. One of these was N. A. Berdyaev (1874–1948), who understood the deeper sources of Russian communism. His forthrightness and insight made him unpopular among his fellow émigrés, who preferred to settle down in a comfortable hatred of communism rather than engage in disquieting self-analysis. His voice was not heard inside Russia itself until the days of Khrushchev and Brezhnev. By then the experiment had come to fruition and much of what he said was highly applicable to it. Not everyone admits this, however, which is a further reason for us to consider his views.

These were expressed in his classic work *The Origin of Russian Communism* (1932; English translation 1937), but also, many years before, in a contribution to *Iz Glubiny (De Profundis)*, a collection of essays by disillusioned intellectuals written in Moscow in 1918.[1] In it we read:

> Gogol's Russia is not only a picture of our society before the [nineteenth-century] reforms; it portrays the metaphysical character of the Russian people, and is reflected in the revolution itself. The crass, inhuman boorishness that Gogol saw around him was not the product of the old regime or of social and political causes; on the contrary, it was the source of everything bad in the old regime, and imprinted itself on political and social forms. . . . People have become accustomed to blaming everything on the autocracy, ascribing to it all that is evil and benighted in our lives; but in talking like this, Russians are only denying their own responsibility. We have done away with the autocracy, but the evil and benightedness remain. They do not reside in outward social forms, but in the inmost hearts of the people. . . . The old autocracy has gone, but absolutism still prevails in Russia . . . : there is still no respect for man, for human dignity and human rights. . . . The revolution is a great developing agent, and it has only brought to light what was hidden in the depths of Russia.

In order to fully understand the unpleasant truth, however, not only a "developing agent" but a fixative was required. It is noteworthy that other writers in *De Profundis* also used a photographic metaphor. Berdyaev himself wrote: "Great sins can only be committed by a nation of great potentialities. The negative is a caricature of the positive." S. N. Bulgakov, echoing this, wrote: "What is happening now is, as it were, the negative of Russia's positive."

Now that we have reached the present state of stagnation, it is unmistakably clear that the "eternal Gogol" is the positive and not the negative. We can no longer deny that the revolution and its consequences are national in character. To explain it as chance or malevolent interference is implausible when the so-called "chance" has made so deep a mark on a country's history. The idea of a splendid "positive," a sudden change from the prevailing evil to a new state of sweetness and light is a starry-eyed patriotic dream and is likely to remain so.

Gogol's characters with their phoniness and brutality are still all around us: Khlestakovs with their boasting and romanticizing (which we have to accept with feigned admiration), Chichikovs on the make, Skvoznik-Dmukhanovskys on the lookout for bribes, Derzhimordas who order about and bully to their hearts' content. Despite the new phraseology, present-day Russia is no more different from the imperial regime than, let us say, Petrine Russia was from the old Muscovy.

We have had the revolution, the civil war, the NEP,[2] industrialization, and collectivization. Then came a reign of terror, lasting for decades, with periods of special severity, and the Second World War, the most ruthless and destructive in our history. All this strained us enormously. We felt as if the whole order of the universe was collapsing. The illusion of progress was replaced by an illusion of regression. How were we to realize that in fact there was no change at all?

The dramatic events of those years distorted our impressions and made it possible for ignorant self-seekers and crooks to pose as champions of humankind's welfare. For the past two decades we have been in a state of more or less peaceful international coexistence, yet none of us, whether supporters or opponents of the regime, have acquired a proper understanding of history. We still debate about whether Marxism is right or wrong, whether communism is humanistic or antihuman, even though few people take Marxism and communism seriously or even read books about them.

We have hardly begun to reflect on the two decades since Stalin's death. We still argue about Lenin and Stalin, although Khrushchev and Brezhnev have given us ample experience of a more candid system under a thinner veil of demagogy. For the past ten years a struggle has been going on for human rights—all that was, and still is, so lacking in "Gogol's" Russia—but this has somehow been marginal to our consciousness.

We pay a great compliment to Russia's present leaders to regard them as dogmatic followers of Marxist-Leninist teaching. In so doing we help them hide their true faces under a mask, all the more convenient since it is the only one they can possibly wear. It is a good deal more impressive to be a crusader for communism than a vulgar Derzhimorda.

But it is not just a tactical calculation. Having realized that our present rulers are identical to the Derzhimordas of the past, we naturally wonder how this can be. We must confront the unpleasant truth that, while Brezhnev and the rest are ugly customers, we ourselves are not very handsome either. By a curious paradox, we embellish the regime we hate for the sake of embellishing ourselves. Does this not mean that we and the regime still have too much in common?

The October revolution was a misfortune in our history. Russia might have developed differently. A country's future depends on itself, as does an individual's, whatever the past has been—that is the meaning of freedom. But our position now is immeasurably worse than it was at the turn of the century. Then the state was just beginning to show the first signs of respect for human dignity, granting the first rudiments of law and liberty. But all this was swept away by the fury of the national outburst. It would be strange to underestimate the scale of crimes committed under Lenin and Stalin that continue uninterrupted at the present time. But scale depends on a standard of measurement, arrived at by intellectual effort. Cannibalism, no doubt, is taken for granted by cannibals; a man does his best to avoid being eaten, but would eat his neighbor without a qualm of conscience. Perhaps crimes would never be committed if men possessed the faculty of seeing them in their true light. When atrocities as great as those in Soviet history are committed in any society, it is a sure sign that people are failing to see and understand.

Fear denotes a higher degree of awareness than moral insensibility. It is the first result of perceiving reality as it is. Fear arises when the mind becomes aware that everyday life is both monstrous and unchangeable. The individual is terrified of being isolated from the dumbly suffering crowd and subjected to a ruthless fate. He knows, moreover, that the masses will be the first to cast stones at him. They may not join actively in terrorizing him, but they will be indifferent to his sufferings, preferring to look on in silence when a victim is dragged from the herd to be torn to pieces and destroyed.

The scale of Leninist and Stalinist crimes is proof that there must have been a multitude of both passive and active participants. Someone had to arrest and guard prisoners, carry out shootings and expropriations. Crowds of people approved and demanded all this, and not all of them were coerced. Let the accuser of the Soviet regime look into his own heart: when the communists are overthrown, wouldn't he like to see them all in jail or shot? Does he long to return evil for evil? But evil, whatever its motives and whoever its target, is the basis of terror. Reasons and excuses can always be found when there is a predisposition to violence or an indifference to its use.

We should not nostalgically depict pre-revolutionary Russia as an earthly paradise. True, all its worst features are many times worse still under the Soviet regime. But is this not because Russians before the revolution had too little respect for law and human dignity, too little sense of the enormity of arbitrary power even when exercised on behalf of the majority and with its consent? And does not the same reproach apply to those who cannot currently perceive the element of stupid cruelty in the Tsarist autocracy?

History might have taken a different course, but we have to deal with it as it is. And the reason for what happened is that men shut their eyes to the metaphysical danger through which they were steering. Even today, after all we have gone through, Russians are averse to looking truth in the face. Nothing changes in history without human initiative and goodwill; we must confess that these are still scarce among us.

There is nothing fatalistic in what I am saying. The evils that Berdyaev wrote about were not eternally ordained and need not exist forever. To suppose this would be as wrong as to believe that God himself endowed Russia with special virtue for all time. This, it is well known, is an ancient tradition of Russian Orthodoxy, which proclaimed itself for centuries to be more Christian than other Christianities. The special association of God with the Russian people, and then with the Russian state, is curiously analogous to the doctrine of the "chosen people," but, unlike Judaism, it excludes personal responsibility: to be a good Christian, it was only necessary to be and remain Russian.

All this has been described by authors far better versed in theology than I, among them, the great Russian philosopher Vladimir Solovyov. I am not suggesting, however, that all Russian religion was so crudely nationalistic. Indeed, it seems to me that the fault lies not with religion as such but with a weak and superficial form of religious faith. The deficiency of personal responsibility was not a result but a cause. Russia failed to develop such a sense because of its slowness to discover individualism and its corollaries—philosophy, art, and self-examination in general.

Under these circumstances, and in the absence of a sense of history, there arose the dangerous illusion that good is somehow "given" and can be preserved by sticking to the same pattern. Thence there grew the extreme dogmatism of religious faith and custom in early times. In our own day, it is manifested in a dogmatic worship of communism. This should not be an offensive comparison, as it has nothing to do with true religion or even true communism—only with lack of initiative, an undeveloped sense of responsibility, and a failure to appreciate the values of freedom.

Evil cannot be "given" in advance any more than good, for it exists only in and through us, through our choice and our freedom. But the difference is that evil will happen if we do nothing, while good has to be worked for. Passivity is evil and cannot become good. Good has to be chosen and created; evil comes about of its own accord. Evil chooses us; we do not necessarily choose it, though of course we may deliberately do so. In Russia's case, however, such a deliberate choice is rare. Evil and darkness spring from the false conviction that good will happen whatever we do or refrain from doing. However wretched our lives, and however conscious we are of this, we expect that one day the bad dream will end and we shall wake up on a bed of roses. We believe, against all evidence, that Russia can do no wrong, and if something unpleasant happens we blame it on an adventitious cause. In this way, unconsciously and irresponsibly, we make our choice in favor of evil. And we fall lower and lower until we find ourselves in the first socialist state in the world, which again is supposed to be a guarantee of perfection.

The only way out of the vicious circle, as far as I can see, is by a self-analysis mentally separating us from the masses. There is nothing either good or bad about the "people" as such. To "go among the people" is a pointless exercise. It only means fleeing from oneself and associating with others who have not found themselves and are unaware of the need to do so. For the same reason the Russian intellectuals' obsession with finding "roots in the soil," which began when they became aware of themselves as a class, is not a salutary impulse but a pernicious one.

This is not merely an abstract, philosophical conclusion. "Going among the people" led our Slavophiles into chauvinism and wild dreams of conquering Constantinople, and it led our Westernizers into "a Russian revolt, meaningless and merciless." Our present system is nothing more nor less than the combination of these two elements.

It is no good blaming others: as long as we remain what we are, the kingdom of our communism is within us. And we may be sure that it will flourish whenever and wherever there is no freedom or sense of personal responsibility. Whether this takes place under the Marxist or the nationalist banner, that of Christianity or any other, is of secondary importance.

The meaning of what took place in our country long remained hidden under the cloak of ideological and political forms. In actual fact, however, it belongs to layers of social consciousness where ideology and politics are irrelevant. For politics to be more than mere competition for power requires the conscious participation of a public that knows what it wants and how it expects to get it. For an ideology to be taken seriously, people must be free to adopt or reject it, recognizing that other ideologies have a right to exist. The fact that Soviet society has no power of choice, and no tradition of tolerance in political and ideological matters, means that it lives with crude imitations of the real thing. We use them as window-dressing for foreigners, pretending for some reason that we are just like everyone else. But why should we deceive ourselves?

At the conclusion of his article in *De Profundis,* Berdyaev wrote:

> The new Russia which is being born with fearful pangs is still mysterious. It will not be such a country as the leaders and ideologists of the revolution imagine. Its spiritual structure will not be uniform. Christian and anti-Christian principles will be more sharply divided and opposed within it. The anti-Christian spirits of the revolution are giving birth to a kingdom of darkness, but

Russia's Christian spirit must display its strength. If the majority falls away, that spirit can be active in a minority.

These words have proved prophetic. The majority did not have to abandon the spirit, but the minority had to break away in order to understand what the strength of the spirit meant. The intelligentsia, not the masses, developed a sense of responsibility, a desire for freedom and an appreciation of its values. This feeling and this desire were combined with a sense of guilt—chiefly the intelligentsia's own guilt—for what had happened and was still happening in Russia.

Soon there was an open clash between the conscious intellectual minority and the authorities—but was it only with the authorities?

Ten years ago the writer Yuly Daniel, on trial with Andrey Sinyavsky for publishing their joint work abroad, gave the following explanation of one of his short stories:

> The idea of the story, according to the indictment, is that we are all guilty, that there was the cult of personality and the mass repressions. I agree with this interpretation, but not that it deserves the epithet "slanderous." I believe that every member of a society is responsible for what goes on in that society; and I include myself in this. I wrote "All are guilty," as there was no other answer to the question "Whose fault is it?" No one has ever said publicly who was to blame for these crimes, and I shall never believe that three men—Stalin, Beria, Ryumin—could have made the whole of our country's life hideous. But no one has yet answered the question— Whose fault was it?

This was a frank statement, and an unusual one. The question "Who is to blame?" has been heard before in Russia,[3] but it is rare for anyone to say "All are guilty" and include himself. The prosecution, too, applied its old-fashioned logic in describing this idea as "slanderous." How can it be right to indict a whole nation?

It was pointed out long ago that, in Russia, the guilty man is not the arsonist but the one who shouts "Fire!" Accordingly, Daniel and Sinyavsky were scorched by the "people's" court. But the trial was a moral defeat for the court and the authorities who inspired it. The arrest of Sinyavsky and Daniel was the beginning, not the end, of a fight that has continued to this day. It is a cause taken up by a wretched minority, a handful of individuals, but invincible since it poses no political or ideological issues, only moral ones. It makes plain the difference between good and evil, and calls on us to choose. The members of the minority have made their choice and, by the openness of their actions, have driven the materially omnipotent but spiritually bankrupt authorities into a corner.

The actions of Sinyavsky and Daniel, and many others since, have demonstrated the great and simple truth that the victory of good over evil occurs on a totally different plane from the attempts of evil to conquer good. Their stand: demolish the edifice of communism stone by stone. It corrodes the basic, essential communism that is within us and not just the bogus kind that fills the newspapers and runs the machinery of state.

Spiritual obstacles, however, remain in the way. They must be tackled cautiously and need to be explained by referring once more to the past.

# A spiritual malady

In the *History of Russia* by the nineteenth-century scholar Vasily Klyuchevsky, there is an interesting passage on the state of culture during the late eighteenth century under the empresses Elizabeth and Catherine. To all appearances, Russia had made considerable strides in assimilating foreign languages and literatures, the humanitarian ideas of the Enlightenment, and an elaborate code of etiquette. But, on the other hand,

> The educated Russian moved and had his being in Russian conditions; his shoulders were burdened with the weight of the Russian past, from which he could never escape, as the facts of that past were part of himself; but the contents of his mind were of a completely different origin, borrowed from another world. . . . The educated eighteenth-century Russian was in a tragicomic situation: he knew the facts of one reality, but was nourished by the ideas of another; his principles and conclusions did not and could not agree. This was the origin of the intellectual disease or intellectual failing,

if one prefers the term, which afflicted many generations from then on, even if we do not admit that if afflicts ourselves. . . . Ideas and stereotyped feelings had no effect on people's attitudes and actions. . . . The educated man in Elizabeth's reign [1741–62] existed at two levels, one of ideas and one of actions; on the upper, intellectual level, the *bel étage* of his mind, he was a highly cultivated European, but on the lower level he exemplified the witty French saying "Scratch a Russian and you'll find a Tatar." The callousness of civic and moral feeling—such is the sad phenomenon encountered by anyone studying the social manners of the period.

"Callousness of civic and moral feeling"—can Klyuchevsky really be describing eighteenth-century Russia, or is he not talking about us today?

We have long been sensitive to literary works that appear to criticize or comment on our society. When Hamlet says "Denmark's a prison," or when Sophocles' Antigone retorts to Creon "These people think as I do, but they dare not tell you so," the reader's mind flies out to meet the "allusion," like an arrow from a bow. Editors, censors, and others in authority make it their business to prevent this from happening, and keep a sharp eye out for "unsupervised implications" (the official term). They reluctantly allow performances of Gogol's *The Government Inspector* or Griboyedov's *The Misfortune of Being Clever,* but do not permit a film based on Dostoyevsky's *A Nasty Story* (directed by Alov and Naumov) to be shown. Similarly, it is impermissible to write about the Nazi treatment of the Jews or Hitler's policy toward art; Saltykov-Shchedrin may not be quoted; the Tsarist censorship may not be mentioned, and the very word "censorship" is being banished from the official vocabulary altogether.

Of course, to ferret out double-entendres one has to have a good notion of what they are—mine detectors must have some affinity to mines; but this is only an argument for caution in filling certain posts. The supervisor or ideologist must have a mind that functions on several levels—simple, ingenuous devotion to truth (supposing this exists anywhere) will not do at all; but at the same time he must take care to keep the various ideas in watertight compartments.

Thus the spiritual malady referred to by Klyuchevsky, which

afflicted the Russian educated class throughout the eighteenth and nineteenth centuries, has become a mainstay of the ideological system in Soviet times.

Klyuchevsky illustrated the phenomenon with some brilliant sketches of curious life-stories. He has been succeeded by some of our contemporaries, who combine tale-bearing and squalid persecution of the best living exponents of Russian culture with a genuine love of that culture and an epicurean taste for its deepest and subtlest manifestations. The grandees of Catherine the Great's time did not bother their heads about the contradiction between admiring Voltaire, Rousseau, or Diderot and flogging male serfs or raping female ones. In Soviet times we have refined techniques for evading the logical professional consequences of passing impartial judgment on a reality no less barbarous than the old regime's. Our ideologists are past masters at justifying cruelty, violence, and injustice by espousing humanism, progress, and the future welfare of humanity.

Other nations used to a different set of values (all except possibly the Chinese) must find it hard to understand Russians. How is it that our people, living in terror under the watchful eye of the police, threatened with "social condemnation" at every turn, avoiding their closest friends if the hue and cry turns against them, extolling what they despise and trampling on what they love—can be the selfsame people who admire Shakespeare and Goethe, debate the subtleties of Plato and Kant, invoke the principles of justice and human rights, and produce immortal poetry and art? How difficult it is to explain that 1937—an appalling St. Bartholomew's Massacre multiplied a thousand-fold—was remembered by sane people for the adoption of the "most democratic Constitution in the world," or for the centenary of Pushkin's death? At a time when one person in ten was being dragged off at night to torture, execution, or death in a concentration camp, millions were bawling out the song: "I know no other country where man can breathe so free!" Even in jail, even when tortured, even when entangled by monstrous and absurd accusations, people went on believing that they had built the most equitable society on earth. They shouted Stalin's name in joyful loyalty until they were killed by a bullet in the back of the neck. And later, after the war, when the peasants were trying to escape by any means from a life of semistarvation in their ruined villages, people flocked to see films like *The Kuban Cossacks,* in which collective farmers fairly burst with prosperity.

I myself was no longer a child in those days. I could have tried to reconcile my orthodox convictions with what I saw around me, but I must confess I did not. I can still hardly explain to myself how all these things coexisted in my mind in a more or less harmonious state.

It was not hypocrisy, cynicism, or lip-service under coercion—how easy an explanation this would be! No, it was rather that the "spiritual malady" of the old intelligentsia had, with the elimination of illiteracy, become a country-wide epidemic. Perhaps this split-mindedness has now reached its apogee and a glimmer of truth is dawning at last.

The disease in question, "doublethink," was rediscovered by George Orwell in *Nineteen Eighty-Four,* a popular book in *samizdat* circles about ten years ago. Orwell's conception of the "power of holding two contradictory beliefs in one's mind simultaneously, and accepting both of them" was based on an analysis of Soviet ideology and Soviet practice, but he generalized it into a means of keeping human beings in subjection under any totalitarian regime. Transposed into English terms by the author, "doublethink" became an artificial creation, as though it were deliberately invented by the propaganda apparatus and forcibly imposed on the rest of the people. It thus appeared to be an offshoot of the system rather than basic to it. No doubt it would be such an offshoot if a Soviet-type system were established in England. We see this happening, for instance, in Soviet-occupied Czechoslovakia. But the situation in the Soviet Union is less rational. The term "doublethink" is almost inappropriate there, for it suggests that the individual concerned consciously shifts from one "register" to the other. It implies only a sphere of thought, a logical apparatus of arguments and conclusions, which makes it possible to move in two independent, mutually exclusive directions.

A usual fallacy in critiques of the present phase of our official ideology consists precisely in treating it as the outcome of more or less conscious doublethink—of the coexistence in a single person of two thought-complexes, each with a separate field of application and expression. The two are kept apart, it is often supposed, by worldly cunning or terror. A wise man knows when to speak out and what to say, or when to be silent. This implies that he is equally at home with "official" or "unofficial" thought and language, and can switch over with all his faculties from one to the other at will.

If things were so simple, we could depict a hypocrite and deceiver who departs from the truth as much as he thinks necessary to achieve some specific practical aim. This would not impede his taking a sober view of reality, and it might even give him the kind of advantage a rogue enjoys over an honest man. In such a case, those in authority would know the true state of affairs, what to conceal and what to tell the public. Meanwhile, of course, the latter would also know the truth and would only pretend not to.

This would mean that as any official statement was made, it would be possible, in theory at least, to discover the secret intentions behind it, to understand why it took the form it did and how far it deviated from the truth known to the originators of the statement. This assumption is sometimes made by Western experts seeking to analyze the Soviet government's moves at home or in foreign policy. But in doing this they unconsciously project their own mental habits into the minds of Russians who are affected by doublethink. A foreign observer cannot admit the possibility of blindness in a case where he himself would be clearly aware of the motives at work and the expected results. Consequently, he adds a dimension to doublethink by postulating a third element, that of sober, pragmatic, unambiguous thought.

Doublethink, however, is not really a function of consciousness but of unconsciousness. It involves not only deception, but self-deception as well.

It may be useful here to recall the classic Marxist definition of ideology as the product of a "false consciousness" (a definition naturally never heard today in the Soviet Union). According to this theory, ideology is related to people's existence but prevents their forming an adequate view of it. One cannot judge a society by what it thinks of itself. An ideology based on a given reality distorts it because, for instance, any particular generation regards its own aims as absolute, universally intelligible, and valid for all mankind. Man may not be able to bear constantly thinking of himself as mortal, or of the relativity and corruptibility of all his achievements. At the same time, it is impossible to form a coherent system of the whole detailed complex by which a given generation is surrounded, for this could hypothetically be achieved only by synthesizing the experience of all humanity.

The only way out of this impasse seems to be to apprehend one's place in history, in the unbroken evolutionary chain of generations pursuing their collective task. A sense of historical continuity at least affords some possibility of seeing oneself with detachment. But this, as we have seen, is the Achilles' heel of the Soviet mentality, and the traditional Russian one in general. It is difficult for us to correlate the past, present, and future and to combine them mentally into an evolutionary continuum. We are inclined to see our own historical past not as a series of transitions but as a number of sudden, arbitrary changes: from Kievan Russia to Muscovy,[4] from the old Moscow tsardom to Peter's empire, from the Romanovs to the Soviet Union. But by chopping up our history in this way we lose the sense of our own continuity, and are apt to imagine ourselves starting from zero and suddenly achieving the absolute.

Ideology is a form of consciousness which, though linked to the problems and tasks of only one or two generations at most, aspires to a self-contained wholeness. Rooted in actual social experience, it actually distorts the content of that experience in the minds of those directly concerned. On the other hand, the adherents of a particular ideology could not be part of their own reality if it did not appear to them in a distorted form.

Since ideology is not a product of individual human experience, and cannot be so in view of its claim to absoluteness and universality, it presents itself to the individual readymade. Furthermore, it must be identical for all members of a given society. It cannot allow any other ideology to exist alongside it, as this would diminish its own universality. Any other views, even those not pretending to universality, appear to ideologists as constituting a rival ideology.

On the other hand, an ideology appears to the individual professing it as something external to himself. His internal world cannot coincide with the ideology, however much he may wish it to. He soon finds that he cannot live according to its rules, and he therefore cheats on it, as one might cheat on an unloved wife. Or, more commonly, he is not actually unfaithful but only casts glances at other women and others' wives—which of course is a sin too, but is much less noticeable even to the sinner.

For this reason it is better, in my opinion, not to speak of "doublethink" but of "dual consciousness," as O. Altayev did in his article "Pseudoculture and the Dual Consciousness of the Intelligentsia." All mental faculties and spiritual strengths are capable of this duality: not only thought but feelings, inclinations, imagination, will, and action. The individual concerned is completely disoriented, lacking any standard by which to correct the judgments he forms and professes. He is, in the strict sense, not answerable for his behavior.

To avoid deluding ourselves, we should remember that dual consciousness is the outcome of a particular set of traditions, and that given this traditional inclination, the difficulty is to cure people of this defect and instill a consistent approach to questions of truth and reality.

The "spiritual malady" is contagious. Its essence lies in intensifying self-delusion, in defending misapprehensions by one subterfuge after another. Dual consciousness reaches its acme whenever it becomes possible to seduce a new victim, for the more an ideology spreads, the more it is convinced of its own rightness.

A dual consciousness is most deceptive when it behaves to itself and others as if it were not divided. It can create the impression of being monolithic more successfully than any other sociopsychological structure. For one side of the divided consciousness can shut the other out. More open-minded people, on the other hand, present a picture of irresolution and doubt as they move from one accepted conclusion to another that excludes it. It is not surprising that dual consciousness has a dazzling effect on the beholder's eyes, similar to that of op art.

The Marquis de Custine, a famous observer of Russia in the 1830s, remarked that the country was like a theater in which the audience dutifully watches the stage although it is well aware that the main action is going on behind the scenes. But the situation is even more ironic: the spectators are actors too, and they perform behind the scenes while imagining that they are on stage. This is well illustrated by the "Potemkin villages" that Catherine the Great's favorite constructed along the empress's triumphal route to the Crimea, with an exuberance of décor that still does honor to the Soviet ballet. The only difference nowadays is that the "villages" are erected by the people and their rulers, not for the benefit of anyone in particular but *pour l'amour de l'art,* out of sheer joy in mutual deception.

Take, for example, the work system known as "Lenin's Saturday."[5] It would be unthinkable not to turn out for work on that day. It is at least as compulsory as any other day, and truants' names are reported to the authorities. Yet everyone proclaims at meetings, and complacently reads in the newspapers, that the universal turnout is a wonderful demonstration of popular enthusiasm for labor and the Soviet system.

Without going further into such fascinating details, let me note that dual consciousness has the power to delude us even when we think we have shaken off its spell and are able to view it dispassionately. It can still delude us in two opposite ways. We may unsuspectingly look only at the bright side—the stage, as it were—and ignore what is behind the scenes; or we may concentrate on the hidden actions and imagine that the brightly lit stage is only a malicious lie. In the first case we see exactly what official propaganda wants us to see; in the second we pay no attention to it even when it really does express mass feelings. Either we believe that the regime is firm as a rock, or we expect it to collapse any moment; either we believe the slogan that "the Party and people are one," or we delude ourselves that the eyes of the oppressed populace need only to be opened to reality, and then—!

The truth, it appears, lies elsewhere. Dissecting dual consciousness and its mechanisms should help us avoid many errors in analyzing Soviet reality and the fate of the Soviet people. We should learn that the "dispassionate observer" is a far likelier victim of naiveté than any brainwashed target of doublethink. Dual consciousness, indeed, is hypocritical, but in a sincere sort of way—not the mendacity of a Munchausen, but the cheerful romanticizing of Gogol's Khlestakov, whose imagination is more real to him than life itself. It is a system of lies that everyone has reason to believe in, for it justifies a sole pragmatic course of action in any given set of circumstances.

It cannot be denied, for instance, that at present communism plays the part of a credo genuinely accepted and professed by the great majority. Many repeat the phrases that fall from above, not because they are intimidated but because they believe them. Everyone in Russia is aware of this consensus, and chooses his company carefully before speaking out against communist dogma. Not only is he certain to be denounced, but he also knows that such utterances will fall on stony ground. Blasphemy against the "ideals of communism" is seldom tolerated even in private conversation, let alone in public.

But it would be hasty to conclude, as some superficial foreigners do, that communism is a national faith in the full sense of the term. No one, from the top down, knows precisely what communism is, nor does anyone care to know when it will become reality. The party has solemnly declared that the present generation will see communism in action any day now, and it has been drummed into everyone that this means "From each according to his ability; to each according to his needs." Why, then, are people concerned about pension plans? Even in mental homes, almost everyone carefully plots his pension prospects for the next ten or twenty years.

Faith in communism is highly necessary, to make the present more or less endurable. Without it one cannot get on in life, cannot make a career, and will probably be virtually destroyed. Doubting weakens resistance and increases vulnerability. Inversely, one can rise to great heights by dint of "sincere faith" and nothing else. Intelligence, knowledge, and skill are unnecessary. All one needs is the ability to ceaselessly parrot the right phrases. What is the point of having doubts, anyway?—at most they lead only to idle chatter about things that all sensible people are well aware of. Consequently, to believe the most obvious nonsense is to obey the dictates of common sense, sober calculation, and ordinary Russian mother-wit. All of these can be transmuted into a very good likeness of sincerity, or even into hysterical fervor.

# Indifference to ideas

Dual consciousness is based on the "indifference to ideas" noted with concern by Berdyaev, which excludes any valuation of ideas for their own sake. No one dreams of examining them for truth or falsity. Individuals unquestioningly adopt those ideas most effective in practice, which enable them to adapt painlessly to the circumstances of life. An idea thus appears as something readymade, prescribed, given from outside. As necessity dictates, it may be either rejected or accepted with every sign of devotion that ingenuity can summon. It is either absolute, unique, and unshakable, or it does not exist at all. Investigation, exploration, the formation and critical development of ideas—all these are excluded in advance as a matter of principle.

Careful inspection generally reveals the reasons why a particular idea prevails under given historical circumstances, e.g., why Russia adopted Marxism (in a simplified form) sixty years ago and not some other doctrine. But the explanation relates to the outward trappings of an idea and not to its essential kernel. Once the idea is adopted—by society *en bloc,* and by order from above—it begins to ossify. It also becomes distorted, simply because no one troubles to penetrate its real essence. But however far this process goes, an appearance of absolute fidelity is kept up. Before long, its truth will be attested to principally by its familiarity and the authority of custom. Obedience to the tablets of the law and to the faith once handed down replaces personal experience or the ability to explain why the doctrine is believed to be the right one. It is not defended by arguments but by police measures, government power, censorship, and the extirpation of dissent. In this way, ardent faith becomes first cousin to skepticism; slavish protestations of loyalty to an idea are akin to disrespect for it. Meanwhile, a great gulf opens between official statements on the one hand and real life on the other: in theory everything is splendid, in practice it is miserable.

There is no way out of this contradiction, because the theory is used expressly to cover up the reality.

In *The Dragon,* a play by Yevgeny Shvarts (1896–1958), there is a dialogue between a cat and a donkey which runs:

CAT: What about meat?
DONKEY: What do you mean, meat?
CAT: Have you tried eating it?
DONKEY: Meat isn't food, silly; meat is a load. They put it in the cart and you carry it.

Many Russians view ideas as the donkey does meat. The authorities load ideas on our backs and we carry them, but it never occurs to us that they are meant as food.

It is generally held that the dualism of Russian life and consciousness dates from Peter the Great's reforms and the forcible introduction of alien elements from Western civilization. To some extent these reforms may indeed be blamed for the spiritual malady of the eighteenth and early nineteenth centuries, as described by Klyuchevsky. But to understand fully the historical background of Russian doublethink, which so plagues us today, we cannot abruptly swing from a Westernizing to a Slavophile point of view and idealize everything in pre-Petrine Russia. It was precisely in old Muscovy that the seeds of dualism were first sown.

The forcible methods by which Peter sought to implant Western culture and the remarkable docility with which Russians accepted forms and principles alien to them hint at already established gaps between private and public life, between practical experience and official ideological forms. In the course of the eighteenth century this gap widened. There was no dramatic break or interruption of the natural course of events, but only a fresh instance of the same process in new circumstances of close contact and conflict with the civilized West.

Centuries before, the possibility of dualism was created by Russia's adoption of Byzantine Orthodoxy. Gospel precepts were superficially imposed on barbarism and heathendom without undue difficulty.[6] Christian philosophy and theology, developed by the Greeks to a high degree of subtlety and inspiration, were neither adopted nor even understood. And little attention was paid to Greek literature and poetry. Apart from the church's moral teaching, the Russians took over dogma and ceremony above all else. Moreover, it was considered pious to accept the faith readymade and not test it against reason and feelings. This inevitably led to a formalistic attitude, and a confusion of the outer attributes of faith with its spiritual and moral core. This fatal tendency to identify what is Russian and customary with what is Christian and universal continued for centuries and is not quite extinct today. Moreover, having received Christianity ready-made, the Russian people developed a haughty and condescending attitude toward those who had bestowed it on them. Greeks were the people of history, development, and speculation, and in Russian eyes these were all signs of imperfection and impurity.

G. P. Fedotov pointed out the ambiguous part in the development of Russian culture played by the invention of a Church Slavonic script,[7] which cut Russia off from Greek sources during its formative stage. For a thousand years the Cyrillic alphabet formed a barrier to free exchange of spiritual experience with other Christian peoples. At a very early stage, the idea arose that the faith of the Greeks was one thing and that of the Russians another. It was held more and more firmly that the latter was absolutely sacred and perfect. The German traveler Olearius remarked in the seventeenth century that "Although the Russians boast that they were visited by the old Greeks and originate from them, they do not resemble them in any way, and in their language and arts they have taken nothing from that gifted people."

Olearius was not completely right in this. Byzantine Greece did exercise a huge influence on Russian culture. But the paradox and ambiguity of the situation lay in the fact that Russians unjustifiably looked down on their masters. Even Greek monks were viewed as impure by the early Russians. The deep-rooted superstition that it is unlucky to meet a priest may well be a survival of the days when priests in Russia were Greek missionaries. Even as late as the reign of Tsar Aleksey (1645–76), when some Ukrainian monks who observed the Greek rite were invited to the Iversky monastery in northwestern Russia, some of the Great Russian monks reacted by leaving the monastery. Those who remained appealed to the patriarch of Moscow, saying, "We have no priest here of our own Russian faith, and are condemned to die unshriven."

Russian contempt for Greek literature is illustrated in a seventeenth-century manuscript in which we read: "Russian writing is more worthy of honor than that of the Hellenes because it was created by a holy man, Cyril the philosopher, while the Greek alphabet was made by the Hellenes when they were still heathen."

Thus imitation was exalted above creation, and the acceptance of faith became far more important than the search for it. The effect of this attitude, however, is to ascribe ideal perfection to an unideal reality. The community demands too little of itself and of life, settling for blind self-satisfaction.

The identification of imperfect reality with an ideal is an infallible recipe for dual consciousness. However cruel and loathsome empirical reality may be, this is simply not perceived by those who are embedded in it.

The monk Arseni Glukhoy, whom we have already met, complained of seventeenth-century ecclesiastics that "in reading the church books they pay attention only to the ink and to the letters, understanding nothing of the sense. They know nothing of orthodoxy or heterodoxy and only scan the ink of Holy Scripture, paying no heed to its meaning." This can hardly have been an exaggeration, for the tragic schism that broke out in the middle of the century originated in the worship of ceremonial and liturgical forms.[8] They were revered not because of their true meaning but because they were familiar from childhood. It is perhaps understandable that the ignorant, superstitious populace, to whom Christianity was no more than a superior form of paganism, rallied to the cause. But it is especially sad that the whole hierarchy, both before and after the deposition of the patriarch Nikon, was unable to rise above the formalistic, pagan approach to religious ceremonies and practices. When Nikon declared, "I am a Russian, but I am Greek by faith," he showed as little understanding of the universal nature of Christianity as did his adversaries, the Old Believers.

The schism would have been impossible had there been even an embryonic sense of history enabling people to distinguish the relative from the absolute, the temporal from the eternal, the local from the ecumenical. Only the historicism of the Christian consciousness makes it possible for the spirit, by unceasing creative activity, to aspire toward a higher goal. Only thus can a bridge be built between our human and divine natures, so that existence is transformed into action and exaltation. Without this sense of evolution, all is stagnant and rigid. And since Christianity not only presupposes history but is the necessary background to historicism in the modern European mind, a nation professing Christianity but devoid of historical sense is bound to suffer from many forms of dual consciousness.

The Russian schism indicated that Christianity had, by and large, been adopted only superficially and not in its essence. Its core can be understood and assimilated only by personal and historical experience, by free and conscious choice. The absurd but widespread tendency to talk about "the Russian faith" instead of Orthodoxy leads some zealots, even today, to brand Chaadayev an arch-heretic merely because he did not believe in all aspects of the special sanctity of old Russia. The same attitude leads to mistrust of critical thought and philosophy altogether. It is also linked with an almost physical aversion and suspicion toward anything foreign. This feeling, even when repressed and driven inward, prevents any contact beyond superficial borrowings and makes it impossible for foreign spiritual experiences to affect Russia's subconscious deeply.

In the seventeenth and eighteenth centuries, generations of budding Russian scholars were exposed to such maxims as: "Brothers, do not seek to be over-wise. If anyone says to you 'Do you know all philosophy?' you should reply: 'I have not studied Hellenic niceties, I have not frequented learned philosophers.' " Given this built-in suspicion of independent thought, Nikon's reforms, intended to combat the spirit of "the Russian faith," were successful not because of any inner conviction of their rightness but because they were rigorously enforced by the secular power (though this did not prevent a schism with the Old Believers). Changes were not the outcome of a spontaneous movement of minds but represented instead an abrupt break with the past, intensifying the duality that already existed.

This state of affairs prepared the way for the reforms of Peter the Great. From then on, any and every action by the autocratic state was automatically accepted, with no doubts, as sanctified by all the canons of Orthodoxy.

Peter's plans were not distinguished by subtlety. He wanted to surpass Europe in military power as fast as possible, and improve the standard of material comfort and pleasure in his gloomy, backward country, by borrowing the end products of Western civilization, especially industry and technology. His reforms were conducted on the basis of the sly Russian saying: "The German [i.e., foreigner in general] does the thinking; all the Russian has to do is look." Neither the reforming Tsar nor his advisers realized the complexities of the historical, political, social, and cultural roots of European civilization. He could not know that the achievements and practical applications of natural science that so excited his envy were based on the age-long development of social institutions that ensured personal initiative and intellectual inquiry. He saw the value of the fruits, but did not appreciate the cultivation that had gone into them. The philosophical revolution of the seventeenth century, which transformed the world's view of itself and opened the way to advances in the exact sciences, was outside the mental horizon of Peter and his Russian contemporaries. It is hard to imagine any of them reading Descartes or Leibniz.

Science in Russia turned into a new branch of state service, staffed by individuals specially trained for the purpose. The ideas that "studies serve for delight" as well as for use, and that free intellectual inquiry is a means of developing the whole personality, were totally absent under Peter's system. European civilization was imposed from above, by the absolute will of an autocratic sovereign. His aims and methods were those of an Oriental despot. They were incompatible with notions of individual dignity or initiative.

I have recalled these historical facts to show the deep roots of certain typical aspects of Soviet reality. In the Soviet Union at present, we perceive at first glance such features as contempt for knowledge in itself, crude utilitarianism in estimating its value, slavish imitation of foreign techniques, amounting at times to theft, arrogance and ill-concealed envy where foreigners are concerned, and the subordination of all culture to arbitrary and despotic authority. The Bolshevik revolution was not a break with the past, but a reaction of old Russia against the incursion of genuine Europeanization.

My comparing a superficial Orthodoxy to a no-less-superficial Marxism, the Tsarist to the Soviet regime, is sure to arouse the anger of both parties. They detest each other, believing they have nothing in common. This, however, only serves to prove my point, since a typical effect of dual consciousness is that "those of a kind do not recognize one another."

Spiritually, the revolution has set us back a long way. By physically destroying the old intelligentsia, the only source of true progress, and uprooting every vestige of spiritual continuity, it has forced the country to begin all over again. Today's newly burgeoning intelligentsia has a difficult path to tread, and can hardly be blamed if its steps are sometimes uncertain, if it stumbles and shrinks from the tragically momentous choices that lie before it.

# The Russian intelligentsia

The corrupting and debasing spiritual disease of a split personality accounts for the predicament of the intelligentsia both in Tsarist and in Soviet times. As long as culture is confined to a privileged area of the mind, whatever outward refinement it may display, one can hardly say that an intelligentsia has come into being. Education is not the same as intellectual attainment, though the two ideas are often confused. The state assigns an ancillary role to education, maintaining and developing it according to its own needs. But true education inherently breeds freedom and independence of judgment, a desire and an inner compulsion to evaluate the condition of society and one's own relationship to it. When education thus refuses to remain in bondage and wrests the initiative from the state, we may speak of the birth of an intelligentsia.

To belong to the intelligentsia means, if not to be cured of the spiritual malady—from which few people in Russia can recover—at least to combat it within oneself and one's surroundings. The Russian intellectual is a sighted person among the blind, responsible and accountable for his acts while those around him are not. His state is a tragic one, but he can recover his serenity only by undergoing spiritual death.

The present stagnation epitomizes his fate. It has finally become clear that the intelligentsia must be defined existentially, rather than in terms of its place in the state hierarchy, or on the basis of educational qualifications.

In our great country almost everything repeats itself. Perhaps we may be moved by the topicality and pathos of the following passage from Leskov's novel *No Way Out,* a book written over a century ago that discusses unsympathetically the emergence of the intelligentsia in the nineteenth century:

> All these were not "knights without stain or blame." Their past lives, for the most part, conformed to the aspirations of the milieu from which they were now detached. The young officials had sullied their hands with bribes; the teachers had gone on their knees to obtain particular jobs, and some of them had written odes to the most despicable personalities; the young noblemen had thrashed their serfs and squandered the hard-earned coppers of the peasantry; the other classes were no better. They were all people whose fathers and mothers had impressed on them that "You can't earn stone palaces by honest labor." All of them had carried away from the parental home a single blessing, "Be rich and respected," and a single commandment, "Get on in the world." True, some of them had also been told "Try to be an honest man," but what was honesty and how did one go about acquiring it? There were of course exceptions, but they were a few drops of fresh water in the salt sea of Russian life. Lepers climbed into the cleansing font. All this crowd were demoralized from the beginning; they were all brought up to lies and trickery; all were taught the arts of ingratiation, remembering the proverb "A calf that behaves itself can suck two mothers." They all did, until they suddenly ran away from both mothers to one whose udder was dry after years of famine.
>
> This time of rebirth, led by people who had not received a penny by way of inheritance, not a single good counsel to speed them on their way, must truly be regarded as one of the great dramatic ages of our history. What inspired these independents except the love of virtue and justice? By whom were they led? Who suppressed in them, even if only for a time, the spirit of selfishness, duplicity and venality that held the nation in its grip? . . .

Remember that recent time when a handful of "people corrupted before their time" awoke, took thought, and began to step out
falteringly, young as they were in terms of civic development. . . .
Knowing the sordidness and corruption of the past, realizing that
inaction was accursed, they united under a single banner all who
spoke of the need to wipe out the stains of impurity and to march
forward. They knew that the past had left them little worth
preserving, and they did not know that almost the whole blame for
the accumulation of lies with which our age is encumbered would be
laid upon their shoulders.

As Khomyakov[9] put it, the country was "black with the
judgments of unrighteousness, branded with the yoke of slavery;
full of impious flattery, pernicious lies, dead, shameless idleness and
every kind of abomination."

Apart from a few small details these words, written in the
early 1860s, are no less true today. And Leskov's title, *No Way
Out,* is no less appropriate. The belief that there was an escape
route accounts for many of the false starts of the intelligentsia.

The Russian intelligentsia of the past suffered from the fact
that no section of society was capable of appreciating its efforts,
assimilating its achievements, supporting its creative activity, or
judging its ideas and intentions. Attempts at practical action
always collapsed. Culture existed in a vacuum. The intelligentsia
aspired to belong to the whole nation, but was condemned to
remain an élite.

Spiritual activity seethed in narrow intellectual circles, where
inherited values were discussed and reappraised. Opinions were
hotly debated, and many suggestions were put forth as to how the
intelligentsia's ideas and theories could be translated into practice. These hopes proved illusory, however, and led to results
diametrically opposed to expectations. The history of the Russian
intelligentsia is covered by a pall of tragedy.

An interest in refined cultural problems appeared incongru-
ous in a country lacking the most elementary sense of law. It was
a society where personal violence and other outrages against
human dignity were constantly perpetrated not merely by hooligans but by the state, and where millions spent their lives fighting
for land, food, and the bare necessities of existence. In the cold
expanses of Russia, cultural impulses expired like the heat from a

stove placed in the middle of a field. Culture and Russian life remained in watertight compartments.

Culture is not simply a collection of poems, pictures, sculpture, and music: it exists in and for human society. Its role is to serve as a guide to man in his contacts with society and nature, enriching his mind, forming his tastes, and directing his will. It is not something to be relegated to particular times in a daily or weekly schedule. Culture is the whole man, the sum total of his physical and mental demands on life, the whole complexity and individuality of his practical behavior. It accumulates from one generation to another, forming custom, tradition, and national character. By its nature, therefore, it cannot be the exclusive property of a few highly cultivated individuals. It can normally exist and develop only as a national inheritance, and thus as the patrimony of all humanity.

Russian culture answered to this description only in part. It was shut up in the intellectual sphere as in a prison. It could direct mind and feelings, but not will. It formed the character of a thin layer of the intelligentsia, but not that of the people. The intellectuals longed to play their part in daily life, but were constantly thrust aside from it.

In the words of the leading Symbolist poet and philosopher Vyacheslav Ivanov, written in 1909,

> The intelligentsia is not content to remain within its own isolated sphere of thought and life. It has stirred up the church, and perhaps awakened it to some purpose. It has not ceased to desire contact with the people, though its efforts in this direction have often been platonic and nearly always ineffectual. While its more active sections have devoted themselves to solicitude for the people in a material sense, and have operated from the outside, the leaders of our intellectual and spiritual culture have endeavored to transcend individualism in this sphere and create forms of art for the whole people. They have tried to approach the people in all openness of heart, proclaiming on the one hand a nationwide spirit [*vsenarodnost'*]—feeling, rightly perhaps, that there is no barrier in principle between the final simplicity of those made wise by tradition and others' wisdom, and the wisdom of the simple among us—and, on the other hand, a new populism [*narodnichestvo*],[10] as if to show that even the most preeminent intelligentsia is only an intelligentsia, and must either become something else or perish.

This is still true today, and so is the following passage by Ivanov's contemporary Lev Shestov, who was perhaps the severest critic of the intelligentsia's efforts to break loose from its isolation.

> His [Ivanov's] whole endeavor is to divorce ideas from reality altogether and inspire them with an independent life of their own—a full, luxuriant life, adorned with all the autumnal beauty in which Ivanov's prose and poetry are so rich. To achieve this, ideas must cease to be nourished with the sap of everyday life. . . . There is no room in his designs for simplicity or intelligibility. In this respect, like the whole school of modern writers who derive from Dostoyevsky, he makes a complete break with Russian literary tradition.

The cultural isolation of what Ivanov called "leading spiritual forces" was part of life and reality. Attempts were made to break out of this isolation through mysticism and the arbitrary coinages of Futurist language. To preserve the spiritual values achieved by its own efforts and suffering, Russian culture had condemned itself to extreme individualism. When it endeavored to escape from this, it lost all its value, ceased to be culture at all and became incomprehensible, impossible, and meaningless. This fate overtook even the great Tolstoy when he decided to adopt a rustic life and "go among the people."

The Russian intelligentsia endowed its native land with its own faith and ideals and the complexity of its rich nature. Russian culture—the heritage of Pushkin, Gogol, Tolstoy, Dostoyevsky, and Vladimir Solovyov—was genuinely national, and it was natural to believe that the country's soul was mirrored in this culture rather than in debauchery, drunkenness, and affronts to human dignity.

Russian culture evolved with an awareness that it was rooted in the nation. The leading intellectuals judged the nation's soul by what they found in their own, to compensate somewhat for their tragic isolation. But this desperate faith turned into pessimism and skepticism when it confronted the hard crust of everyday Russian reality. Poverty and gloom, savagery and oppression, a life cut off from knowledge and civilization, without social culture or respect for human rights and freedoms—all this filled the intellectuals with sadness and compassion and obliged them to make a difficult choice: to return from spiritual wandering of happier times to the bosom of their own unhappy country. A dying invalid, tired of the unequal struggle, may abandon himself similarly to the inexorable course of his disease.

Sometimes this heartrending love of their native soil led Russian intellectuals to trample on themselves in a kind of inverted aestheticism and to renounce all feelings dictated by moral sensibility. The poet Blok, for example, saw Russian life in all its sadness, darkness, and poverty. He expressed his vision in the lyrical language of the Symbolist school, but exulted in its very sordidness. The glaring duality of style and sentiment in this perfervid patriotism was characteristic of the milieu that formed Blok's poetic temperament.

Intellectuals alternated between sober or ecstatic faith in Russia and black despair, like divers plunging into an ice-hole straight from the sweat-room of a Russian bathhouse. The intelligentsia's reaction to the defeat of the revolution of 1905 was expressed by Merezhkovsky in his bitter article "Our Heads Are Bowed." Not long before, he had written in a triumphant and optimistic vein, prophesying Russia's millennium and the role the intelligentsia would play in leading the country to the light. Now, in the grip of an all-encompassing skepticism, he piled up bitter epithets. He saw writers, publicists, and political, religious, and cultural leaders tending Russia's sick body as one would a dying child's—trying to brighten its spirit, plying it with spiritual nostrums, endeavoring to save it from a fatal reactionary delirium. But nothing helps: ideas and philosophical projects are of no avail. Russia, like the child, is in a state of mortal decline:

> In other countries, reaction springs from revolution, but with us revolution, or what seems like it, springs from reaction. The noose is pulled too tight, and we struggle feverishly; then they pull it tighter still, and we become rigid again.
>
> In other countries, reaction is secondary and derivative. With us it is an active, primary agent; not something taken away but something added; not a minus but a plus, though of course a revolting, abominable plus.
>
> It sometimes seems as though reaction is the *prima materia,* the primal substance of Russia, as though disintegrating radium is the

heart of our hearts and the marrow in our bones; as though Russia *is* reaction, and reaction Russia.

It sometimes seems that in Russia there are no revolutions but only unsuccessful revolts: that of January [1905], that of December [1825], the Chuguyev revolt, the cholera riots [of 1830–1], the Pugachev rebellion[11]—eternal rebellions by eternal slaves. We are like a weighted doll—whenever the revolution overturns us, reaction sets us straight again.

The curse of spiritual and practical isolation that weighed on the most cultured segment of the intelligentsia imparted a special tension to its mental life. Unhampered by any link with practical affairs, this part of the intelligentsia could follow either path open before it, to extremes. The exalted proclamation of ideals alternated with extreme nihilism. Dreams of the regeneration of all mankind gave way to extreme subjectivism, individualism, and introversion. Nothing was held dear or cheap in practical terms. The search for truth alternated with listlessness; the image of Christ coexisted with that of Antichrist, and the two merged into a monstrous synthesis. The ideal and the abyss were confounded; the spirit, left to itself, ran to extravagance in all directions.

This tragic situation was keenly felt by many prominent figures in the Russian cultural renaissance of the years before 1914. Some attempted to view it as a praiseworthy feature of the Russian character, while others criticized it strongly. Merezhkovsky, for instance, wrote:

> "A Russian is terrible when he is free"—so said Dostoyevsky of Peter I. This strange freedom of the spirit, this ability suddenly to abandon one's roots and one's history, to burn one's boats and break with one's past in the name of an uncertain future—this arbitrary rootlessness[12] is one of the profoundest Russian characteristics.

And Ivanov:

> The main feature of our national character is the urge to divest ourselves of all disguises and to strip from the naked truth every kind of disguise and adornment. . . . From this tendency springs the skeptical, realistic attitude of honest Russian thought, the ruthless consistency with which it follows every path to the end, its abhorrence of any contradiction between thought and act, the

mistrustful severity of its judgments, and its urge to depreciate values.

Such references to "national character" should be taken with reservations. The subject of discussion was the "Russian spirit" that the intelligentsia believed it embodied. Its distinct features were derived not from the depths of the national soul but from the intelligentsia's isolation from any kind of "depth" outside itself.

"Rootlessness" was a characteristic trait of the Russian people. Russians did not feel they were masters in their own land, the ancient Tsarist patrimony. Hence the general disorder and slovenliness of life. The most active felt the urge to "cut and run" from the centers of fixed habitation. This form of rootlessness produced the arch-rebels Razin and Pugachev. It was accompanied by a fierce contempt for traditional values, whether material or spiritual, and a readiness to go berserk on slight provocation. This was the "nihilism" that united the autocracy and the people in spiritual kinship and, as we saw, aroused the alarm and indignation of the intelligentsia. It burst with the energy of a compressed spring suddenly released in the Bolshevik revolution.

But the intelligentsia had a special rootlessness of its own, described by such Dostoyevsky characters as Ivan Karamazov, Stavrogin, and the two Verkhovenskys. This was a mental rootlessness, caused by eyeing life as an outsider and attempting to define one's own position on a purely intellectual basis, according to one's own conscience and feelings.

The Russian intellectual was rarely troubled by the "contradiction between thought and act," because his acts remained suspended: they went no further than an acute desire to put his ideas into practice, and a firm conviction that they were practicable. The desire and the need for action did not proceed from external social reality, which the intellectual regarded as hopelessly ossified, but from a subjective internal impulse. He could not reconcile himself to reality. It frustrated and hemmed him in at every turn, stifling every move toward spiritual independence and self-expression as a matter of course. This ingrained Russian reality was a challenge to "do something," and something radical at that.

Thus the intelligentsia's impetuous and ill-planned activity was motivated by internal stimuli. Formed against the background of highly impersonal or antipersonal surroundings, they were highly restless. This extreme dichotomy generated an intellectual torrent, surging toward its goal with the "ruthless consistency" of which Ivanov spoke.

The paradox lies in the fact that Russia never provided conditions under which individuals could participate in public affairs. The traditional foundations of the state simply did not allow for this. Every subject (a more accurate term than "citizen") was obliged to conform to administrative dictates and to bear his "load" *(tyaglo)*, i.e., to render any service that an autocratic government chose to demand of him. The moment he stepped outside this framework, he was deprived of the protection of the "law," which in any case was more a figure of speech than a reality.

Theoretically and historically, the intelligentsia were well aware of this sad state of affairs, and had analyzed it extensively. Berdyaev, for example, wrote in 1915:

> The Russian people has created a state on an unprecedented scale and has exhausted itself in the task. The Russians are made helpless by the vast extent of their territory and their defensive position in the world. The crushing size of the state apparatus with its historical protective mission has brought about a curious parasitism and vampirism on the state's part, which in turn has bred various false ideologies. . . . To the misfortune of the Russian people, so unhappy in its historical situation, the state system has turned from a means into an end and has acquired a fictitious, self-sufficient life of its own. Hence the vast development of bureaucracy and the feeble development of social and personal independence. . . . This fatal characteristic of the Russian state keeps us all in permanent tutelage. It is because Russian people have been crushed by the self-sufficiency of the state that they have been prone to espouse ideal systems involving its abolition.

Thus the Russian intelligentsia, despite its firm desire to take a hand in public affairs and transform Russian life, felt acutely its exclusion from practical activity. Its hatred of the existing system increased its longing to take action, but not in the ordinary political sense. Even Berdyaev, while chafing at the state of perennial adolescence, was averse to any kind of political activity. The action that the intelligentsia dreamt of was not the practical, Western kind, but involved an outpouring from the depths of the individual consciousness. The idea of uniting for a "common cause" was present in some of them, some of the time, but they refused to use any existing organizations or institutions or to be guided by the limited interests of a particular group. The first priority was to make a clean sweep of the old Russia, and create a new and wholly different one that would be in complete accord with their ideals.

Moreover, the old system involved too much crude oppression for intellectuals. However ideal and far-reaching their plans, they were unwilling to contemplate any restriction on personal liberty. The intelligentsia itself was free in the realm of the spirit, where neither the government nor the people could dictate to it, and where it could indulge its anarchist speculations at will. The experience of the revolution showed, of course, that when anarchism came up against the elemental realities of Russian life, its advocates had either to practice violence with the rest or become its victims; but this could not have been foreseen.

A part was played by the historical conditions that had formed Russian intellectuals and Russian culture in the second half of the nineteenth century and the early twentieth. These were studied with classical lucidity by Gershenzon in his *History of Young Russia,* published in 1908. In this work he remarked that during the whole eighteenth century and the first quarter of the nineteenth, advanced Russian circles had been unafflicted by "tormented moral searchings and the tragedy of the spirit. . . . As a cloud is formed by exhalations from the sea, so the condition of society gave rise to a philosophy of life which was broadly the same for all and was not the result of any one person's sufferings." The change came, in Gershenzon's opinion, after the defeat of the Decembrists,[13] who were not an intelligentsia in the later sense but were part of the "establishment" and thought of themselves as primarily men of action. Culture was not yet divorced from life, and the integration and equilibrium of the cultivated Russian mind was reflected, for instance, in the incomparable harmony of Pushkin's poems.

The Decembrists' generation was also the first to break with the prevailing system of "doublethink," but without realizing how monolithic that system was. The confusion of the revolt and its bitter suppression taught them and all thinking people that the peculiar ills of Russian society could not be cured by ordinary Western means. As Gershenzon goes on to observe:

> It is very probable that even without the shock caused by the Decembrists' failure, the old outlook would not have prevailed much longer; but the catastrophe naturally hastened its collapse. . . . Thought, artificially disjoined from action, was turned back upon itself. . . . The old philosophy disappeared; the great current of Russian thought began to flow, like a river in springtime. There began a period of theoretical work, highly unnatural in its one-sidedness but most fruitful in its results.

Thus the distinctive feature of Russian intellectual life in the nineteenth and early twentieth centuries was the withdrawal of the mind into itself, the transformation of outward-directed energy into arbitrary subjectivity. It was a culture founded on individualistic self-study, made possible only because individual personalities already existed. Conversely, it provided the only ground in which personality could flourish, and when it was destroyed, personality vanished also.

# "Landmarks"

At the present time, this process is repeating itself. The Russian intelligentsia is not being born, but reborn. It would do well to study its own past, to recognize its achievements and avoid old pitfalls.

In 1975, a hundred and fifty years after the Decembrist rising, a group of intellectuals assembled on Senate Square in Leningrad under the banner: "Long live the Decembrists—the first Russian dissidents." Our intellectuals have always been "dissidents," but this term has come into use just as the full tragedy of their fate is becoming perceptible. It is also a time for profitable rereading of *Landmarks* (*Vekhi*, 1909),[14] an imposing tribute to Russian intellectuals' powers of self-examination.

This work is especially full of lessons for our day. Our intellectuals are stifled by life's grayness and the despairing realization that things may not right themselves in our lifetime, that we are blundering about like lost children. In our helplessness we may well need to listen to the prophetic voices of our spiritual forebears of seventy years ago.

The Russian mind, just barely freed from the thralldom of official verbiage, is now being flooded by ideas of eminent early-twentieth-century thinkers ignored by previous generations of the intelligentsia. This serves to heal and restore our violently disrupted tradition; and it enables us to deepen our understanding through assimilation of the thought of master intellects, and to avoid the hackneyed, "respectable" judgments of the conventional wisdom.

However, while doing our best to assimilate the ideas of Berdyaev, Bulgakov, Semen Frank, Petr Struve, Fedotov, and other contributors to *Landmarks,* we should approach these thinkers fully conscious of our own subsequent experience. We have seen things that they could not have imagined. We must not simply repeat the ideas they developed and expressed so clearly, but apply them creatively, and above all critically, to our present situation. The old positions, in all their coherence, are less important to us than the principles which led to their formulation.

The present tendency to repeat monotonously and uncritically the ideas of the "religious renaissance" (the revival of interest in Orthodoxy by several writers and thinkers in the early twentieth century) is symptomatic of a lack of historical sense. It is as though people had forgotten the experience of their own lives and the evidence of the present day. One is sometimes amazed that those who swear by *Landmarks* should act, think, and feel in ways that are completely out of tune with it. But this, alas, is inevitable as long as we suffer from dual consciousness and until our ideas possess existential integrity.

The essays in *Landmarks,* like other writings by members of this group, were pioneering efforts, and it is for us to blaze the trail further. The neat categories of the past no longer apply without qualification to a world that has moved onto a different existential plane.

*Landmarks* is described in its subtitle as "a collection of essays on the Russian intelligentsia." The authors, writing from a liberal national standpoint, subjected the radical intellectuals—to whom the term "intelligentsia" was traditionally restricted—to an impartial analysis, pointing out faults that appeared dangerous to the country's future. Now that the work has been rescued from oblivion and slander, it is seldom read with indifference and never, perhaps, with the blindness which once precluded all understanding of its intentions.

If the authors' criticisms were once greeted by an explosion of moral indignation among intellectuals, who regarded them as insulting, it has now become commonplace to criticize the revolutionary-democratic tradition. "Socialism" was once the password whereby intellectuals recognized one another in the crowd, but now things have changed completely: anyone who professes socialist ideals, even if only for the sake of his career, is unwelcome in decent Moscow society. Belinsky, Chernyshevsky, and Dobrolyubov are no longer intellectual idols, and Marxism is not mentioned, just as one doesn't talk of rope in the house of a man who has been hanged.

The tradition associated with Dostoyevsky's *The Possessed* finds no favor with today's intellectuals. Appeals to "do something, no matter what" arouse ridicule. Moralistic judgments do not satisfy. The passions of cliques and coteries have set our teeth on edge, and we have begun to develop a taste for tolerance. Respect for law and order, the demand for legality, and the sense of legal principles are prevailing trends among the intelligentsia of our time. It is more and more clearly understood that cultural activity is our immediate business. Voices urge us to appraise our own history with a critical mind. Finally, with old-fashioned intellectual materialism clearly worn out, there is an unmistakable interest in religion and a return to it or to other forms of idealism.

All these present trends can also be found in *Landmarks*. But how slowly, superficially, and uncreatively its lessons are being absorbed, and how timid we are in applying its religious and philosophical principles to our own lives! Even when we have learned something from it, we remain unprepared for the blows of life and fail to understand where they come from. And, as before, we look on with helpless bitterness when a friend is sucked under by the quicksands of life.

Perhaps a rapid, surreptitious reading of free literature is not enough to make it a mainstay of our lives and a means of transformation. Or perhaps it is not enough to read it privately. Maybe we need to discuss questions crucial to the intelligentsia's existence as a spiritually mature force in public, on the widest possible scale.

Our culture is like a human body that has been beaten and battered: it is numb and swollen, the blood cannot flow properly, and all its functions are agonizingly painful. But this is not all. Not only is the body covered with welts, but its soul suffers from an inveterate disease—which was to some extent diagnosed by the authors of *Landmarks*—and our sick society feverishly rejects the salutary truth of self-knowledge.

The modern intellectual, no doubt, understands the critical side of *Landmarks* without difficulty, but not its constructive program. As in the past, the intelligentsia becomes aware of its unity on a basis of rejection. The intellectual is one who finds the burden of the times intolerable and demands to be rid of it, no matter how. For the time being, at least, his spiritual being does not focus on positive impulses or the desire to build and create. Thus, although the intelligentsia has seen enough to be convinced of the justice of the criticisms in *Landmarks,* it has scarcely overcome any of the faults to which that work drew attention so forcefully. This is an extremely important fact.

As Semen Frank wrote in *Landmarks:* "Revolutionism is only the reflection of the metaphysical absolutization of the values of destruction. . . . Hatred is always the psychological spur and accompaniment to destruction, and, insofar as destruction supplants other forms of activity, hatred will take the place of other impulses in the make-up of the Russian intelligentsia." Today, perhaps, it would not be an exaggeration to say that the "reflection" has receded while its metaphysical basis remains intact. Revolutionism has lost its attractiveness, at least in the old Social Revolutionary–Bolshevik sense. The modern intellectual looks back with horror at the revolution and all it brought with it. But a deeper, more fundamental feeling remains: the sense that it is impossible for things to go on as they are, the urgent longing for the existing order to crack up or at least be so shaken that it becomes possible to breathe. Hatred remains too, but it is blinding and debilitating, the eternal companion of weakness. Moreover, it is hatred directed precisely at that object which intellectuals of former generations ardently desired and would have made any sacrifice for. This, perhaps, has opened up the modern intellectual to the criticisms in *Landmarks,* which feed his hatred by their clear formulation of his suppressed anguish and the causes of his pain.

If the intelligentsia had heeded *Landmarks* in the first quarter of the century, they would have felt duty-bound to criticize themselves, to do penance and undergo a psychological transformation. Instead of righteous hatred, they would have had to cultivate a sense of their own responsibility, a sentiment incompatible with hatred of any sort. They would have had to forget the bullying, the humiliations, and the very real horrors of life, and to concentrate on themselves. Only by self-inspection could they have recognized and eradicated the causes of the general evil— not only its direct and open manifestations, but its indirect ones. They would have been forced to grasp that a mere change of circumstances, and even the attainment of external freedom, is no cure for the troubles of society as long as people's souls, and especially the souls of the intelligentsia, still bear the marks of hundreds of years of slavery.

However, the pre-revolutionary intelligentsia was not discontented with itself but only with a state of society diametrically opposed to its ideas of goodness, justice, and humanity. It regarded itself, by and large, as the embodiment of truth and virtue, destined to fulfill the country's aspirations and give it the future it deserved. It imagined that only the sordid state of Russian reality prevented it from using its accumulated knowledge and abilities to solve the problems of Russia and all humanity.

The modern intellectual derives solace from *Landmarks* because he thinks its strictures apply only to a past generation and not to him. They nourish his hatred and flatter his complacency, giving him a false sense of superiority over the men and women of earlier days who led the country to an impasse.

So, if we look closely, there is little difference between today's intellectual and his pre-revolutionary forebears. By a curious aberration he misinterprets the counsel of *Landmarks* as they did. He sees in it a condemnation of all forms of public activity and the call to withdraw into a world of "sweet harmony and prayers," as Pushkin once put it. This type of quietism appears in a different guise in present-day Moscow, where "revolutionism," now a term of abuse, is applied, with conscious reference to *Landmarks,* to all those who resist the prevailing conformism in any way. In exactly the same way as sixty or seventy years ago, the authors of *Landmarks* are misrepresented as preachers of conformity; a minority reject them on this account, while others admire their worldly wisdom. In other words, today's intellectual, like his predecessors, can conceive of no form of social action except the destruction of the existing order, in Bolshevik style. The only difference is that the old generation did not know what this would mean in practice, while our generation does.

A sense of confusion and disappointment, exacerbated in our case by the experience of the last two decades, is the common element of the atmosphere of Russia in the 1970s and that of the years following the debacle of the 1905 revolution. *Landmarks* appeared in 1909, but the following description of the situation by Gershenzon could have been written yesterday:

> The intelligentsia understood, not only with its mind but with its whole being, that the reason for failure lay not in programs but in something else. . . . In the first place there was a panic of purely personal, almost physical self-preservation when it turned out that society had failed to cure itself and that each one of us would have to drag out his painful existence for an indefinite time. Up to then, with public opinion in a state of hypnosis, people had endured their lives in the hope of a political panacea; but now, when hope was defeated for the foreseeable future, they lost heart and felt unable to endure any longer. . . . The fanatics of social action are astonished at the passivity and indifference of the mass of the intelligentsia with regard to politics and social questions generally. Reaction triumphs, the executions go on and on—and the public maintains a deathlike silence.

Also in *Landmarks,* Bulgakov wrote: "The future of Russia is a matter of despondency and the deepest doubt." So it is today. Gershenzon's reference to "executions" should, it is true, read "arrests" as far as we are concerned. This is a mercy we are duly thankful for, but in the present state of things, can we be sure that it will continue?

However, the strength of *Landmarks* in its own day, and its current importance, does not lie primarily in the accuracy of its gloomy descriptions or even in its frank acknowledgment of political defeat. Russia in those days was rich in essayists who could eloquently describe the intelligentsia's disarray. But their main effort was directed toward keeping hope alive. The defeat of the revolution, it was thought, should be a call to revise and improve tactics, to "draw the moral" and learn the lesson of events, but not to alter course, or criticize the historical role of the intelligentsia and the country, or adopt a radically different view of the intelligentsia as such.

Among the rival collections of essays which appeared at this time was *"Landmarks" as a Sign of the Times* by the Socialist Revolutionaries (SR). The SR writers, like many others, regarded *Landmarks*'s criticism of the intelligentsia as defeatism, loss of faith in socialism, and reluctance to endure any longer the burdens and sacrifices of the road to freedom. The years of reaction would pass, and, it was argued, there would be a new political upsurge undermining the grounds for defeatism. The SR, the Social Democrats, and the Constitutional Democrats ("Cadets") all appealed to the intelligentsia to bear the dark days with fortitude. The parties should remain faithful to their different programs, and build up strength for the next onslaught on the autocratic citadel.

The intelligentsia sought to minimize the discouraging aspects of their recent experience. They wished to believe that everything was not yet lost—for otherwise there seemed no reason to go on living. To their thinking, the actual state of Russia afforded firm grounds for hope, popular feeling made it possible to bridge the gulf between past and future, and Russia and the intelligentsia as well were "holy." Intellectuals were united against *Landmarks* by their determination to have faith, their reluctance to look truth in the face, and their fear of departing from customary methods and objectives.

In those pre-revolutionary years, as again today, the intelligentsia—a small island of consciousness lashed by a turbulent sea of despotism—was afraid to renounce the illusions that constituted a thin defense line against the cruel necessity of choice. The left-wing SR Ivanov-Razumnik, for instance, wrote:

Here, perhaps, is the profoundest divergence between us and them [the authors of *Landmarks*]. We believe in the "immanence" of man, not the transformation of mankind, and we expect to conquer on this basis. In this respect we are "realists," whatever the mystic tendencies of some of us. They, on the other hand, believe only in the transformation of mankind by a miracle, and see no hope of salvation otherwise. From this point of view it is they who are "mystics." . . . They believe in the transcendent, we believe in the immanent. They live in the absolute, we in the relative.

It should be pointed out for the sake of objectivity that *Landmarks* spoke less of man's transformation than of the need to transform the intelligentsia. Before teaching others and calling on them to make sacrifices and join in the fight, it behooved the self-appointed leaders to examine themselves and their own responsibility. It was their duty to rise above the daily turmoil to contemplate the absolute. Thus, they would swim above the misguided relativism in which noble ends are used to justify ignoble means, and the empirical ego is finally crowned with an undeserved halo.

*Landmarks* pointed the way to a longer and more difficult road than the intellectuals customarily envisaged; it did not encourage the illusion that they had only to stretch out their hands to grasp the moon. It called on the thinking part of Russian society to undergo serious self-analysis, the fruits of which, though taking long to appear, would be ripe and edible. It is not our fault if, in the Russian climate, fast-ripening fruits go bad, while evergreen plants fail to take root.

It may indeed be regarded as a miracle, that the ideas of *Landmarks,* which were misunderstood, misrepresented, or ignored for decades, appear sharply relevant today. Once dismissed as "unrealistic," they now seem like a helping hand stretched out at a time of tribulation. Who could have foreseen this truly miraculous state of affairs?

The main point is not, of course, that the efforts of the *Landmarks* authors are vindicated today, when they are all dead. Their philosophy did not include the idea of "fertilizing the soil of history" and sacrificing oneself on the altar of the future. Their activity was rooted in the problems of their own day and was an answer to its cry of pain. They were animated by the same self-consuming spiritual fire, perhaps, that animates our own existence. It is precisely because their work was self-sufficient in its time that it has contributed to history.

The ways of history are not known to us in detail; we cannot foresee the future as it will be. But it is nonetheless *our* history, formed entirely by our own efforts; it is determined by our choice of personal and social behavior, it is burdened by our mistakes and illuminated by our insights. Man's contact with history transcends his immediate experience both in scale and qualitatively, but for that very reason it is a real contact.

In calling on the intelligentsia to make a conscious effort to transform itself—a task suited in the first instance to thinking men and women and not to "humanity," the "people," or any such abstraction—the authors of *Landmarks* gave a critical review of the intelligentsia's spiritual background. Knowledge of the past was necessary in order to arrive at true self-knowledge. A sober, sensible look at beliefs that might have rigidified into "behests" or "testaments," was required to make amends for anything in them that was superstitious, irresponsible, or unworthy. The intelligentsia must look into its own soul and pass impartial judgment. This meant a true spiritual revolution, in which the traditional ethic of groups and parties would give place to free knowledge and action.

But the intelligentsia shrank from this task. To cut loose from the past seemed to it as dangerous as to abandon coastal sailing for the open sea. *Landmarks*'s appeal to the intellectuals to transcend their past seemed to them, in their confusion, retrograde. They were traditionalists, but their tradition was revolution and thus the revolution they sought was conservative and tended to follow principles of group ethics over personal ethics, party politics over individual aspirations. Like hidebound conservatives, they refrained from taking the trouble to understand *Landmarks*'s closely reasoned arguments. "Immanence" and "realism" consisted in a rigid attachment to the past. Their response to criticism was emotional and instinctive rather than rational; and their faith in the past caused them to treat the present with reckless arrogance.

Merezhkovsky, who inveighed so bitterly against Russia's "essential reactionism," nevertheless declared: "We must either abandon ourselves finally to Egyptian darkness, bowing our heads and saying adieu to Russia, or else we must resolve to find in the past, no matter what it was, not only a provisional but an eternal truth linking it with the future." Or, as Ivanov-Razumnik expressed it more directly:

> Belinsky, Herzen, Chernyshevsky, Lavrov, Mikhailovsky—such is the unbroken tradition of our covenant, in sharp opposition at the present day to Petr Struve and his associates [i.e., *Landmarks*]. . . . The road we must tread is still the ancient road of the Russian intelligentsia, illumined by the testaments of the past and leading us to achievements in the future. For these achievements are built on testaments which will lead us to fresh searches and fresh achievements.

But the intellectuals' attachment to the past, and their piety for even nihilistic leaders, meant that they had no more to offer than stale formulae and a despondent return to ancient ways. To find "eternal truth" in "the past, no matter what it was" meant throwing in one's hand before the future, committing oneself to accepting whatever it might bring even though it simply repeated the past, returning to the old equilibrium like a weighted doll. . . .

Here, however, we should pause for a moment. The intelligentsia's blame for the calamitous events of recent Russian history has been greatly exaggerated, both by the intelligentsia itself and by its enemies. This is the reverse side of the intellectuals' baseless claim to represent the "people," which invariably ends in self-styled leaders' noticing that the "people" has not budged, and their rushing round to join the tail end of the procession. The destructive role of the progressive intelligentsia, on the other hand, was a figment of the frightened imagination of the reactionaries under Nicholas I and Alexander II. Seeing that the country was in trouble, they did not have the wit to ascribe this to anything but the plots of malefactors. Their Soviet successors raised this attitude into a pathological suspicion of omnipresent "wreckers" and "enemies of the people,"[15] the consequences and cost of which are only too well known.

Actually, the intelligentsia had no decisive or even noticeable effect on political events, either before or after 1917. Certainly, they were occasionally involved in the assassination of public figures, who were by no means all among the most harmful.[16] The short period between the February and October revolutions, when the intelligentsia was at the helm, does not rank as a bright spot in its gloomy history.

The intelligentsia was and is the only social class that is seriously concerned about Russia's fate and that writes, thinks, and talks about matters that citizens in general are not supposed to discuss. It "dares to have its own opinion," in Griboyedov's phrase—an attitude which strikes the rest of the country as dangerously frivolous and even infantile. The unruly habit of criticism, so foreign to the rest of Russian tradition, has often led the intelligentsia into self-delusion and has also deluded the authorities into thinking it more formidable than it is. Amid the deathlike silence and torpid indifference of society as a whole, the voice of a few intellectuals, by natural acoustic contrast, rings out like a thunderclap; but no great good or harm ensues. The surface of the stagnant pool ripples for a moment, then the weeds close over again.

The intelligentsia's mistake was not that it was deluded by false political ideas of socialism or parliamentary democracy, but rather that it concentrated on politics and absolutized them as the sole and sufficient answer to its agonizing problems. It was observed long ago that the politicization of the intellectual consciousness was the result and reflection of the age-old character of the autocracy. It had only one problem and one point of reference—its own preservation—and therefore regarded all social phenomena, including philosophy, art, and culture of all kinds, from a political point of view.

In any case, the intelligentsia from time to time cherished dreams of seizing the existing power and using it as a lever to transform society. The confusion between political, social, and spiritual aspects of public life is the saddest feature of Russian cultural development in the past hundred and fifty years. The intelligentsia did not love and respect humanity enough to avoid violence. With few exceptions, it also had too little of the joyful play of mind that goes with intellectual freedom. Consequently, from whatever point of view it considered itself, the "people" or the state, its ideas were prejudiced and its actions overhasty.

The intelligentsia was to blame, for the most part, for being ashamed of its intellectual standing and for trying to hide it as some unseemly defect. It abounded in self-depreciation, which, it has been said, is "worse than pride," and often seemed to model itself on the character in Dostoyevsky's *Notes from the Underground*. It surrendered to relativism, and appeared to consider it almost disgraceful to do otherwise. It was constantly endeavoring to see some higher meaning in the "people," in ideals, in the state, or in a national church, which by definition laid no claim to universality and was neither spiritual, rational, nor fully accountable for its actions. The intelligentsia ran away from freedom, choosing rather to suffer and to serve. It was captivated in turn by the people's humility and submissiveness and by its wild anarchistic instincts. It forced itself to delight in abominations that it should not have even tolerated.

In spite of its self-sacrifice, disinterestedness, and on some occasions outstanding heroism, the intelligentsia found itself in the end defeated. Wanting everything at once, all it got was humiliation, exile, and death. Extravagant historical aspirations often end in a return to the status quo. Despising evolutionary methods and daily constructive work, that continuity of human effort which is the weft of history, the intelligentsia was confronted again and again by stagnation or paroxysms of reaction. It was repeatedly thrown back to the starting point, its discomfiture thinly veiled by periodic changes of ideological raiment.

. The fundamental offense of the intelligentsia was an offense it committed against itself; in the last analysis, it was not too intellectual, but rather insufficiently so. The characteristics analyzed at length in *Landmarks* all stem from this: the intelligentsia's indifference to truth and philosophic diversity, its pragmatism and utility-worship, its nihilism and masochism, its contempt for law and implicit faith in collective discipline, its intolerance and sectarianism, its unwillingness to listen, and its compulsive desire to preach.

# "Landmarks" and "From Under the Rubble"

*Landmarks* itself, however, suffered from a contradiction due to the limited and specific nature of the problems of its day. Its authors, to varying degrees, wrote from a partisan point of view, directing their fire against the part of the intelligentsia that embraced a revolutionary and atheistic position in the early 1900s. Some of the authors of *Landmarks* still believed in the Russian people as the "elect of God," and they accused the intelligentsia of having been seduced by crude materialism into losing sight of this divine mission and favor and thus becoming what Petr Struve called "renegades." (By a curious coincidence, half a century later the Soviet press began to apply this term to present-day dissidents.)

The authors of *Landmarks* sought to redefine the term "intelligentsia" so as to cover only socialists and atheists. Thus Berdyaev, on the first page of the book, writes as follows:

> I am speaking of the intelligentsia in its traditional Russian sense: our clique-intelligentsia, artificially separated from the life of the community. This curious world of its own, living a self-contained life under the pressure of a double conventionalism—externally the force of reaction, internally the weight of conservative feelings and mental inertia—is called, not without reason, the *intelligentshchina**  by contrast with the intelligentsia in the broad, national, historical sense of the term.

The distinction between the intelligentsia and the educated class as a whole was drawn even more sharply by Struve, who wrote:

> We are not talking here about this [educated] class and its historically intelligible and most obvious role of disseminating culture and enlightenment. The intelligentsia in Russian politics is a

---

*The suffix -*shchina* is pejorative: cf. note on *obrazovanshchina*, p. 77. —Translator's note.

factor *sui generis,* whose historical significance derives from its relation to the state as an idea and as embodied in actuality.

Struve's view, in other words, was that the Russian state, whatever its form, must be regarded as a realization of the "Russian idea," and that the intellectual forces of society were duty-bound to serve that idea by collaborating with the state and not opposing it.

According to the authors of *Landmarks,* the "intelligentsia" whose sociopsychological portrait was drawn in the book bore no relation to those—philosophers, scholars, writers, painters, public servants, priests—who made a positive contribution of any sort to Russian culture. An illusion became prevalent, although perhaps the *Landmarks* group did not fully share it, that enlightened and constructive cultural activity was not subject to interference in Russia, and that any deviation from this tolerant system was due to the errors of the intelligentsia. Alas, history decided otherwise, for after the Bolshevik victory most of the *Landmarks* writers were expelled from the country, which took little note of their disappearance.

*Landmarks* contained a deep and bitter truth. While its authors wrote from different points of view, their common theme was summed up by Gershenzon in a short preface to the first edition:

> The recognition of the primacy both in theory and in practice of spiritual life over the outward forms of society, in the sense that the inner life of the individual is the sole creative force of human existence, and that it, and not the self-sufficing elements of some political order, is the only solid basis for every social structure.

It followed, in these writers' view, that the cure for Russia's age-old ills must begin with the self-styled physicians, by curing them of superficiality, self-assurance, and irresponsibility. Political changes could not be fruitful as long as life was entangled in petty everyday affairs and transient historical circumstances governed by despotic caprice. All the intelligentsia had to offer was abstract moral schemata with no firm basis of personal freedom and maturity. Concentration on the externals of political order, and the belief in instant solutions for all the difficulties of historical development—such had been the foundations of the intellectuals' hopes for many decades, but all they proved was that the intelligentsia had too little sense of the importance of freedom and too little concern for spiritual problems. Freedom was not to be achieved by removing this or that external obstacle to action. There must be a rich, specific, integrated content to life, seeking its realization in action, and the only possible source of this content was personality. Neglect of the principle of personality was the main fault of the Russian intelligentsia and the source of its historical impotence.

But here the *Landmarks* authors added a further point, switching their criticism from the underdevelopment of personality to the nature of the intellectuals' world-view—as though the deficiency could be compensated for by changing from a wrong philosophy to a right one, or as though the vacuum in the soul could be filled by simply adopting a Christian outlook. Instead of proclaiming that a chosen social behavior pattern must remain a matter of individual conscience, they gave the impression that such a choice was already predetermined, as though one's spiritual being could be located in the "state" or the "people" or anywhere outside personality. It was as though words and arguments were sufficient to turn the intelligentsia from its atheist, socialist, and revolutionary ways and make it occupy its assigned place in a developing social system.

In *Landmarks* the attempt was made, as it had been so many times before, to discover a "positive principle" outside the individual, the intelligentsia, or the culture. The authors laid too little weight on individualism, although they drew attention to the baneful consequences of shifting the locus of consciousness to a crowd or group. Their view of Russian history and of the intelligentsia tended to establish a polar opposition between "self-perfection" and "patriotism," the latter meaning constructive work for the country's good. This was pointed out in 1918 by Pavel Novgorodtsev in the symposium *De Profundis*,[17] which attempted to apply the ideas of *Landmarks* to post-revolutionary conditions. He observed there that "certain disagreements among the authors of *Landmarks* were responsible for the fact . . . that, although ardent patriots, they were reckoned among the preachers of personal self-improvement." Combating Gershenzon's view of "the primacy of spiritual life over the outward forms of society," which he regarded as inadequate, Novgorodtsev supported Struve's viewpoint in the following passage:

> P. B. Struve's article, it seems to me, expresses most accurately the basic feature in the consciousness of the intelligentsia that has led to its downfall, namely its irreligious desertion of the state. Using the customary forms of philosophical language, we should say that the basic manifestation of the consciousness of the intelligentsia which has led to its downfall consists in rationalist utopianism and the endeavor to organize life on a basis of reason divorced from objective historical principles, the organic foundations of social order, and the life-giving sanctities of the nation's being.

In 1918, when the civil war was only just beginning, it was possible to romanticize the recent past and to suppose that the Tsarist regime had embodied these "organic foundations" and "life-giving sanctities," and it was possible to hope that they were still present somewhere and could be invoked to correct the mistakes of the apostate intellectuals. But much has changed since then. As early as 1921, a group of émigré intellectuals produced a symposium entitled *Smena vekh* ("Change of Landmarks," or "New Bearings")[18] promoting the view that Soviet Russia was henceforth the only Russia that existed and was itself the realization of "objective historical principles." In full accord with patriotic tenets expressed by some writers in the original *Landmarks,* the writers of this school proclaimed their readiness to return home and serve the new Russia. However, their zealous resolve to break with the old "apostasy" did not meet with a friendly response. Their attitude contained too strong an element of freedom, independence, and individualism to please the new regime, and most of them ended up as "wreckers" and "enemies of the people." Those who were lucky enough to escape this fate were soon submerged in a faceless mass, with no incentive to think about bearings, old or new, or to do anything but parrot the injunctions of the "leader of all times and peoples."

Many years later, when the intelligentsia started to reawaken, the first thing it became aware of was its alienation from the people and the state. At the time of *Landmarks,* no doubt, the situation was less disastrous and irrevocable; but now the isolation of the intellectuals was a basic fact, regardless of what they thought of it or whether they liked it. Today one can hardly speak without irony of the "life-giving sanctities of the nation's being," with which we are supposed to harmonize our subjective efforts: what were those sanctities, and what has become of them?

Nevertheless, we presently feel the criticisms leveled by *Landmarks* at the isolation of the intelligentsia all the more sharply. The disease of isolation has not been chosen voluntarily, but was brought on by circumstances. The alternative to isolation is conformism, a still-worse disease. By refusing to conform in present circumstances, as in the pre-Bolshevik era, we appear as outsiders and are condemned by all who feel warm and comfortable in the dense, indiscriminate mass. But as soon as we take a few first steps to freedom we are harassed by the government and exposed to popular hatred (by no means inspired only from above). It is at this stage that we fail to maintain our independence of mind. Having summoned up the courage to form and express opinions freely, we become dizzy from the unfamiliar sensation. We acquire a false sense of uniqueness and heroism, and this leads to facile and radical judgments, moralizing, intolerance, and the urge to impose our will on others. Our isolation is a disease that we cannot help, but if we abandon ourselves to it we shall commit spiritual suicide. Having taken the first step toward freedom, we must take care not to forfeit it at the second step, falling into authoritarianism by our own will and choice. History supplies us with a warning here, and so do the counsels of *Landmarks*.

When the dividing line between bondage and freedom has been crossed, and the foundation stone of personality laid, the conflict becomes internalized instead of externalized. What was previously the rejection of something objectively bad becomes, or should become, a debate within oneself. In traditional Russian circumstances, spiritual development is like a geometrical line drawn perpendicular to the base, which is personality. But the line is faintly traced and may break off altogether if the dynamic impulse fails, and the base acquired with such difficulty will then be lost also.

The problem lies not in the character of the abstract principles an immature personality may regard as the only true ones, but rather in the immature personality itself. The operative principles of the era of *Landmarks* were atheism and socialism, which the intelligentsia took up not for their own sake but in opposition to the state ideology—they were a kind of fashion or epidemic. In our own day, the same logic of repulsion might lead the intelligentsia to espouse Orthodoxy, autocracy, and nationality. In either case the individual substance in which convictions are rooted remains the same, and a change of convictions makes no more essential difference than shuffling a deck of cards.

I find striking confirmation of this in the collection of essays *From Under the Rubble,** published at a time when most of the present work had already been written.[19] As a matter of fact, the unhealthy symptoms connected with our first uncertain steps toward freedom had appeared earlier, but in the moral rather than in the intellectual sphere. They were seen in the haughtiness of some newly revealed "heroes," in their facile teaching and prophesying in the scramble for high rank and status among the dissidents, in a certain laxity of behavior (as "anything goes" in a situation of constant danger), and in a contemptuous attitude toward less daring intellectuals, glibly dismissed as "riffraff" (the Russian term is stronger). This mood was exemplified at the height of the protest campaign of 1968: the idea of publishing the names of those who had refused to sign was suggested, so as to hold them up to ignominy. Freedom was thus transforming itself into a categorical imperative. In justice, however, to our immature band of independent spirits, it should be noted that most of them resisted this temptation. The crisis within our ranks passed, and seemed to have resolved itself by the time of the scandalous trial of Yakir and Krasin. Fortunately the "organs" had not been clever enough to exploit it; it provided us with an important lesson for the future.

A few years later, we are presented with a talented literary expression of precisely those dangerous features of the isolated consciousness against which *Landmarks* directed its warnings. Not all the essays in *From Under the Rubble* are equally open to this criticism. The authors are united in being drawn toward a

---

*The quotations from this work on the succeeding pages are all taken from the English-language edition published in Boston by Little, Brown in 1975.—Tr. note.

religious outlook, as a rule that of Orthodoxy; but, as I have tried to show, in our circumstances this outlook can be and is combined with a variety of personal and existential attitudes. From this point of view, the collection bears out Berdyaev's warning in *Landmarks:* "I fear that even the most metaphysical and mystic teachings will be converted to domestic use; and this will not cure the Russian evil of despotism and slavery, which is not to be conquered by extreme doctrines."

Berdyaev's stricture does not, of course, apply to all those who have reverted to Christianity, or to all the writers in *From Under the Rubble.* In any case, it is not my purpose here to review this book as a whole; instead, I want to direct attention to Solzhenitsyn's essay "The Smatterers." It begins by lamenting that the intelligentsia of the time did not pay sufficient attention to *Landmarks,* and continues: "Even after sixty years its testimony has not lost its brightness: *Landmarks* today still seems to us to have been a vision of the future. And our only cause for rejoicing is that now, after sixty years, the stratum of Russian society able to lend its support to the book appears to be deepening" (pp. 229–30).

However, when Solzhenitsyn proceeds to lend his own support to *Landmarks,* we rub our eyes in astonishment. First, he maintains that the "faults of the old intelligentsia" as described by *Landmarks* have faded away for the most part and are now merely of historical interest (then why is *Landmarks* "a vision of the future"?). Second, he regards these faults as a source of pride, since "The Russian intelligentsia cannot have been so base if *Landmarks* could apply such lofty criteria in its criticism of it" (p. 232). Third, he identifies a still more gratifying category of "Faults at the time, which in our topsy-turvy world of today have the appearance almost of virtues" (ibid.). When we read the list of these, we are even more astonished:

> The aim of universal equality, in whose interests the individual must be prepared to curtail his higher needs. The psychology of heroic ecstasy, reinforced by state persecution; parties are popular in proportion to their degree of fearlessness. . . . A personal sense of martyrdom and a compulsion to confess; almost a death wish. . . . The heroic intellectual is not content with the modest role of worker and dreams of being the savior of mankind or at least of the Russian

people. Exaltation, an irrational mood of elation, intoxication with struggle. He is convinced that the only course open to him is social struggle and the destruction of society in its existing form. (Pp. 232–33.)

Yes, this is indeed a fairly complete list of the faults criticized by *Landmarks!* In our topsy-turvy world, as Solzhenitsyn calls it, we are not only failing to advance but are reverting to an anti-*Landmarks* position.

It is true that Solzhenitsyn goes on to list a fourth category of faults criticized by *Landmarks* that, he says, have persisted to the present day. These include: "An exaggerated awareness of [intellectuals'] rights. Pretentiousness, posturing, the hypocrisy of constant recourse to 'principles.' . . . An overweening insistence on the opposition between themselves and the 'philistines.' Spiritual arrogance" (p. 233). But I am prepared to wager that Solzhenitsyn will not find in *Landmarks* any condemnation of the intellectuals' "exaggerated awareness of rights," or of anything that might derive from this. The suggestion that *Landmarks* made such an accusation is Solzhenitsyn's own contribution and, like the rest of his article, seems inspired by hostility to the *Landmarks* standpoint.

I have noted only one criticism leveled by *Landmarks* which Solzhenitsyn quotes and which may be applied with some justice to intellectuals today, viz., that they "live in expectation of a social miracle" (p. 233). As we might expect, this very defect can be found in Solzhenitsyn's article itself. The *Landmarks* criticisms are coherent, and the attitude of "heroic ecstasy" goes along with "expectation of a social miracle." But Solzhenitsyn appears to display this expectation in a far more naive way than the intelligentsia ever did when he says (p. 250) that "Two hundred such men [namely, 'distinguished people'] (and they number half a thousand altogether), by coming forward and taking a united stand, would purify the public air in our country and all but transform our whole life!"

Of course, neither Solzhenitsyn nor anyone else is obliged to take *Landmarks*'s criticisms to heart—that is a matter of personal taste and opinion. But why quote authorities if one is immediately going to interpret them at random and without discernment? Have we not seen enough of this procedure in our time?

I would not take issue with Solzhenitsyn this way if he did not himself exemplify the old faults. They are breeding and reproducing before our eyes, and the lack of freedom and respect for human personality exacts its price. We are still involved in a vicious circle whose exit is not ideological but existential.

Berdyaev wrote in *Landmarks* that the Russian intelligentsia had not learned to respect truth as such, regardless of its social and practical applications; that its love of truth had been "paralyzed by the love of egalitarian justice, the good of society and the national welfare," and that this disrespect for knowledge had led it to profess superficial ideas and anticultural aims. And now Solzhenitsyn condemns the intelligentsia for claiming that its status as an educated class raises it above the "simple, suffering people," and for refusing to abandon its creative mission in philosophy, art, and science. Berdyaev expressed the hope that the intelligentsia would gain a "new soul," while Solzhenitsyn wishes to destroy what is, with all its faults, the only intelligentsia we have.

Bulgakov wrote in *Landmarks* that the Russian intelligentsia had launched a heroic challenge, and that the abstract, inhuman character of its demands, pitched at the highest level, inevitably caused their proponents to become intolerant, uncritical of themselves, and prone to pass judgment on others. Heroic self-denial was a divisive principle even when based on ideals of community and public interest. "The obverse of the intelligentsia's maximalism is historical impatience and lack of sobriety." All this is far removed from a sense of evolution and the gradualness of progress, as illustrated in Solzhenitsyn's writings.

Gershenzon, also in *Landmarks,* pointed out that the intelligentsia's eternal concern with social problems led it to despise everyday work and ordinary duties, proclaiming transcendent ideals and neglecting the individual. The effect was that

> no one *lived*—they only served social causes, or pretended to. They did not even live selfishly, they took no joy in life and its pleasures. . . . The house was full of poverty, dirt and disorder, but the master did not care. He was out saving the people, and that is far easier and more distinguished than doing dirty work at home.

But now Solzhenitsyn reproaches the intelligentsia because, with the wretched means at their disposal, they do their best to put their own home in order, to bring some beauty and gladness into life and art.

A. S. Izgoyev, another writer in *Landmarks,* attributed the irresponsible, slovenly habits of the intelligentsia to its preoccupation with the ideas of death and sacrifice for the sake of society. "People cannot live properly on the mere thought of death, making their willingness to die at any moment the criterion of every action. One who is willing to die in this way will of course attach no importance to conditions of life, manners and morals, philosophy, art, or literature for their own sakes." Yet Solzhenitsyn makes the curious statement that "people may pass into the spiritual future only one at a time, by squeezing through. By deliberate, voluntary sacrifice" (op. cit., p. 272). This is echoed by his fellow contributor Igor Shafarevich: "Russia's fate is in our hands, it depends on the personal efforts of each and every one of us. But the essential contributions to the cause can be made only through sacrifice" (p. 291). Izgoyev pointed out that this antihuman and anticultural spirit of self-sacrifice had a devastating effect on the family, the upbringing and fate of children, and the formation of stable family traditions. Solzhenitsyn's comment (p. 249) is:

> But the chief justifying argument is: children! In the face of this argument everyone falls silent: for who has the right to sacrifice the material welfare of his children for the sake of an abstract principle of truth?! That the moral health of their children is more precious than their careers does not even enter the parents' heads, so impoverished have they themselves become.

And elsewhere (p. 272) this "supporter" of *Landmarks* throws in the Russian proverb: "Bread and water make fine food."

Bogdan Kistyakovsky contributed to *Landmarks* an article, "In Defense of Law," that is perhaps especially important to the formulation of principles of democratic protest in the post-Stalin era. He observed that the intelligentsia had always regarded law as too formal and unconstructive, and that this depreciation of legal knowledge and culture had weakened the spirit of responsibility and self-discipline and encouraged a predisposition to violence. But Solzhenitsyn in *From Under the Rubble* is at great pains to belittle the importance of legal norms, arguing that democratic principles are illusory and that the demand for intellectual freedom is insufficiently spiritual. Taking issue with Andrey Sakharov, he even writes on page 24: "The state system which exists in our country is terrible not because it is undemocratic, authoritarian, based on physical constraint—a man can live in such conditions without harm to his spiritual essence."

Struve, emphasizing the isolation of the intelligentsia, wrote in *Landmarks* that this could be overcome only by creative work, practical participation in the education of the people, and the gradual but thorough transformation of political institutions. Solzhenitsyn, however, in *From Under the Rubble*, is full of sarcasm at the present intelligentsia's efforts to pursue scientific studies, to know as well as to act. He is especially vexed by the idea of scientific and technical progress.

Finally, Semen Frank's brilliant essay at the conclusion of *Landmarks* emphasized the danger of nihilism as a denial of highly developed cultural values for the sake of an equalization and standardization of culture, of dissemination instead of creation. This led, he argued, to a state of affairs in which the personality was undeveloped and dependent, and individual freedom was replaced by the stereotypes of a group morality imposed by pressure of public opinion. Frank's analysis serves as an apt commentary on Solzhenitsyn's position as set out in *From Under the Rubble,* as this is essentially a moral attitude based on nihilism.

To sum up, the three essays by Solzhenitsyn and the three by Shafarevich in *From Under the Rubble* must be regarded as "anti-*Landmarks*," the more so as these articles mention every single point or idea contained in the earlier work. True, I have left out the religious theme, which might seem to provide a thread of continuity between the epoch-making symposium of 1909 and that of 1974. But, as I have tried to show in my comparison, a religious attitude in itself does not necessarily lead to similar conclusions and need not stem from the same personal and existential basis. Religion is one thing, ideology another.

*Landmarks* analyzed the intelligentsia from within: its authors were primarily intellectuals, and their criticism was the more severe because it was also a confession and an act of penance. However much they condemned the intelligentsia's isolation from the state and people, they still appealed to it as the keeper of the nation's conscience. Bulgakov's words on this subject must be especially offensive to Solzhenitsyn:

> The soul of the intelligentsia, Peter I's creation, is also the key to the future of the Russian state and society. For good or evil, the fate of Petrine Russia rests with the intelligentsia, however much it is harried and persecuted and however weak and helpless it may appear at a particular time. It is the window that Peter opened onto Europe, admitting the Western air that brings with it both life and death. This handful of intellectuals has the monopoly of European education and enlightenment in Russia, it is the chief agent transmitting these to a nation of a million people; and if Russia cannot do without enlightenment on pain of national and political death, how lofty and important must be the intelligentsia's historical mission, how frighteningly great its responsibility for our country's immediate and distant future!

Solzhenitsyn does not like the intelligentsia, and judges it from outside. This greatly weakens the moral force of his call to repentance, as he does not accept any responsibility for the sins of intellectuals although, as we have seen, he displays many of their inveterate weaknesses. To criticize the real or imagined faults of the cultivated part of society from the abstract point of view of an idealized "people"—i.e., its uncultivated part—is an old Rousseauian device: it leads the critic into a nihilistic rejection of cultural values, and into the questionable position of identifying his own viewpoint with that of the "people." This error was often committed in the past by Slavophiles and Westernizers, populists and Marxists, and today's "national leaders" continue to sin in the same way. Criticism of this sort does not purify or clear the air, but rather the reverse.

But one might object that Solzhenitsyn is not criticizing the intelligentsia as such but only the Soviet intelligentsia, the "smatterers." He denounces those who sell their knowledge and ability for a mess of pottage, who take part in brainwashing the public and receive fat rewards for doing so. Is he not right to call on these people to repent, and why should he feel responsible for their sins?

I do not think these objections are well founded. The "smatterers," if this term has any meaning, are more an emanation of the people than of the intelligentsia. They may aspire to high office, but not necessarily. In a country where secondary education is compulsory, the masses absorb the poison of official propaganda and, to a great extent, take part in spreading it. Our leaders show that they are well aware of the difference between true intellectuals and "smatterers" when, for instance, they send members of the KGB, duly equipped with academic degrees, to international conferences of learned bodies, while our real scholars and scientists are told to report sick.

Solzhenitsyn lumps the two categories together and, without seeming to be aware of what he is doing, attacks the "smatterers" in order to demolish the intelligentsia. This is hard for foreigners to perceive, as the various shades of intellectual attitudes are not properly reflected in literature and elude the untrained observer. It is also not obvious to people inside the Soviet Union, for those who read Solzhenitsyn's criticism are themselves intellectuals. They are the only class in the country conscious of responsibility, torn by remorse and by a sense of isolation, and therefore prone to accept any rebuke directed against it.

There is one indisputable though external sign by which the real target of Solzhenitsyn's polemics can be identified. None of the writers he inveighs against in *From Under the Rubble* have been officially published or received rewards in the form of royalties, distinctions, or foreign travel—they are, in short, all *samizdat* authors. In his Foreword, Solzhenitsyn makes the curious statement that "It is from out of those dank and dark depths, from under the rubble, that we are now putting forth our first feeble shoots." This, I should point out, was written in 1974, when *samizdat* already constituted a literature of considerable size. "Feeble" it may have been, but it existed, and still does. How can we pretend that it does not? Yet how can the above words be understood except as a claim that *From Under the Rubble* is the first literature of protest? This is all the stranger since at least some of its contributors had already made a name for themselves in *samizdat*.

Another curious fact is that, as future students of Solzhenitsyn will no doubt notice, his ideas in *From Under the Rubble* have much in common with those of certain authors slighted in the book. To mention only one point, Semen (Semyon) Telegin, the author of an article "What Is to Be Done?" is dismissed (p. 254) as "a breezy, pushing know-it-all, quick at side associations and with a familiar, low wit." But if we disregard these epithets and look at Telegin's text as quoted by Solzhenitsyn himself, we find that his precept of "nonacceptance" is virtually identical with Solzhenitsyn's command "not to take part in the lie" (p. 274). The only difference is that Telegin said it first, and that many people began years ago not only to reject the lie but to live according to the truth, without waiting to be admonished in prophetic tones.

This is especially important, because we find no mention in *From Under the Rubble* of that truly spiritual effort of resistance which has been going on for at least a decade, working out a clear notion of its objectives, rich in heroes and, alas, already too rich in victims. True, Solzhenitsyn writes, on page 269:

> I can testify . . . that during the last few years I have seen these modest and valiant young people with my own eyes, heard them with my own ears; it was they who, like an invisible film, kept me floating in air over a seeming void and prevented me from falling. Not all of them are still at liberty today, and not all of them will preserve their freedom tomorrow. And far from all of them are evident to our eyes and ears—like spring streams they trickle somewhere beneath the dense, gray, hard-packed snow.

On page 271 he adds:

> Not only is this nucleus not yet a compact mass, as a nucleus should be, but it is not even collected together, it is scattered, its components mutually unrecognizable: many of its particles have never seen one another, do not know of one another, and have no notion of one another's existence.

We are not concerned here with individual acknowledgment or recompense. But it is a little over ten years since the first demonstration on Pushkin Square in Moscow in support of Andrey Sinyavsky and Yuly Daniel, as they awaited trial. And there have been many subsequent acts of protest on different grounds, including the invasion of Czechoslovakia. There were and still are collective and individual declarations, protests, demands by hundreds of persons whose acts and names are, or should be, "evident to our eyes and ears." There is the Action Group for the Defense of Human Rights, most of whose members, it is true, either are under arrest or have emigrated; but their names and their tragic fate are not hidden "beneath the dense, gray, hard-packed snow." There is the Moscow branch of Amnesty International, which has made itself known despite persecution. Solzhenitsyn mentions (p. 257) the names of some journals which "sprang up in *samizdat* for a brief period." He emphasizes their futility, but for some reason says nothing about the *Chronicle of Current Events.* This *samizdat* journal has been appearing continuously since 1968, and has thus far produced forty-four issues despite the war it wages against the KGB. It aims, not without success, at bringing the components of the "nucleus" together, and has played its part in creating the "invisible film" that has saved Solzhenitsyn and many others from falling. Sergey Kovalyov, a member of the Action Group and the Moscow branch of Amnesty International, was sentenced to seven years in strict-regime labor camps and three years of exile on charges that included the dissemination of *The Gulag Archipelago.* And, finally, is Solzhenitsyn's category of "modest and valiant young people" meant to include General P. G. Grigorenko, the late writer Aleksey Kosterin, A. S. Yesenin-Volpin, Lydia Chukovskaya, Professor Andrey Sakharov, and many, many others?

I repeat, we are not concerned here with individual reputations. But Solzhenitsyn only indicates obliquely, in *From Under the Rubble,* whom his argument is really directed against. On page 20 he writes:

> Among Soviet people whose opinions do not conform to the official stereotype, there is a well-nigh general view [in short, there is not only an unorthodox view, but it is practically universal—B.S.] that what our society needs, what it must aspire to and strive for, is freedom and the multiparty parliamentary system.

Naturally anyone is entitled to think that democratic freedoms are unnecessary and pernicious and that a one-party system is the political bulwark of national concord. But the question is, how do we then avoid intolerance, intransigent narrow-mindedness, and the deliberate depreciation of those who think differently from ourselves? How can we avoid "taking part in the lie" if we do not love, respect, and value the only true freedom, that of others?

Neglect of the past and its lessons, the determination to start everything off again from the beginning—i.e., from oneself, making one's own opinions the basis for an overturning of all values, treating those opinions as the absolute expression of national unanimity—these are familiar symptoms of the unconscious self-isolation of the Russian intelligentsia. It is easy enough to speak in the name of the dumb masses: as we know, "the people keeps silent."[20] But the intellectuals, seduced by their own false claim to represent the people, lose touch with their own proper tradition. The result is that despite radically rejecting the past, stowing old banners in the attic, adopting new jargon, manners, and dress, they find themselves essentially repeating the same thing over and over again.

However much they may invoke the spiritual principle, it is outweighed by the undiminished burden of corporeality. For the spiritual lives and breathes only by individuality, and the latter, even though it be national or confessional, is something unique and specific. It can exist only in meaningful association with other equally unique individuals, who must not be elbowed aside and treated as objects.

These simple truths, which have cost the Russian intelligentsia so dear, have come to light in our day in an existential manner, if not in an explicit philosophical form. As a result we have what are called "dissidents." The challenge of the spirit begins with the embodiment of these truths in social behavior, and *Landmarks* provides us with an arsenal of critical concepts, necessary in evaluating our present stagnation.

CHAPTER V

# The Dissidents

## By way of definition

The term "dissidents" came to us from the West. It was first used in Russia by foreign journalists confronted by a new phenomenon. Like all such terms applied by outsiders, it is not a good description of what the people concerned feel about themselves. It suggests a desperate minority which has parted company with the mass of orthodox believers, who toe a common line out of conviction. No doubt this is how the foreign journalists saw it. As Andrey Amalrik has noted, the arrival of "dissidents" on the scene had the same interest for them "that a fish would have for an ichthyologist if it suddenly began to talk."[1]

The contrast with the silent millions certainly points up the phenomenon of "dissidence" with special emphasis.

When "Soviet people" confront foreigners, they appear as uniform as a single person. Any divergence seems due only to lack of "finish" or incomplete rehearsal. The Soviet citizen presents himself to foreign eyes not as Comrade So-and-So but as a representative of the great Soviet Union—not simply a human being, but "Soviet man" personified.

This stereotyped figure is constructed with regard to foreign opinion. He is designed to create the best possible impression on foreigners. His inventors have a pattern in their mind's eye of the average Western man, and adjust their efforts to it as well as they can. By studying the variations of "Soviet man" from decade to decade we can follow the evolution of the official Soviet conception of the West.

"Soviet man" as presented to foreigners is supposed to be an image of Western man without the latter's faults. The Westerner, looking upon him, is expected to contemplate his own radiant future.

In the latest version, great emphasis is laid on decorum in dress, manners, and convictions. Soviet man, on show to foreigners, conforms strictly to the etiquette believed typical of the West. His suit is well pressed, he wears a clean shirt and a tie, and is altogether antiseptically clean. He does not drink excessively or frequent pornographic films, nor is he attracted by Western trumpery. Before he is displayed, he must get a signed and sealed certification of his moral and ideological soundness. He must never look disreputable. He is decently conservative—not merely bourgeois in his manners but steeped in bourgeoisdom—without of course stooping to individuality, cupidity, or religious superstition.

He is simple, democratic, just, and rocklike in his convictions. He is always prepared to help the humble and oppressed, expecting no return but proper gratitude and devotion. On all questions—political, technical, or whatever—Soviet citizens have a common point of view. They are open to argument, but only for the purpose of setting errant foreigners on the right path. If others persist in disagreeing, they are at once suspected of evil machinations. Soviet man is uncompromising in discussion, not out of obstinacy but because he alone knows where truth and justice lie. He is happy and harmonious in a world of distortion and contradiction.

All this, of course, is a façade. The harder the Russians try to convince outsiders, the more they are assailed by secret doubts. The effect is like a waxwork, and tremendous effort is spent preventing foreigners from getting at the real truth. Not surprisingly, the deception is often successful. It is hard, when people appear to wear their hearts on their sleeves, to suspect them of brazen, almost contemptuous hypocrisy. An excess of uniformity in behavior and opinions is easily ascribed to the peculiar historical features of this strange culture. Visitors to the Soviet Union, moreover, are often weary of their own multiple-choice civilization and are relieved and pleased to find people who seem happier than themselves.

It is hard for outsiders—and not only for them—to understand why a whole nation should form a conspiracy to deceive. Soviet people lie to foreigners with the facility of singing birds. Pretense is as natural to them as eating and drinking. Moreover, they are convinced in their inmost hearts—and how should they not be?—that foreigners are as deceitful as they.

Visitors, without suspecting it, are drawn into the same game. They are seduced into making statements confirming the impressions the authorities are trying to create. Their polite remarks are often taken as heartfelt admiration. Whatever they say about the Soviet Union is as thoroughly censored as the thoughts and utterances of Soviet citizens. Only favorable comments are published; others are either suppressed or denigrated as anti-Soviet propaganda. Soviet propagandists, venal themselves, are ready to accuse everyone else of venality. The mixture is completed by a shrill display of hurt feelings, an almost sincere note of generosity betrayed—so *this* is the foreigner's gratitude for a Soviet welcome!

In view of all this I am not inclined to judge too harshly those who are taken in and used by Soviet propaganda. Nothing in their previous experience leads them to imagine that a whole nation can be dedicated to lying. The more open-minded, the more easily they are bamboozled. The remarkable thing is rather that some do notice something amiss.

The national habit of lying is not solely due to threats from above. Of course, there is a huge bureaucratic apparatus concerned with arranging contacts between Soviet people and foreigners. It uses both stick and carrot, either permitting contacts as a mark of special confidence or punishing unmercifully those unauthorized or those that become too sincere. Acquaintances whom the foreigner believes to be ordinary citizens are often KGB agents who are trained to lie skillfully as part of their duties. They are well paid for doing so. Nevertheless, the whole system of official control is supported by a basic disposition of the

Russian people, dating back so far that its strength makes it seem a moral imperative.

The façade is kept up not only by paid officials but by innumerable zealous volunteers, acting for the mere fun of it or out of a sense of duty. Typically, Soviet crowds become genuinely indignant when some unfortunate foreigner takes a picture of an old-fashioned house or some other sight not on the prescribed list. Generally the tourist has no intention of showing Soviet conditions in a bad light, but simply finds them interesting or picturesque; but the ordinary citizen cannot understand this. He knows what sort of pictures appear in propaganda journals, what scenes the foreigner is supposed to admire and photograph, and what he should ignore out of politeness. He strongly believes that dirty linen should not be washed in public, and he does not let the foreigner transgress this rule.

The Marquis de Custine, an eminent French traveler, described Russia in 1843 as an "empire of façades," and observed that "the *corps diplomatique,* and Western people in general, have always been considered by this Byzantine government, and by Russia in general, as malignant and jealous spies. . . . There is this similarity between Russians and the Chinese, that both one and the other always believe that strangers envy them: they judge us by their own sentiments."[2] Custine's remark was based on the way he himself was treated in Russia: government spies gave him what appeared to be a cordial welcome, but saw to it that he was under constant supervision; his conversations were reported; he was shown what they wanted him to see and prevented from looking below the surface. Reading his account today, we are struck by the way the country of victorious socialism has reproduced in every detail the peculiarities of the despotic regime of Nicholas I. Herzen remarked of Custine that he had noticed more clearly than anyone "the artificiality that meets our gaze at every turn, and the habit of boasting of elements of European life that are only there for show."

The morbidly suspicious attitude to Westerners, the desire to impress and attract them by make-believe, and the immense care taken to conceal the true situation in Russia, were traditions that provided fertile ground for a specifically Soviet hypocrisy and pretense. For decades the slightest connection with foreigners, correspondence with émigré relatives, or even the existence of such relatives with whom one was afraid to correspond, or any casual unauthorized meeting, was punished by sanctions that could ruin a Soviet citizen's whole life. The seeds of xenophobia grew majestically. Bureaucratic prohibitions became deeply rooted custom; perverted moral norms were erected into a barrier separating the Soviet Union from the outer world.

This complicated phenomenon has many different consequences. It has become interwoven with every other aspect of Soviet life, either as cause or effect. Its particular relation to the question of "dissidents" lies in the fact that the oppression of Russians by their own government has always been concealed from foreigners with special care. As Dostoyevsky observed, the absoluteness of the government's authority is based on secrecy. Effectual terror depends on imagination rather than knowledge, and therefore needs an atmosphere of mysterious uncertainty. By blocking all channels of information within the country, the government creates a basis for the consolidation of its authority; but this is shaken if the regime's ferocity to its own subjects becomes known to the outside world.

For the regime to have absolute control over its own people, its reputation abroad must be unblemished. Neither the Soviet state nor Tsarist Russia could afford complete indifference to foreign public opinion. For instance, Prince V. P. Kochubey, a minister under Nicholas I, advised that the proposal to deny education to the children of serfs should be enacted by a secret rescript; he wrote on this occasion:

> I venture to think that this course would be more convenient as it would attract less publicity. A law promulgated by the Council would become known to all Europe, there would be various comments, etc., and, although we are differently placed from other European states as regards our internal arrangements, we cannot despise their opinion or the state of feeling in the country itself.

"We cannot desist from wicked ways, but we must not upset Europe"—in these words a "high dignitary" in one of Leskov's stories described the crafty tactics Russia's rulers use to veil its spiritual suffering. They create a façade of loyal unanimity, concealing the measures by which it is enforced, and on the basis of this deception they demand undeserved respect from the outside world.

The Soviet regime, with its camouflage of communist rhetoric, managed to avoid "upsetting Europe" for decades. The "wicked ways" and their perpetrators were supposed to be a thing of the past, and Europe rejoiced at our happy state. No one in the country dared utter a sound, and foreigners almost envied our singleness of mind. The delusion that arose was highly dangerous to the fate of humanity, and is still not entirely dispelled. We may recall the final scene of Solzhenitsyn's *The First Circle,* where prisoners are jammed inside a Black Maria on the side of which the word "Meat" is painted in four languages. A foreign journalist, remembering that he has seen several similar trucks that day in different parts of Moscow, takes out his notebook and writes: "Food supply to workers improving." A bitter joke, the more so as we ourselves have helped to spread the pernicious lie.

But it would seem that the days of easy deceit are over. The world has become a smaller place, and we can no longer do without Western contact. How, then, are we to prevent inquisitive foreigners from approaching so close that the illusion vanishes, and the beautiful picture dissolves into blood, mire, and desolation?

It is in this genuine contact, as opposed to make-believe encounters with the West, that the dissidents play their historic role. These are men and women who have conquered the ingrained habit of secrecy and have performed the most courageous feat possible for a Soviet citizen: speaking out and not caring who may hear. Moreover, their express purpose is to be heard, at home as well as abroad—for their fellow countrymen, if not absolutely deaf, have been hard of hearing for a long time.

Western observers have duly noted that there are Soviet citizens who speak out despite persecution, but they are mistaken in ascribing to them the characteristics of a Western opposition. Misled by the Soviet practice of "doublethink," they pay undue attention to the outward differences between the "dissidents" and the rest of society. These are real enough, but reflect deeper and more complex relationships. The essential point, however, is not that the "dissidents" hold different views from the majority, but that they speak and act in accordance with what they think.

Andrey Sakharov has remarked that the "dissidents" should not be called *inakomyslyashchiye* ("those who think different-ly"), but rather *svobodomyslyashchiye* ("those who think freely") or simply *myslyashchiye* ("those who think"), to distinguish them from a majority afraid to think and intent on ignoring the truth they all know in their hearts. A man becomes an apostate and a pariah the moment he speaks his mind on questions of vital interest to society.

The term "dissidents" suggests an opposition group with a definite political program and tactics based on its lack of mass support. But this is perhaps too Western an idea, based on the standards of a democratic society in which political life exists and the influence of social movements is directly proportionate to the numbers involved.

The "dissidents" are aware of the same facts as the majority of thinking people, but, unlike this silent majority, they speak out concerning what they know. They do not, as they might rationally do, refrain on the ground that it's no use running your head against a brick wall. They concentrate on those aspects of contemporary Russian life that the majority think it more prudent to ignore. This is the source of their strength and, despite everything, their growing influence. Their strength lies in the truth, as they and their persecutors are equally well aware.

Hence attempts to define the program of the "dissidents" or to identify them as a political party are doomed to failure. The character of an opposition depends on that of the society that gives it birth. Thus in medieval Western Europe the opposition assumed religious forms and was inseparable from them. In the same way the "dissidents" are not to be understood in the abstract sociological terms of a political opposition on modern Western lines, but against the background of the spiritual stagna-tion of modern Russia.

On closer examination it may be seen that the "dissidents" vary in their political, philosophical, and religious ideas. But as far as their position inside the country is concerned—I am not speaking of émigré circles—these differences are not so prominent as to lead to clear demarcations or the formation of sects. The appearance of "dissidents" represents the first steps toward freedom, and it is only after a longer period of development that the differences in their views might lead to the formation of diverse parties.

This does not mean, of course, that ideas and views do not play a part in inducing individuals to join the "dissident" movement. Some approach it by way of a Marxist critique of the Soviet system, others because they belong to a persecuted faith or an oppressed nationality. But, for example, adherence to Orthodoxy and the devout performance of its rites does not make a man any more of a "dissident" than the profession of Marxism. The Soviet Union is seething with national loyalties that present many possibilities of alienation, but the nationalists include a great many who are not "dissidents."

What distinguishes the "dissidents," in any case, is not their convictions as such but the fact that they defend them openly, breaking with the tradition of doublethink. They demand the right to be independent of official ideology. In other words they are distinguished by freedom of action, for under Soviet conditions, speech is a form of action. Again, the nature and momentum of their oppositionist activity may vary: a signature on a collective protest, an outspoken book, the publication of documents, participation in a forbidden demonstration. Such acts are not necessarily committed systematically, so as to constitute a "life's work." The behavior of a "dissident" is determined by his personal motivation and cannot be imposed by external discipline. His action may be due to a nonrecurring combination of personal circumstances. Hence it is absurd to say, as people sometimes do, that So-and-So has "left the movement."

Finally, the circle can with perfect justification be widened to include those who make clear their sympathy for those who act openly, without doing so themselves, or who distribute and read *samizdat* literature, or collect money to aid political prisoners and their families. Without the help of this class of sympathizers, to which it is also dangerous to belong, the "dissidents" could not have survived the totalitarian persecution that has been going on for decades. And perhaps their chief victory inside the country, and the chief defeat for official repression, is that they are no longer successfully isolated and turned into untouchables, as was the case in Stalin's day. Nonetheless, it is still a valiant deed to visit the wife or mother of a political prisoner, to look after his children and to help them morally or materially, in defiance of what is selectively called "socialist" or "revolutionary" humanism. Acts like these, unknown to society at large and not publicized abroad, are often punished more harshly, as the authorities feel freer to deal with the offenders as they wish.

But however much we widen the category of "dissidents," it will not include all those who are discontented. Great numbers of them pay strict obedience to the rites of "doublethink": for the most part, they make no secret of being afraid, and of course they cannot be blamed for this. There are, however, more complicated cases. A man may hate the existing order so much that he is obliged to conceal the fact, as his opinions would otherwise lead him to acts punishable by law in any society, not only a totalitarian one. He may harbor dreams of terror, violence, or armed rebellion; decades of enforced duplicity have created a store of pent-up hatred that could explode at any moment. But he must conceal all this and be silent. Radicals of this sort regard the "dissidents" almost as collaborators with the regime, since the latter act openly and in accordance with laws that are violated by the authorities. There are times, however, when such intransigence serves as a pretext for keeping away from "dissidents," and consequently away from danger.

Some of the discontented rationalize their silence on the ground that resistance should lead to some practical result and that the dissidents are too "idealistic." They argue that open acts of defiance only irritate the authorities and provoke countermeasures. They think it best not to challenge the stability of the existing order, even its moral stability. Often they pursue orthodox careers in the hope of rising to a position in which they can help the cause of reason and progress. But it is a long way to the top, and somehow their efforts fail to pay off. Meanwhile, however, they have an excellent pretext for not sticking their necks out and for preserving an outward appearance of propriety and even zeal for the regime.

Doublethink is not the product of official ideology as such, for that is uniformly one-sided; it results from the individual's effort to adapt to official ideology. For this reason people go to enormous trouble to shield themselves from the truth and to observe the prescribed bounds of social relationships without becoming too contemptible in their own eyes. One may say that there are as many formulas for this as there are people. Paradoxically, one's whole personality is expended on becoming a conformist.

Doublethink by no means excludes an anti-Soviet consciousness beneath a Soviet exterior, as was well shown by Orwell in *Nineteen Eighty-Four*. Official ideology divides and polarizes the world: it must constantly invent an enemy for itself, because it has no positive content and consists wholly of opposition and denial. It can assert itself only against some adversary, and the effect of its educational activity is also mainly negative.

The Soviet system is the center of the Soviet citizen's mental universe, whether he is in favor of it or not. He believes that contemporary Russian socialism is the purest form of the doctrine, as he has been told in countless educational sessions, newspapers, and propaganda booklets. He has no doubt that the international prestige and popularity of the Soviet Union are growing steadily, as he learns from the same media, and this will delight or horrify him according to which side of his divided soul receives the information. The system, even to those who hate it, is the basic point of reference for all judgments; and the more they hate it, the more unshakable it seems to them. A Soviet citizen measures the standard of living of Western workers by Soviet criteria and wonders why they are discontented. He also firmly believes that the West has, or should have, no other ambition than to destroy the Soviet system.

To be anti-Soviet does not in itself afford an escape from doublethink. As long as the person concerned is in the Soviet Union, he will be more submissive than ever. If and when he emigrates and becomes openly anti-Soviet, his example helps keep his fellow countrymen in order; all his acts and judgments go to confirm the official Soviet myth of "anticommunism," as he transforms himself in accordance with the accepted parameters of the myth. Enslaved only yesterday to Soviet ideology, today he vies with *Literaturnaya Gazeta* in proclaiming the dissoluteness of the West; he demands more censorship and less sexual freedom, more frequent death sentences, bigger arms budgets, and military training for the young. All these complaints and appeals are ideally calculated to help the Soviet authorities persuade those under their care of the rightness of the Soviet system and the belligerence of the West. What they reflect, of course, is simply the fact that Soviet man, much as he may detest the system, is conditioned by its way of thinking—another illustration of the truth that "extremes meet."

To break out of this vicious circle, we must have real faith in freedom and human rights, and not merely use them as sticks to beat our political opponents with. To escape from the bonds of official ideology we must cure ourselves of doublethink, which is what the "dissidents" attempt to do.

The most accurate account of the "dissident" viewpoint was given in an article, "The Ideocratic Consciousness and Personality," by Dmitry Nelidov, in a collection of essays entitled *Samo-soznanie* ("Insights"—reprinted in New York in 1976). He wrote:

> Thus it went on: phrases about freedom and democracy were repeated day after day in the calculation that they would be understood within the framework of previously instilled reactions. When some people tried to understand these words differently, having first overcome the reactions in question and then pretended that they did not exist, they were of course committing an act of unheard-of impropriety. . . . Whatever their particular intentions, they were struggling out of the context of doublethink in which such terms were normally embedded, and this changed the scene completely, showing up the whole spuriousness of our constitutional forms, solemn proclamations, and ritual. A flood of light was thrown on the ideological machinery which had been used to create conditioned reflexes and sclerotic habits of regimented thought.

The "dissidents" were bound to do things in the open, for only thus could the spell of doublethink be destroyed. Their openness is not merely a demagogical device to create maximum annoyance to the powers that be. (This is a criticism leveled by some who sympathize with the "dissidents" but are themselves still rooted in doublethink.) It is necessary as a means of regaining possession of one's own mind and restoring the integrity of its reactions, just as a person recovering from paralysis slowly learns to walk. Only in this way can a spiritually corrupted society be reeducated in the ordinary norms of human thought and behavior.

But, in Soviet conditions, "doing things in the open" means doing them so that they become known outside the Soviet Union. This is true in the most elementary sense: if events are not reported in the foreign press, they might as well not have happened as far as publicity is concerned. One can parade with banners on Red Square, but unless foreign reporters chance to be present, passersby will be aware only that some hooligans are being rounded up and beaten by policemen and plainclothesmen. One may write open letters to Brezhnev or Kosygin, but unless the foreign press lends a hand they will reach only the KGB, which will wreak its vengeance without inhibition.

The phenomenon of *samizdat,* which is now well enough known for this term to be used in foreign books and articles, could not have developed if manuscripts had not been printed abroad and introduced to the Soviet public in Russian-language radio programs.

As long as Soviet society is cut off from outside contact, the most daring statements can have no effect except on the offender, who will be summarily dealt with. The few who hear about it will take extra care in future. It is particularly dispiriting when the West will not or cannot hear the voices of those crying out within Russia. When secrecy at home is matched by inattention abroad, those imprisoned in Soviet doublethink feel as if they are in a leaden coffin. And, conversely, when they hear a word of encouragement from the West, thousands inside the country breathe a sigh of immense relief.

Instinctive awareness of this state of affairs is an important factor in the universal doublethink. The regime does its best to close off the country so that objective information cannot filter through in either direction. But, as it cannot completely achieve this aim, it uses the so-called détente to stop those who might tell the truth to foreign and Soviet audiences.

Ever since the "dissidents" came into being, they have waged a war against the state to reach the Western public. Their whole existence as a group depends on the fact that they have managed to secure a small bridgehead to Western interest, and are gradually enlarging it despite heavy losses.

The dignitaries of the regime resort to every possible dodge to silence witnesses inside the country; those outside can more easily be denounced as slanderers. They are afraid to recognize the hand of fate in the accumulation and disclosure of discreditable facts. In their attitude to the "dissidents," they are like bullies who kick, slap, and trip up their playmates and, when called to order by their parents (or in this case by world opinion), mumble sulkily, "Well, what are they howling about? Who wants them anyway?" And then they go on terrorizing, blackmailing, and intimidating, in secret as far as possible, but in a way that leaves no doubt whatever of their blackguardly nature.

For these reasons, I do not agree with the conclusion of Howard L. Biddulph's article "Protest Strategies of the Soviet Intellectual Opposition"[3] that

> The dissidents seemed to overestimate both the willingness of the external publics to intervene and the susceptibility of Soviet leaders to foreign influence on such issues. This tactic provided ammunition for charges of disloyalty, which undoubtedly exercised a persuasive appeal against them in public opinion. The overreliance on external communication with third parties was therefore not only unproductive but counterproductive to the objectives of the movement.

The appeal of the "dissidents" to Western public opinion is no more a "tactic" than a drowning man's cry for help; it is the only course open to them.

But, while the term "dissident" covers several shades of meaning, it has the merit of indicating to Russians, by its foreign origin, that the movement of resistance and nonconformity has aroused interest and sympathy abroad. In official Soviet circles the dissidents are referred to, in terms of purely Russian origin, as "slanderers," "apostates," or "renegades." The Soviet public, on the other hand, orally uses such terms as "revolutionaries" and "democrats," with a connotation of hostility and incomprehension.

The "dissidents" do demand that the state observe democratic norms such as freedom of speech and conscience, national self-determination, freedom of the press, the rule of law, and the right to hold meetings and demonstrations. Not only do they demand such rights, but as far as possible they assert them in practice, as though taking permission for granted. But the term "democrat" hardly seems appropriate to those who protest on an individual basis, with little thought of leading a party or influencing the masses.

It is true, too, that certain "dissidents" coined the term "Democratic Movement" to describe themselves. But this was partly due to an illusion that the movement was rapidly increasing in size, and partly to a somewhat disingenuous attempt to foster such an illusion when it was apparent to the "dissidents" themselves that this assumption was becoming less and less well founded.

Some Russian émigrés use *inakomyslyashchiye* ("otherwise-thinking" or "heterodox") as a translation of *dissidence:* it is apparently meant to suggest greater intimacy with the movement, but is no more familiar to its members than the latter term. It also has the disadvantage of suggesting "thought" to the exclusion of action (cf. page 198 above). Consequently, in spite of all objections to the word "dissident," I shall henceforth use it without quotation marks.

# Opposing good to evil

The story of the dissidents is not yet written, although their desire for publicity has created a great deal of documentation. It is not my purpose here simply to cite examples from the existing wealth of material, but rather to elucidate the origins of the dissident movement.

As others have pointed out, the first significant event was the trial of the writers Sinyavsky and Daniel. Their arrest in September 1965 was the opening shot of Brezhnev's regime against the emerging movement for a freer society. A major complaint of the party bureaucracy against Khrushchev, who was ousted in 1964, was that he had let the intelligentsia get out of hand. The ruling clique, all former henchmen of Stalin's, were frightened by the disclosures, expurgated though they were, of crimes in which they themselves had participated. They had had to play a wily game, making semiliberal speeches and pretending to ignore the intellectuals' increasingly searching criticism. Their desire to put a stop to it was restrained by Khrushchev's flirtation with liberalism. As soon as Khrushchev was disposed of, the arrests began.

At about the same time as Sinyavsky and Daniel, the authorities arrested a group in Leningrad who had circulated a typewritten journal entitled *The Bell*,* as well as some "nationalists" in the Ukraine. These moves had evidently been prepared in advance, for security organs clamped down on the victims as soon as the taboo on repressive action was lifted.

However, as the ancients knew, "one cannot step into the same river twice." Russian intellectual society, just reliving the shocking truth of its own recent past, was not prepared to make such an instantaneous return to habits from which it had been set free by the voice of conscience. It showed neither approval of the arrests nor submission. The accused, shut off from the world in the old style and "worked over" for many months, refused to admit their guilt or do penance and recite the tale of their imaginary crimes in public. Friends rallied to their cause instead of shunning them, as well-behaved Soviet citizens were supposed to do. The investigators were unable to hire a sufficient number of false witnesses; those called on to give evidence were less afraid of official threats than of harming the accused. Soon they too began to invoke the law, demand their rights, and call upon the authorities to observe that "legality" so recently and loudly trumpeted in the press.

These normal human reactions to the authorities' lawlessness seemed to the KGB little less than surrealistic. Spoiled by so many years of connivance on the part of institutions and private persons, they complained in puzzled and reproachful tones: "You don't want to help us." No, that was precisely what the public did not want.

Agents of "state security" could not remember a time when they had encountered such resistance. In the thirties, agents had needed no skills except a total lack of conscience. They arrested innocent people by the thousands and invented cases against

---

* *The Bell (Kolokol)* was originally the name of a journal founded and edited by the nineteenth-century liberal humanist Aleksandr Herzen. The Leningrad group's choice of this name presumably reflected their identification with the same general outlook.—Tr. note.

them. For decades they had been let loose on nameless, mute, defenseless victims ignorant of what was really wanted of them. Finding itself up against real resistance within the law, the KGB was confused and lost its bearings. In Stalin's day the legal system was hypocritical enough to enact harsh penalties—for espionage, "diversion," and conspiracy—against law-abiding citizens. It now turned out that the basis for prosecution was so insufficient that the state would have destroyed the thin partition on which the system of doublethink depended by merely devising *ad hoc* laws. It is easy to bring a charge of espionage, but how do you convict a man for writing unorthodox novels or short stories?

The KGB, already discredited in the eyes of thinking people, was dealt a further moral blow by the arrests of 1965 and trials of 1966. It has yet to recover. Formerly it had unlimited power to tyrannize, and it was accommodated by a servile press; but now the lies were met with contempt instead of credulity.

The moral impasse into which the government had blundered became a major factor in the country's internal life. As soon as people appeared prepared to tell the truth aloud, the supposedly omnipotent regime was obliged to hide. The huge apparatus of repression was no longer serviceable. Its creators had never meant the clumsy machinery to be exposed to public view. From 1965 onward, the KGB was on the defensive, with no appropriate means of safeguarding either the regime or itself. The chain reaction that began then is still in progress.

On December 5, 1965 (Constitution Day), the first demonstration was held in Moscow. The demonstrators demanded that the trial of Sinyavsky and Daniel be open to the public; one of the slogans was "Respect the Soviet Constitution!" The demonstration was dispersed, of course, revealing what the authorities thought of the Constitution. After Sinyavsky and Daniel were sentenced—the trial was not held in public, only falsely reported in the newspapers—Aleksandr Ginzburg published an accurate account of the proceedings under his own name. He too was arrested, and his trial was conducted in the same way; this time the truth was published by Pavel Litvinov, who was subjected to penalties in his turn. . . . In this way the dissident movement grew.

The infertile minds of the nation's defenders could think of nothing better than to accuse the dissidents of "slander." But, as the information they had divulged was fully documented and above doubt, the government's reaction sounded like hysterical self-accusation. The authorities deprived themselves of the possibility of admitting openly what they had been up to. Accused of breaking their own laws, they answered by breaking them again. Instead of rebutting the charge, they confined themselves to bald assertions, endeavoring with dull-witted persistence to keep their punitive measures from becoming public knowledge.

Of course, the struggle was and is an unequal one. A small band, numbering only hundreds during the most vigorous protests, stands against the millions who are silent with fear or indifference, who look on at persecutions or abet them. But the moral strength of the few hundred compensates for their numerical disadvantages.

The dissidents have suffered many heavy losses. It does not require much ingenuity to cause them difficulties. It is easy to arrest a man when there are no sanctions against repressive measures and when he does not conceal the evidence, but actually publishes it. But all the arrests and sentences to jail, labor camp, or exile, the confinement of healthy people in prisons for the criminally insane, the innumerable acts of arbitrary power against the dissidents' right to work and move about freely, the secrecy of their correspondence and the privacy of their homes—all these and similar crimes neither solve the problem nor drive it underground. Violence and blackmail do not wipe out a criminal's misdeeds but only add to them.

For this reason it is wrong to say that the resistance has weakened or proved a failure, or that the government is getting the upper hand. Such conclusions are due to an imperfect understanding of the present situation in Russia or of the dissidents' aims.

Even the tightening up of repression and its increasingly illegal character indicate that the dissidents are getting stronger rather than weaker. It is noticeable, for instance, that the KGB tends to avoid publicity by having people tried in provincial cities instead of Moscow, where the resistance is especially active and foreign observers can see the barbarous proceedings at first hand. Grigorenko and Gabay were tried at Tashkent, Amalrik at

Sverdlovsk, Superfin at Orel, Kovalyov at Vilnius. All these trials violate a Soviet law which stipulates that accused persons must be tried at their place of residence. The authorities added to their list of crimes the monstrous stratagem of imprisoning the most obdurate dissidents in lunatic asylums. A person declared incompetent to answer for his acts can be tried *in absentia*—a relief to investigators who have trouble cooking up false accusations. This course was widely adopted at first, but the KGB has come to regret it, as even the most hard-boiled Western communists look askance at it.

Bukovsky, Gluzman, and others are tortured in jail for spreading information about the regime's use of psychiatrists to fight the opposition; but, far from quieting the situation, this has produced a fresh outcry.

The conflict that began with the arrests of 1965 is a moral and spiritual one, not political or ideological. It takes place on a level which Brezhnev's stagnant regime does not belong to. The authorities began by imprisoning the refractory, but they can no longer afford this luxury. At the outset, two writers were charged with publishing uncensored works abroad under pseudonyms; by now there is a whole library of artistic, historical, and political literature, and the lovers of violence are obliged to hold their hand.

The irrationality of the regime has affected the nature of its opposition. It arose from rejection not of its deceptive appearance but of the reality. The opposition may appear lacking in form and overall purpose, but that is its strength and not its weakness. From the very beginning of the dissident movement, Soviet propaganda endeavored to ascribe to its members such motives as would justify the KGB campaign against them: they were accused of wanting to overthrow the existing order, of being agents of anti-Soviet organizations abroad suborned by foreign money. The most recent claim—that they are insane—was intended to appeal to the common man, who could not imagine anyone deliberately defying the norms of Soviet ethics. And indeed, they are insane from the point of view of the present heirs of the revolution. They have nothing in common with the regime, either positive or negative: their ideals are on a completely different plane. Hence the regime's action against them has absolutely no legal or moral foundation.

At the trial of Sinyavsky and Daniel, the prosecution and the court—which, of course, were the same thing—were surprised to find that authors could not be jailed simply for the books they wrote, and that the political significance of a work of fiction is a question for subjective appraisal and not a point of law. They quoted repeatedly from the words put into the mouths of these authors' characters, displaying both their own ignorance and the court's incompetence to judge literary matters. They found the authors guilty and sentenced them to jail, but this was—and remains—an act of unconcealed lawlessness.

A similar situation has occurred in other clashes between dissidents and the authorities. On each occasion it becomes clear that the dissidents are not members of an anti-Soviet organization or exponents of a hostile ideology, but are simply individuals who wish to follow their consciences. They are willing to abide by the law of the land, which, despite its vagueness and loopholes for arbitrary application, does not in fact forbid the dissidents' activities. The use of criminal sanctions against them becomes increasingly absurd. Thus it has been empirically shown that the dissidents have found not a political or social, but a spiritual and existential, way of escaping from the country's present stagnation.

The dissidents include people of various ages, differing in their opinions, life history, and social position. The single point they have in common is that in one way or another they have stepped out of the magic circle of doublethink. General Grigorenko stated at a party conference that the Communist Party of the Soviet Union had departed substantially from communist theory; Father Dudko preached to his flock in favor of Orthodoxy and against atheism. In any other situation these two men would probably have found no common ground, but in present Soviet society it is enough that they dared to be themselves, unlike ordinary members of the party or the church. General Grigorenko devoted all his energy to defending the Crimean Tatars in their fight for national existence. Father Dudko celebrated a requiem for Gabay, who was not a member of the Orthodox Church and had committed suicide. The differences that arise when personality is overshadowed by its alienated social role lose their meaning in the face of the universal evil of contemporary Soviet society. The dissidents have joined hands not because they think and feel alike, but because they respect one another as free men and women.

The dissidents have come to know one another as the result of persecution and violence. The camps for political prisoners are an important meeting-place, and the friendships formed there extend to the prisoners' families and friends. Thus the arrests have helped to weld together forces that the authorities can no longer control. But however widely the circle spreads, it is not a rigid, formal organization but a network of personal contacts. When someone is in trouble, others do their best to help morally and materially, defending him by all possible means and especially by publicity. Such actions are not planned or directed from a single center; they are a matter of personal impulse and individual conviction in each case. No one dictates to anyone what risk he shall run or what sacrifice he shall make: each does what he feels he can, and he is not reproached if others do more. There have been exceptions to this rule, but with sad consequences, as people broke down or were faced with situations they could not handle. In this way experience has taught the dissidents to treat one another with tolerance and magnanimity.

For the same reason there are no "leaders" among them. Some are especially brave, some have suffered more cruelly than others, some are writers noted for their talents and honesty. For such reasons one or another dissident may be better known than the rest; but the most respected among them cannot and do not teach, admonish, instruct, give orders, or sit in judgment. It is contrary to the dissidents' moral system to suggest that there should be a leader, to put forward any name, or to speak of rivalry in this respect.

The nature of the links between dissidents is well illustrated by *samizdat*. An author decides to write an open letter, an uncensored article or book. He types it with as many carbons as possible, usually five to eight, and gives them to his friends. Anyone who finds the material interesting recopies and distributes it in the same way. Before long an uncountable number of copies are circulating by hand throughout the country. Like all other links among the dissidents, *samizdat* is a polycentric activity. As far as composition and distribution are concerned, individuals act on their own initiative and not under any pressure of discipline or group ethics. Their motives, too, are internal rather than external: the object is not to propagandize but to share with others what one finds important and interesting, just as we are pleased when a close friend reads a book or sees a film that we have enjoyed.

The authorities have the same trouble with *samizdat* as in their other efforts to crush the dissidents. In the first place, it is not clear on what principle the state can forbid citizens to express their thoughts on paper for their friends to read. Secondly, even if, like the KGB, we overlook this legal nicety, there is a practical problem. The author generally does not try to hide, but repression arouses such a stormy reaction that security agents proceed as gingerly as possible. As to the distributors, who are more in the shadows and not protected by publicity, they may be arrested or hounded, but this does not put an end to *samizdat*.

The personal and informal nature of the links among dissidents has another important consequence. In previous Russian history, all opposition groups have been infiltrated by the police; but this is not the case with the present dissidents, despite their apparent weakness as a social group. There have been cases where the KGB has beaten a confession out of someone or made them give information compromising a friend; but this was due to violence and not to premeditated treachery. Those broken down in this way feel remorse and often try to atone for their guilt; but their comrades do not judge them with fanatical severity. Relations among dissidents are intimate, friendly, and based on a degree of mutual understanding far beyond that required by any "cause." They are not particularly concerned with numbers and therefore do not seek proselytes, so that the moral level of the group remains fairly high.

The dissidents are the only movement in the history of the Russian intelligentsia that has concentrated on the defense of human rights. The law, to them, is not a means but an end, for it is only on a basis of respect for the law, and for human beings as its subject, that further objectives can be set.

The phenomenon of dissidence cannot be understood outside the framework of previous Russian history. If its present condition is to some extent a direct consequence of the past, the attempt to escape from it is inseparable from a critical understanding of experience. Having cast out "Soviet man," the dissidents have to exorcise other, less clear-cut forms of the same entity. The faults of the pre-revolutionary intelligentsia, so penetratingly described by *Landmarks,* are present today in an exaggerated and repulsive form. Soviet intolerance shows up the viciousness of all intolerance; Soviet contempt for the truth brings out its intrinsic value. The degradation of man bears witness to his unique individuality. To anyone who has freed himself from the Soviet ethos, there is no place for any kind of nihilism.

The old specters, it is true, still walk among us. Moral apostasy or lack of self-criticism, relics of inner enslavement or disrespect for others' freedom, still at times give delight to the demons of former days.

In spite of all failures, however, the dissidents have achieved their most important aim: there is now a moral potential in our society that even the state cannot ignore. However much the regime tries to crush it, it comes to the fore and proclaims its existence, and by so doing foils the schemes of petty tyrants.

People sometimes talk as though the dissidents were defeated because many of them have been thrown into prisons or madhouses, exiled, cut off from ordinary life, or forced to emigrate. But this is not a victory for the KGB, not even a Pyrrhic victory. The rulers are determined to destroy the dissidents physically, but with each new act of violence they suffer a moral decline. If violence were the dissidents' weapon as well as that of the regime, it might be said that they were defeated. Anyone who saddles them with physical aims is in fact weakening them. But, in all honesty, one cannot speak of such aims in contemporary Soviet conditions.

It is not to be considered a defeat that the dissidents were and are few in numbers. Big battalions are needed for revolutions or victory at democratic elections; but we clearly do not want the first, and there is no chance of the second in the near future. The dissidents' strength lies in the fact that the regime cannot and will not be able to ascribe to them any evil or subversive intent.

The great poet Pasternak wrote, after living through the agonies of Soviet history:

> Others will follow your fresh trail inch by inch, but you yourself must not distinguish defeat from victory. You must not depart a hair's breadth from your true self, but simply be alive—alive to the very end.

The dissidents are true to themselves; they are alive, and will remain so.

# Epilogue

*The following letter, dated January 5, 1971, was written by the author from Moscow to Larisa Bogoraz in Siberia, to which she was exiled for taking part in a demonstration against the invasion of Czechoslovakia by Soviet troops.*

Dear Larochka,

At last, like our fellow Jew in the story, "I have found a time and place to write to you."[1]

I think I have apologized to you before for my organic dislike of writing letters. As far as I am concerned, all writing is work, and one is usually lazy about doing it unless, of course, one gets carried away. But you can hardly be carried away when you know that alien, unfriendly eyes are presumably going to read what you write, and you have to hint and garble and not say things straight out. I have gotten out of the habit of writing for the censor even when I am paid to: I have been spoiled. And it is hard to combine the sense of work, with all its tension and fatigue, with the pleasure one takes in conversation and the desire to interchange ideas freely.

And so for years I have been silent, though I have not felt happy about it.

But today's opportunity is so excellent that I must use it—especially as I have thought and talked so much, to Natashka[2] and others, about all the sad, complicated, mixed-up things that have been happening: I have thought about you, and all of us, and the past, and the future we shall have to endure (if we live). I have been going more and more deeply into the history of the Russian intelligentsia, which threatens to become my life's work, to use a rather pompous expression; because it seems to me that we need a clear idea of the spiritual foundations on which we stand, and must stand unless we are to act irresponsibly and even irrationally. There is so much at stake, and the sacrifices required from us are so great, that it is an unpardonable luxury for our actions not to be as effective as we can possibly make them.

The problem comes down to this: What kind of country are we living in, and how does its past determine its future? And, on the other hand, how should the intelligentsia, the self-conscious part of society, conduct itself in view of the objective possibilities that history offers?

Thinking over these problems has brought me to some very pessimistic conclusions. Historically the die was cast, it would seem, as far back as the thirteenth century, when Alexander Nevsky allied himself with the Mongols against the Teutonic Order.[3] Russia turned her back on Europe and surrendered to Asia as the lesser evil. She found the Mongols more congenial, and remained their faithful vassal for a long time. This is very important, as it conflicts with our usual stereotype of the "Tatar-Mongol yoke." Just as the early Slav tribes in what is now Russia had mingled with the Varangians,[4] so they now mixed with the Mongols and other tribes of the steppes. One may even say that Russia was the legal heir of the Mongols and the continuer of their empire. As L. Gumilev rightly pointed out, the Russians acclaimed Alexander Nevsky as a saint and thus showed that they wholeheartedly approved his choice.

But the Asiatic social and spiritual structure which we took from the Mongols, and which has virtues of its own, differs from the European in being static and incapable of development or progress. Being part-Asian and part-European, Russia had to adopt certain features of Western civilization, but she did so in order to combat that civilization and prevent herself from being Europeanized. Hence political attempts to Europeanize Russia always led to the strengthening of the Asian element. This was so under Peter and Catherine, Alexander I and II and, finally, the "great founder" of our present polity. In order to achieve so-called industrialization, make the H-bomb, and send men into space, Russia had first to abrogate, for practical purposes, even the halfhearted reforms of the 1860s.[5] As a result, we are closer now to the regime of Nicholas I and Arakcheyev than we were a hundred years ago.[6] Russia's Asiatic side comes out more strongly whenever there is an attempt to weaken it or play it down, and I believe the October revolution was a supreme example of this. What is now called socialism in our country is a typically Asiatic phenomenon, which means that it is partly Russian too. This is confirmed by the fact that only the Russians and the Chinese find this socialism a natural order of things; other peoples can hardly endure it, and do so only under the pressure of overwhelming external force. This, I think, is an essential factor in the national conflicts that are now getting more acute.[7]

The only serious difference between Russia and other Asiatic societies is that she managed to create an intelligentsia that was European in its ideas and education. Naturally enough, however, the cultural characteristics and the position of this intelligentsia were and are highly peculiar. Insofar as it is European, it is alien in its own land; and it is this sense of being alien and rootless that chiefly distinguishes it from the intelligentsia in Western countries. A specifically Russian type of intellectual was evolved, and we may even speak of his possessing a national outlook, though it has little in common with that of the peasant, worker, or bureaucrat. These classes developed their typical characteristics by a process of mutual repulsion, and the bureaucrat is much closer to the worker or peasant than is the intellectual. As Gershenzon remarked, even anthropologically the Russian intellectual belongs to a different type than a man of the people.

Incidentally there may be a key here to the peculiar nature of Russian anti-Semitism, which is directed against the intelligentsia as a class. The intellectual is felt to be alien, and it is natural to label him a "Yid," the embodiment of all that is foreign. It is typical of the intelligentsia, moreover, that it strives to get out of its national shell and to develop cosmopolitan ideas; we see this in both Westernizers and Slavophiles, and in such thinkers, diametrically opposed in many respects, as Tolstoy and V.

Solovyov. In Dostoyevsky's case, too, nationalism took the form of considering the Russian a "universal man."

At the same time, throughout its existence the Russian intelligentsia has endeavored to cultivate a national spirit and to achieve union with the people by cerebral means, thus creating a "soil" in which it could grow. It did this either by presenting itself as the defender and mouthpiece of the social and political interests of the common people, which they themselves could not be expected to grasp unaided, or by embracing the religion professed by the nation at large. The intellectuals attributed to the people the ideas which they had evolved amid struggle and torment, and persuaded themselves that they had imbibed these from the people. They imagined, too, that their own character and the fruits of their creative activity were a realization of powers that lay dormant in the Russian people. The effect of these illusions was to ascribe everything to the people and leave the intelligentsia naked and defenseless before it. But all was in vain, as the people could not understand its own, supposedly self-evident interest, interpreted in European style, nor did it comprehend the humanistic idea of God as developed by intellectuals of genuinely Orthodox convictions.

Thus for a hundred and fifty years, from the Dekabrists onward, the intelligentsia busied itself with the material and spiritual salvation of its people, a task that no one had really asked it to perform. It could be shown how the noblest ideas of Kireyevsky[8] and Khomyakov degenerated into Black Hundred anti-Semitism,[9] how the Bolsheviks appropriated the tradition of Herzen and Belinsky, how the intelligentsia put its own head in the noose (cf. the poems of Blok and Voloshin, especially the latter, in the first years of the revolution), and how finally, infatuated by its own love of the people, it degenerated into the "Soviet intelligentsia." All this has to some extent already been analyzed by Berdyaev in *The Origin of Russian Communism,* which I hope you have read.

The essential feature of our present period since the middle fifties is, it seems to me, that the Russian intelligentsia which dissolved, capitulated, or was physically destroyed under Lenin and Stalin is now being visibly reborn among us. This is happening in several ways: (1) The links of continuity are being restored. Dostoyevsky, Solovyov, Berdyaev, Pasternak, Akhmatova, Mandelshtam, and others are being eagerly read, not only because their works can now be had but most of all because they are mentally within our reach, we can understand the problems that tormented them. (2) Our intelligentsia, having set itself to school again, is catching up with contemporary European culture, not only in technical but in personal ways. (3) Its cultural and ethical potential is being restored, a process of which there are well-known examples.

There is, however, an essentially new factor in the make-up of today's intelligentsia, namely the experience that separates us from the heyday of the so-called Russian spiritual renaissance, the period of Izgoyev's *Na perevale.*[10] That was also the time of *Landmarks,* which ought to be the constant reading of every true intellectual, but which was then rejected by intellectuals of every political, religious, and philosophical shade. The distinctive feature of our own time is that the wisdom of *Landmarks* has become self-evident. We may note sadly that it took a no less talented educator than Stalin to get, or should I say "beat," this truth into our heads.

But there is something to be added to the picture as the authors of *Landmarks* saw it, and that, I venture to think, is the skeptical view of Russian history, and of the future outlook, that I have tried to sketch. I think it is significant that Amalrik takes a similar view, though starting from different premises.

The adoption of this view would really mean going back to the sources of Russian national thought and also raising ourselves to the present European level, since it may be denoted by the single word "existentialism" (in the complex of its various meanings). It is not for nothing that I. Kireyevsky and Dostoyevsky are regarded, correctly, as nineteenth-century forerunners of existentialism; in the twentieth century Berdyaev and L. Shestov, among others, have worked out original systems of existentialist philosophy based on our national spiritual experience.

Lenin says somewhere that Russia "learned its Marxism through suffering." It would be truer to say that suffering has taught it existentialism and the rejection of Marxism, although the latter does have an existential aspect (not in Lenin's version, of course). For example, my own Marxism and that of some others in the fifties was nothing else than a progress toward existentialism and was very like, e.g., the views of Sartre, who at that time was going through a period of enthusiasm for Marx, especially the "young" Marx, while remaining an existentialist. In our circumstances the works of the "young" Marx were in fact the only possible way of gratifying the urge toward a live philosophy. Berdyaev, who is tremendously important to us at the present time, evolved from Marxism to existentialism in the same way.

The existentialist view of history, to put it briefly, denies that it contains any rational or moral significance that is "given" automatically, without the play of personal initiative. Humanity does not become better of its own accord, nor is it necessarily better off in each century than in the one before. And no one can improve humanity in any way simply by relying on the good qualities that it is supposed to possess. Those who try to do this never achieve their object. History, understood in the orthodox Marxist way as a natural-historical process, is without meaning or purpose: it consists of going round in a vicious circle, mindlessly repeating and reproducing the same thing, namely the expression of crude "human nature." And as long as we base ourselves on this kind of history, we cannot answer for the consequences of our own actions. Such history leaves us unprotected against cruelty, absurdity, and the most grotesque surprises.

The point is that when history is understood and made in this way, its agents are the masses (or the people, which is the same thing) and not individuals; and the masses are blind and irresponsible. It may be true that ideas become a material force when they take possession of the masses, but in doing so they cease to be ideas in the proper sense. They become hackneyed and stereotyped, losing their inner consistency and many-sidedness, and therefore it is only in appearance that they govern mass behavior, which is essentially instinctive and irrational. This is why only demagogues can even give the appearance of leading the masses, feeding them with slogans that they have no intention of putting into practice. Ideas have to be presented to the "people" in a specially adapted form—that is to say, they have to be distorted.

From the existentialist point of view, however, this means

that the role of human personality is all the more important and universal. It is the seat of reason, meaning, and conscience, in fact of everything that deceptive philosophical systems purport to discover in the objective course of historical evolution. But not every individual is a "person" in this sense. Personality is not formed biologically or even socially. It is the fruit of culture, as agnostic existentialists would put it, or of divine revelation, in the view of existentialists who are also believers. Hence, if you like, spiritual history, based on the continuity of personalities, is the only truly creative history (Berdyaev called it "metahistory"). It can be neither conceived nor described except in concrete personal terms—like the history of art, literature, or philosophy. The same is true of political history, looked at from the point of view of ideas.

The meaning of that history is not that it benefits ignorant humanity but that it creates and imparts infinite variety to the values which enable the personality (I stress this word again) to attain its highest and only true happiness. The highest significance of personality consists in realizing its creative freedom, which means primarily internal freedom: for external freedom is possible only when internal freedom has been first developed, that is to say the ability to decide and act in accordance with one's personal motivations and not under the influence and pressure of external circumstances. This does not mean, of course, that external freedom is not necessary too: this would be an error condemning the free personality to torment and destruction. For this reason even Berdyaev, while a self-proclaimed advocate of aristocratic thought, was at the same time a democrat and understood the value of legal guarantees of external freedom. However, this in turn is of no use without internal freedom. Amalrik, incidentally, wrote well on this point in his letter to Kuznetsov. But to achieve internal freedom we must cease to put our trust in automatic historical progress or some principle of good inherent in history and independent of our will. As Camus brilliantly said: "History starts with understanding; the world is an absurdity." Berdyaev, as a religious thinker, considered the world irrational in its objectified state. But these views are much the same from the point of view of the inferences to be drawn concerning the basic principles of the realization of freedom.

This kind of philosophy seems to me perfectly organic, especially in the sociohistorical situation in which the Russian intelligentsia has always found itself and in which we are at the present day. In the West too, I would recall, existentialism came to the fore as a philosophy of the antifascist resistance—a resistance that took no account of whether victory was probable or not, and that stood up to the cruelties of the occupation and concentration camps. We in Russia are, so to speak, in an occupied country, and to compare it with a concentration camp is not just a metaphor.

And, sure enough, existentialist tendencies appear among us in all sorts of places as soon as we begin to seek the road to freedom. Solzhenitsyn's novels seem to me to mark a new stage in this development. You will remember, for instance, how the arrested diplomat in *The First Circle,* thrown into an isolation cell and stripped of his clothes and possessions, suddenly feels free from fear and brave enough to offer resistance. I also detect a purely existential note in some of your husband's writings,[11] especially *Redemption* and the poems written in prison. And the stand taken by Andrey and Yulka[12] impressed public opinion precisely because of its existential quality. They expressly did not set out to alter the present system, but asserted their creative freedom—not merely demanding it, but enacting it. And your Red Square demonstration[13] most certainly had an existential significance, as you and others made clear at the trial.

I was greatly touched by what Arkady Belinkov wrote to the PEN Club just before he died. "What do we hope for?" he said in his letter. "We know we cannot alter the present system in our country, and we deliberately do not set out to do so. But we must save that which is alive in Russia." (I heard this on the radio and am paraphrasing it.)

But the trouble is that being, as it were, existentialists by instinct and unawares, we are often inconsistent. Our actions have not always taken the form of a self-realization of freedom. Sometimes their purpose has been to "shake up" other people, to confront them with a sharp moral issue and force them to choose. And at times it has been like a man jumping into an icy river so that someone else would have to pull him out. Perhaps this is a slight exaggeration, but it is not too far from the truth.

An existential act—be it the writing of a book or poem, a demonstration, a public statement, or whatever—is distinguished by the fact that it is *self-sufficient*. It is simply and solely the outcome of inner spiritual and moral promptings. It is the act of one whose conscience, and not merely the judgment of his fellows, commands him to behave in this way and not otherwise. Any external effect is a secondary consideration—the meaning of the act is in itself. Its chief precondition is a high degree of spirituality on the agent's part—a degree of personal development such that he will be prepared to answer for his action, to defy threats and not break under strain.

Often our actions have failed to measure up to this. Sometimes we have been moved by hatred, and not by any wiser or more exalted feeling. Even while realizing that the point of most of our acts is not to achieve a practical result, we have often behaved as though we expected them to. What is more, we engaged in actions that were really practical in purpose as though they were existential, and by so doing have vitiated matters at the root.

Perhaps what we chiefly lacked was awareness of our own motives, which often led and still leads to a confusion that is far from harmless. It was easy for surrogates to be proffered and accepted as true spiritual values. The traditional mechanism of this kind of substitution was analyzed long ago in *Landmarks,* in Bulgakov's article if I remember right.

This is how I see the matter. An existential act requires a high degree of moral stoicism, perhaps even heroism. It has more to do with its own inner significance and possible spiritual consequences than with material consequences for the agent or anyone else. Among us, however, the desperation of an act came to be regarded as a measure of its existentiality. In *Landmarks* the psychological attitude prompting this grave error was summed up in the phrase: "The closer a man is to death, the more right he is."

We somehow got used to valuing a person for what he or she "was doing" or "had done" or "might do"—in short the fact of their "making a stand," or rather the amount of risk involved in doing so, for the substance of the matter was by no means always taken into account. Moral judgments and personal relationships were formed accordingly. Whereas relations among us were supposed to be based on personal sympathy and friendship, in cases like these they became intertwined with the idea of a "cause," and secondary to it: our friends were those who served the same "cause" as we did. Everything became equal and impersonal; the individual's contribution lost its meaning and value and interested nobody. What counted about a man was not how he lived, his professional interests and attainments, but merely what statements he had signed. We were all subordinate to the "cause," which did not care whether we were young or old, clever or stupid, cultured or primitive, insane or in our right minds (I am not speaking of insanity as defined by the authorities), poets or scholars, academicians or demimondaines; and all of us were marked off from society by a kind of special seal.

It was only imagination that made us think we were freely determining our own acts: compulsion lay in the very fact that we had to keep "acting." Actions brought consequences, and these had to be reacted to. If there was a lull it became oppressive, and people would think up something new. For some of us (I shall not mention names, that is not the point) continuous action became a kind of spiritual drug, a way of filling up the emptiness of life, a comparatively cheap form of self-affirmation.

The position became altogether absurd when "organizational" features began to creep in, although they were quite alien to the spirit and circumstances of our community. There were people who were in the know, and others from whom certain details were withheld. Certain actions were performed purely in order to stir up the "intelligentsia," to give it a lead. The term "riffraff" began to be applied to our intelligentsia by people who had no claim to belong to it and no influence over it, not because they themselves were too radical or the intelligentsia too cowardly, but because they were primitive, second-rate and pretentious.

I would also remark that the clarity of our present situation is dangerously deceptive. One might think that not the slightest effort is necessary to identify good and evil, the truth and the lie. But what is on the surface can only provoke a superficial reaction.

I have spoken about these things in the past tense because I think they do indeed belong to the past, to an infantile stage which was apparently necessary but which we have outgrown.

Through this complicated and confusing process the intelligentsia came to maturity in the sense I have described. Now we have reached a time of choice: we must either develop our own personality and its spiritual potential, or be condemned to obviously pointless actions. Along these lines we are already witnessing—thank God!—a sharp differentiation within our "progressive society," in which formerly all cats were gray.

This letter has become frightfully long, and I simply have not the strength to explain properly that nothing I have said involves in any way "coming to terms with reality." I have been talking about the inner meaning and content of an opposition, not whether it should exist at all. To put things as concisely as I can I will refer to the example of Solzhenitsyn, who, in my opinion, is contributing most to the "cause" and is doing so in the right way, namely by writing his books.

My pen has run away with me . . . All the same, you can't say everything on paper. Perhaps Natashka and I can meet you and Pavel one day.[14] I dream of this constantly; I love you dearly and admire you, as I always have done and as everyone does.

Your affectionate<br>Boris.

# Notes

1. This refers to the fact that the Bolsheviks began by exterminating, among others, the intelligentsia of all persuasions except their own—and later, especially after 1936, took to exterminating one another.

2. The slogan of the Czechoslovak Communist Party at the time of the "Prague spring," 1968.

3. From a song entitled "Moscow-Peking," set to music by Vano Muradeli and popular during the period of "friendship" between the USSR and the Chinese People's Republic.

4. The Pushkin quotation is from *The Captain's Daughter* (1836), a story set in the time of the Pugachev rebellion (1773). The passage appears in modern editions, but was not included in the final version published in Pushkin's lifetime.

5. The Tatars conquered medieval (Kievan) Russia in the thirteenth century, and their suzerainty was not thrown off until the fifteenth (by Ivan III, grand duke of Moscow).

6. Stalin died on March 5, 1953.

7. "The Fisherman and His Wife" (1833).

8. From the poem entitled "Night" (1854).

9. People deprived of their jobs for ideological or political reasons are then penalized under the decree of the Supreme Soviet of the Russian Soviet Federated Socialist Republic (RSFSR) dated May 4, 1961, "On Strengthening the Struggle with Persons Avoiding Socially Useful Work and Leading an Anti-social, Parasitic Way of Life" (translated in J. N. Hazard and Isaac Shapiro, *The Soviet Legal System*, New York, 1962). Under this decree, a court or a "group of toilers" in an

office, factory, farm, etc., may sentence offenders to "correctional labor" and banishment.

CHAPTER I

1. The term "cult of personality," first used at the July plenum of the Communist Party Soviet Union in 1953, became an accepted euphemism for the unbridled atrocities of Stalin's rule. Under the Brezhnev regime, the term has gradually gone out of use.

2. Under Article 7 of the Constitution of the USSR (1936), "Every collective farm household, in addition to its basic income from the public collective farm enterprise, has for its own use a plot of land attached to the house and, as personal property, an auxiliary establishment on the plot. . . ." (Text published by Cooperative Publishing Society of Foreign Workers in the USSR, Moscow, 1937, p. 12).

3. The official denunciation of Stalin's misrule, which began in 1956, was continued at this Congress. Cf. Chapter 2, note 11.

4. Quoted from *Resolutions and Decisions of the Communist Party of the Soviet Union*, Vol. 4: *The Khrushchev Years*, ed. Grey Hodnett, University of Toronto Press, 1974, p. 230.

5. At Soviet elections there is always only one candidate for each seat, representing the "communist and nonparty bloc" (a Stalinist term). According to the official count these candidates always get at least 97 percent of the votes cast. In his Report to the Eighteenth Party Congress in 1939, Stalin said: "In 1937 Tukhachevsky, Yakir, Uborevich and other fiends were sentenced to be shot. After that, the elections to the Supreme Soviet of the USSR were held. In these elections, 98.6 per cent of the total vote was cast for the Soviet power. At the beginning of 1938 Rosengoltz, Rykov, Bukharin and other fiends were sentenced to be shot. After that, the elections to the Supreme Soviets of the Union Republics were held. In these elections 99.4 per cent of the total vote was cast for the Soviet power" (J. Stalin, *Leninism*, London, 1940, p. 646).

6. The term "voluntarism" as a criticism of Khrushchev's rule first appeared in the Soviet press at the end of 1964: it evidently meant that he made decisions without consulting his colleagues.

7. In 1957 Khrushchev declared a 20-to-25-year moratorium on the interest due to contributors to previous annual state loans. In 1958 he abolished the Machine and Tractor Stations, so that collective farms had to buy equipment from the state. Prices in general were raised under cover of the monetary reform of 1960.

8. The effect of the new by-laws was that the bureaucrats enjoyed indefinite tenure.

9. One aspect of this is that photographs of Soviet leaders are retouched to conceal the effects of age.

10. The "economic reform" adopted at the Twenty-third Congress (March–April 1966) was intended to "combine the centralized management of branches of the economy with the extension of the rights of Union Republics, to strengthen the role of economic methods in management, to improve radically the planning system, to increase the economic independence and initiative of collectives in enterprises, and to give them a greater material interest in the results of their activity" (*Pravda,* April 9, 1966).

11. This phrase is from a *samizdat* poem by Naum Korzhavin, "A Fable About the Multiplication Table."

12. From a satirical epitome of Russian history, in verse published posthumously, by A. K. Tolstoy (1883).

13. Alexander Solzhenitsyn, ed., *From Under the Rubble* (Boston: (Little, Brown, 1975), p. 96.

CHAPTER II

1. The Mongol-Tatar khan (grandson of Genghis Khan) who founded the Golden Horde and conquered Russia in 1236–40; he also defeated the Poles and Hungarians.

2. Officials of the khan, responsible for tribute and census matters.

3. Literally, a member of the Pioneers, a political organization for children between 9 and 14, founded in 1922.

4. "Volunteer" police units in factories, offices, etc.

5. Article 10 of the Code of Criminal Procedure of the RSFSR states that "In the case of an offense of minor importance or not involving great danger, when the fact of the crime is evident [?] and the offender can be corrected by the application of social measures, the court or the public prosecutor, or the examining magistrate and the investigating authority with the prosecutor's consent, may refer the evidence to a comradely court instead of instituting a criminal prosecution."

6. Another euphemism (cf. Chapter 1, note 1) introduced in Khrushchev's time to designate the Stalin terror. Cf. also note 11 below.

7. The present Constitution of the USSR, formerly known as the Stalin Constitution, became law in December 1936; 1937 was the peak year of Stalin's mass executions.

8. Among Soviet intellectuals, the government is commonly referred to simply as "they."

9. Bryusov (1873–1924), Symbolist poet. He joined the Communist Party in 1920 and became chairman of the Literature Division in the new

Soviet regime's Ministry of Enlightenment. Lunacharsky (1875–1933) was People's Commissar (Minister) of Enlightenment from 1917 to 1929.

10. The Research Institutes of the Academy of Sciences of the USSR produce comprehensive works, usually in many volumes, covering whole branches of learning and compiled by several authors. Their work is made easier by the fact that uniformity of views can be presumed in advance.

11. The first of these disclosures was Khrushchev's report to the Twentieth Congress in 1956, which has never been officially published in the USSR but was read to meetings in all organizations and enterprises.

12. Applicants for jobs of all kinds have to fill in exhaustive questionnaires about themselves, including any information that may be to their discredit from the official point of view. The hero of Chukhray's film *Clear Sky* (1961), an air-force pilot, was victimized by the police because he had been a prisoner of war.

13. Some of the works mentioned were published officially (e.g., translations of Hemingway and Faulkner); others, like Mandelshtam's poems, circulated illegally.

14. In the last decade there has been a rapid turnover of officials in command of Soviet culture: Ilyichev, Yegorichev, Yagodkin . . .

15. This was the term favored by Yagodkin when he was secretary of the CPSU's Moscow committee for agitation and propaganda.

16. Title of a celebrated novel by Ilya Ehrenburg (1956).

17. *Samizdat,* literally "self-publishing": works copied and circulated privately by authors and their friends to evade the official censorship.

18. A *samizdat* journal, circulated in the USSR since 1968, which publishes information about violations of human rights.

19. Alexander Solzhenitsyn, ed., *From Under the Rubble* (Boston: Little, Brown, 1975), p. 252.

20. A term applied to the mentality of the Russian intelligentsia by the philosopher S. Frank, a contributor to the collection *Vekhi (Landmarks):* see Chapter 4, note 14.

21. The organization known as Narodnaya Volya (People's Will, or People's Freedom), after eight attempts, succeeded in assassinating Tsar Alexander II in 1881. After the assassination, one of its leaders, Degayev, became a police agent and betrayed many of his comrades.

22. The Slavophile and Westernizing schools of thought arose in the 1830s. The former extolled the importance of Russian and Orthodox traditions; the latter stood for Europeanization.

23. A group of military officers (also known as "Dekabrists") who stood for constitutional government and attempted to carry out a *coup*

*d'état* in 1825, at the time of the accession of Nicholas I. See also Chapter 4, note 13.

24. Count Uvarov was Minister of Education under Nicholas I (1825–55).

25. In 1721 Peter the Great allowed the Moscow patriarchate to fall into abeyance and placed the Russian church under the authority of a government organ, the Most Holy Synod. This arrangement lasted until 1917.

26. A church congress held in 1917 restored the patriarchate and took various liberal decisions, but the church soon fell victim to Bolshevik persecution.

27. Lenin, *Collected Works*, 4th edition, London, 1964, Vol. 18, p. 26.

28. Article 190(1) of the Criminal Code of the RSFSR prescribes penalties for "the systematic dissemination in oral form of deliberate fabrications which defame the Soviet state and social system, and similarly the preparation or dissemination in written, printed or any other form of works of like content" (Mervyn Matthews, *Soviet Government: A Selection of Official Documents on Internal Policies*, London, 1974, p. 288).

29. Flats inhabited by several families, usually one family to a room, with shared kitchen and toilet.

30. Owing to the shortage of labor, due to its low productivity, students on vacation and intellectuals are often conscripted in this way, to the detriment of their proper work.

31. "Going among the people" (also called Populism) was a widespread movement among the intelligentsia, especially in the 1880s: it involved settling among the peasants, adopting their dress and way of life, furthering their interests in the way of health services, education, etc., and trying in this way to become attuned to their outlook and gain their confidence.

32. Aleksandr Solzhenitsyn, *The First Circle* (New York: 1968), p. 388.

33. Ibid., pp. 388–89.

34. Russian essayist, 1840–1868.

CHAPTER III

1. The "boy in pants" and the "boy without" are characters in a humorous dialogue by Saltykov-Shchedrin, translated by G. Struve in Vol. XVIII of the *Slavonic Review*, London, 1939.

2. Oblomov is a proverbial type of flabbiness and indolence, the chief character in the novel of that name by Goncharov (1859).

3. The spelling of the Russian language was officially simplified in December 1917.

4. Translated from *Za Rubezhom* ("Behind the Border"), in Vol. V of Saltykov-Shchedrin's selected works (Moscow: 1948), pp. 159–63.

5. A cliché used to rebuke writers and artists for not portraying Soviet life in a sufficiently flattering light. The shadows, it is claimed, only appear dark because of the general brightness.

6. A comedy written in 1825; first published without censorship cuts in 1862.

7. Characters in Gogol's *The Government Inspector (Revizor)*, 1836.

8. From *The Misfortune of Being Clever* (note 6 above).

9. This refers in particular to the trials and executions of famous and loyal communists, many of them devoted adherents of Stalin himself, from 1936 onward, as well as a host of smaller fry. The textbook of Soviet history by Shestakov, then in use in schools, contained many illustrations of political and military leaders which the children had to blot out one by one as their subjects proved to be "traitors."

10. Cf. Chapter 2, note 5.

11. This refers to works of so-called "socialist realism," intended as artistic illustrations of the official morality.

12. Tsars Peter III and Paul were killed by palace guards in 1762 and 1801 respectively. Alexander II, the liberator of the serfs, was assassinated in 1881; Nicholas II and his family were murdered by the Bolsheviks in 1918. Nicholas I was removed by natural death in 1855, Stalin in 1953; in both cases the event relieved the country of a weight of oppression. The removals of Malenkov from the premiership in 1955 and of Khrushchev in 1964 were effected without bloodshed.

13. One of Peter the Great's measures; a contemporary cartoon shows him with scissors in hand.

14. Nicholas I similarly ordered the Slavophiles to shave off beards which they had grown as a mark of attachment to old national custom.

15. At the time of the invasion of Czechoslovakia in 1968, the Soviet press inveighed against Czech and Slovak youths for wearing long hair. No beards are seen on Soviet television.

16. The *mir* or *obshchina*, in old Russia, was the village community which owned the land jointly and parceled it out among members.

17. A Soviet official phrase denoting a simulacrum of democracy, generally organized from above.

18. The term "personal record" is the accepted designation in party and Komsomol organizations for examinations or investigations of a member.

19. A. Zhdanov, the ideologist of Stalinism and postwar cultural dictator, spoke as follows in the discussion of a *History of Western European Philosophy* by G. F. Aleksandrov: "In our Soviet society, in which antagonistic classes have been liquidated, . . . the development from a lower to a higher level takes place not, as under capitalism, through the class struggle and cataclysms, but in the form of criticism and self-criticism: this is the true driving force of our development, a powerful instrument in the party's hands."

20. This concept of Stalin's is defined in the *Great Soviet Encyclopedia* (2nd edition, 1954, Vol. 28, p. 275) as "unity of economic and political interests, the community of views and aims and of the moral and spiritual temper of the workers, peasants, and intelligentsia of the USSR, fighting under the leadership of the Communist Party for the victory of communism."

21. See, e.g., Shafarevich's article "Separation or Reconciliation?—The Nationalities Question in the USSR"; Solzhenitsyn on "Repentance and Self-Limitation in the Life of Nations"; and Borisov on "Personality and National Awareness," all in *From Under the Rubble* (Boston, 1975).

22. See Introduction, note 5.

23. The liberal socialist A. Herzen (Gertsen) (1812–1870) lived abroad, chiefly in London, from 1847, and in 1857–67 published *The Bell*, the first uncensored political journal in Russian.

24. Valery Panov and his wife Galina (née Rogozin), artists of the Kirov Theater in Leningrad, had to wait over two years before their applications to emigrate were granted.

25. The landowners' serf-right over peasants was consolidated in the course of the sixteenth century on the basis of common law, and was abrogated by the liberation of the serfs in 1861.

26. This slogan, incessantly repeated in propaganda and party speeches, was coined by Lenin and is quoted by Klara Zetkin: see Lenin, *On Literature and Art* (in Russian), Moscow, 1957, p. 583.

27. *The Correspondence Between Prince A. M. Kurbsky and Tsar Ivan IV of Russia, 1564–1579*, ed. and trans. by J. L. I. Fennell, Cambridge University Press, 1955, p. 215.

28. "Corrupting" is the accepted Soviet epithet for Western influence; it is interesting that it is used in the same way, ironically, by Saltykov-Shchedrin.

29. Satirical descriptions of jury proceedings may be found in Dostoyevsky's *The Brothers Karamazov* and Tolstoy's *Resurrection*.

30. Control over the outlet from the Black Sea—the Bosporus and

Dardanelles—was a longstanding objective of Tsarist policy. Stalin revived the policy after World War II, but later Khrushchev officially renounced it.

31. In the sixteenth century a monk named Philotheus advanced the doctrine that as the original Rome had fallen into heresy and the second (Constantinople) had been conquered by the Turks, there remained Moscow, the third and eternal Rome: "a fourth there cannot be." This became the traditional religious foundation of Russian chauvinism and imperialism.

32. In a speech in 1936, "On the Draft Constitution of the USSR," Stalin said: "We now have a fully formed multinational Socialist state, which has stood all tests" (*Leninism*, London, 1940, p. 568).

33. Marx, *Early Writings*, Penguin Books, 1975, pp. 346–47.

34. Articles 124 and 125 of the Soviet Constitution (*op. cit.*, p. 35) guarantee freedom of conscience (but not of religious propaganda) and of speech, the press, assembly, and demonstrations. Article 125, however, states that these rights are conferred "in conformity with the interests of the toilers and in order to strengthen the socialist system."

35. See Introduction, note 10.

36. In 1957 Khrushchev leveled a number of rather vague accusations against his immediate colleagues and, supported by a plenum of the Central Committee of the party, secured their virtual exclusion from public life.

37. The ideological campaign against "cosmopolitanism"—with its thinly veiled anti-Semitic purpose—lasted from 1949 to Stalin's death in 1953; many were arrested, dismissed, or expelled from the party.

38. Shortly before Stalin's death many prominent doctors, several of them Jews, were arrested for allegedly conspiring to murder Soviet leaders. After Stalin's death the "Doctors' Plot" was declared to have been faked. It was "apparently a first move in an attempt to unleash a new wave of terror similar to the Great Purge of the 1930s" (S. V. Utechin, *Everyman's Concise Encyclopedia of Russia*, London and New York, 1961).

CHAPTER IV

1. *De Profundis* was written and set in type in 1918 but its publication was blocked by the Bolshevik censor. It was printed in 1922, but the plates were confiscated and very few copies were preserved. The work was virtually unknown till it was reprinted in 1967 by the YMCA Press in Paris.

2. The New Economic Policy, instituted by Lenin in 1921, allowed a

small measure of private initiative in order to restore the economy, devastated by the revolution and civil war. Stalin declared it obsolete in 1936, but it had actually come to an end several years earlier.

3. *Who Is at Fault?* is the title of an early novel by Herzen (Chapter 3, note 23).

4. The first Russian state, with its capital at Kiev, lasted from the ninth to the thirteenth century, when it was destroyed by the Tatars. The Moscow principality was founded in the twelfth century and took effective shape in the fourteenth, when it began to throw off the Tatar yoke and to assert its supremacy over the rest of Russia.

5. The Saturday nearest Lenin's birthday (April 22) is a day of "voluntary" unpaid work throughout the Soviet Union.

6. Russia was converted to Byzantine Christianity under St. Vladimir, prince of Kiev, in 988.

7. The Cyrillic script used in Russia and Bulgaria was invented in the ninth century by the Byzantine missionaries Cyril and Methodius. Christian literature was transmitted to these countries in Slavonic translations from the Greek, and Slavonic was the language used in the liturgy.

8. The schism *(raskol)* in the Russian Orthodox Church originated in the seventeenth century as a protest against the liturgical and ceremonial reforms of the patriarch Nikon, which many of the common people of Russia regarded as a blasphemy against their ancient ways. The Old Believers or Old Ritualists, as the schismatics were called, were persecuted for two centuries but exist to this day.

9. A lay theologian, philosopher, and Slavophile, 1804–1860.

10. See Chapter 2, note 30.

11. The Chuguyev revolt in 1819, on a military settlement in south Russia, was cruelly suppressed by Alexander I's minister Arakcheyev (cf. Epilogue, note 6). A widespread peasant revolt in 1773 was led by the Cossack Pugachev, who claimed to be Tsar Peter III. Cf. Introduction, note 5.

12. The term *bespochvennost'* (lack of contact with the soil) was coined by Dostoyevsky in his *Diary of a Writer* (c. 1880) to denote the intelligentsia's lack of national and popular roots.

13. On Decembrists, see Chapter 2, note 23. On December 26, 1825 (December 14 by the old calendar), about 3,000 troops who refused to take the oath to Nicholas I assembled on Senate Square in St. Petersburg. However, they failed to resist the loyal troops and were easily suppressed, after which harsh reprisals were taken.

14. The authors of *Landmarks (Vekhi)*—N. Berdyaev, S. Bulgakov, S. Frank, M. Gershenzon, A. Izgoyev, B. Kistyakovsky, and P.

Struve—were generally liberals and ex-Marxists who denounced the radical intelligentsia for its revolutionary views and its lack of religious and patriotic feeling. (*Vekhi* may also be translated as "Signposts.")

15. Both these terms are associated with the show-trials and purges of the Stalin era, when scholars, doctors, engineers, and industrial managers were accused wholesale of abusing their power in order to commit sabotage and treason.

16. The groups which believed in assassination and terrorism in pre-revolutionary times were the People's Will (Chapter 2, note 20) and afterwards the Socialist Revolutionaries (SR). The latter, a loosely organized populist party, were responsible for the murder in 1911 of the progressive minister Stolypin.

17. See note 1 above.

18. Published in Prague in 1921 by a group led by the historian N. Ustryalov. The writers of this school regarded the NEP (note 2 above) as denoting a return to capitalism, and called on the intelligentsia to cooperate with the new regime. Many of them returned to Russia.

19. This symposium was compiled in Moscow in 1974 and published in that year in Paris after Solzhenitsyn's expulsion from the Soviet Union. The English-language edition was published in 1975.

20. An allusion to the end of Pushkin's historical play *Boris Godunov,* where the crowd is ordered to acclaim the usurper but remains silent. (In Pushkin's original ending, banned by the Tsarist censor, the people do as they are told.)

CHAPTER V

1. A. Amalrik, *Will the Soviet Union Survive Until 1984?* (New York: Harper & Row, 1970), p. 5. Russian-language edition, Amsterdam: Herzen Foundation, 1970.

2. Marquis de Custine, *Russia,* London, 1854, p. 166.

3. In Rudolf L. Tökés (ed.), *Dissent in the USSR,* Johns Hopkins University Press, 1975, p. 115.

EPILOGUE

1. This refers to a joke about a Jew who is urged by the KGB, in line with the new policy of détente, to write to his brother in America. To make sure he complies, they tell him to sit down and write then and there from the KGB office. He begins his letter with the words quoted.

2. The present writer's wife, Natalya Nikolayevna Sadomskaya.

3. The Tatars took Kiev in 1240. In 1242 Alexander Nevsky, prince

of Novgorod in northwestern Russia, inflicted a decisive defeat on the Teutonic Knights in a battle on Lake Peipus (Chudskoye Ozero). His policy toward the Tatars was one of submission and conciliation.

4. The Varangians were Vikings who made their way from Sweden to Byzantium (Constantinople) from about 800 onward and whose leaders played a prominent part in the formation of the first Russian states, Novgorod and Kiev.

5. Besides the abolition of serfdom, Alexander II's reforms included trial by jury, a degree of local self-government, etc.

6. General Arakcheyev, Alexander I's chief counsellor in the latter part of his reign, devised a system of harshly disciplined military-agricultural settlements ("military colonies") in the western parts of Russia: cf. Chapter 4, note 11. His name is a byword for ignorance, reaction, and cruelty.

7. Many of the component nationalities of the USSR take less kindly to its social system than the Russians do. As a result, their hatred of the Soviet regime is expressed in hatred of the Russians.

8. A leading Slavophile (1806–1856).

9. The Black Hundred gangs were monarchist organizations created by the police in 1905–7 under the names of "League of St. Michael the Archangel" and "Union of the Russian People"; they carried out pogroms against Jews and the radical intelligentsia.

10. "The Turning-Point": a series of articles published in the journal *Russkaya Mysl' (Russian Thought)* between 1905 and 1917.

11. Larisa Bogoraz was married at the time to Yuly Daniel.

12. Andrey Sinyavsky and Yuly Daniel.

13. On August 25, 1968, Larisa Bogoraz, Natalya Gorbanyevskaya, Vadim Delone, Vladimir Dremlyuga, Viktor Fainberg, and Pavel Litvinov demonstrated in Red Square in Moscow against the Soviet invasion of Czechoslovakia. On their trial, see Peter Reddaway, *Uncensored Russia*, New York, 1972, pp. 112 ff.

14. Pavel Litvinov. At the time this letter was written, he was also, like Larisa Bogoraz, in Siberian exile.

# Glossary of Names

AKHMATOVA, ANNA (1889–1966). Russian poet who preserved her spiritual independence under the Soviet regime. In the 1940s she was subjected to harsh attacks and for a long time was deprived of the opportunity of publishing her poetry. To this day some of the most important of Akhmatova's works have not been published in the Soviet Union, although they have received wide distribution in typewritten copies.

ALEKSEY MIKHAILOVICH (ALEXIS) (1629–1676). Tsar under whose reign attempts were made to Europeanize Russia and carry out church reforms: these led to the breakaway of the "Old Believers" from the official Orthodox Church.

ALEXANDER I, EMPEROR (1777–1825). Favored liberal ideas during the first half of his reign, but after the defeat of Napoleon he inspired the Holy Alliance for the purpose of consolidating reaction in Europe, and also pursued a reactionary policy in domestic affairs.

ALEXANDER II, EMPEROR (1818–1881). Succeeded to the throne in 1855. Carried out some liberal reforms, most importantly the abolition of serfdom (1861), the introduction of trial by jury, and local self-government (the *zemstvos*). Assassinated by members of the secret revolutionary society Narodnaya Volya ("People's Will" or "People's Freedom").

ALEXANDER NEVSKY (1219–1263). Prince of the medieval city-state of Novgorod. A skillful commander who defended Russia against invasion by the Teutonic Knights, Swedes, and Finns. One of the saints traditionally most revered by Russian Orthodoxy.

ALLOV, ALEKSANDR (b. 1923). Film director and collaborator with V.

Naumov (q.v.). They made several "liberal" films, notably *Peace to Him Who Comes In* (1961) and *A Disagreeable Affair* (from a story by Dostoyevsky). The latter was banned by the censorship.

ALTAYEV, O. Pseudonymous author of the *samizdat* article "Pseudo-culture and the Dual Consciousness of the Intelligentsia."

AMALRIK, ANDREI (b. 1938). Dramatist and publicist. From the beginning of his career as an author he produced works independent of Soviet ideology and had them published outside Russia. In 1970 he was sentenced to three years in corrective labor camps, and in 1973, on the eve of completion of this sentence, to a further three years. In 1976 the pressure of police persecution and threats compelled him to emigrate to the West.

ARAKCHEYEV, ALEKSEY (1769–1834). A statesman and general who exercised much influence on the emperors Paul I and Alexander I (qq.v.); noted for harsh policies and the imposition of military discipline in civilian life.

BELINKOV, ARKADY (1921–1970). Writer and literary critic. Under Stalin's rule, he spent thirteen years in prisons and concentration camps for writing a novel which was suppressed by the secret police. He later wrote two books on the fate of the intelligentsia in Russia and under the Soviet regime, *Yury Tynianov* and *Yury Olesha;* the latter was published posthumously abroad. Emigrated to the West in 1968.

BELINSKY, VISSARION (1811–1848). An important literary critic, founder of the democratic and socialist tradition in Russian journalism.

BERDYAEV, NIKOLAI (1874–1948). Philosopher who created his own original system of religious existentialism. He was exiled from Russia on Lenin's orders early in the 1920s. Berdyaev's ideas have had a great influence on the development of independent thought in contemporary Russia.

BERIA (BERIYA), LAVRENTY (1899–1953). In charge of state security from 1938, he acted as Stalin's tool for the repression and destruction of real or supposed enemies. After Stalin's death, he was executed on grounds of espionage and "breaches of legality," but no public trial took place.

BLOK, ALEKSANDR (1880–1921). Russian poet, the most brilliant representative of Russian symbolism. Blok's search for the sources of poetry in the depths of the national soul led him to an interpretation of the Bolshevik Revolution as a manifestation of the rebellious, anarchic nature of the Russian. Soon, however, he was seized with a disillusion-ment which, according to a widely held opinion, was the reason for his spiritual breakdown and early death.

BOGORAZ, LARISA (b. 1929). Philologist. Married to Yuly Daniel (q.v.). When her husband was arrested and imprisoned in a corrective labor camp and at Vladimir, she was the first to interest the Soviet and international public in the question of human rights in the USSR. In 1968 she took part in a demonstration against the Soviet invasion of Czechoslovakia, and was sentenced to four years' exile in Siberia. Now married to Anatoly Marchenko, author of *My Testimony*, who is in exile in Siberia.

BRYUSOV (BRYUSSOV), VALERY (1873–1924). Symbolist poet. Joined the Communist Party in 1920, and became chairman of the Literature Division in the new Soviet regime's Ministry of Enlightenment.

BUKOVSKY, VLADIMIR (b. 1942). An active fighter for human rights in the USSR. Arrested in 1963 for disseminating a Russian translation of *The New Class* by Milovan Djilas, and confined in a psychiatric prison hospital. After serving his sentence, he organized a demonstration to demand a public trial for the writers Andrey Sinyavsky and Yuly Daniel (qq.v.), and published in the West evidence on the Soviet authorities' use of psychiatry as a weapon against dissidents. Arrested once more, he was sentenced to seven years in prison and labor camps with a further five years in exile. At the end of 1976, he was exchanged for the Chilean Communist leader Luis Carvalán and was forcibly deported to the West.

BULGAKOV, SERGEY (1871–1944). A philosopher, theologian, economist, and publicist; ordained an Orthodox priest in 1918. In early life he was a Marxist and specialized in economics, but by the turn of the century he had reverted to a religious outlook. One of the contributors to *Landmarks* (1909). Deported from Russia in 1923, he became Dean of the Theological Institute in Paris in 1925. Invented the philosophical system of "all-unity," closely interwoven with Orthodox theology.

CATHERINE II, EMPRESS (1729–1796). Known as Catherine the Great. While professing adherence to the ideas of the French Enlightenment, she strengthened serfdom in Russia and pursued an active policy of conquest. She seized power in 1762 by organizing a conspiracy against her husband, Peter III, who was killed immediately afterwards.

CHAADAYEV, PETR (1794–1856). A philosopher and political thinker, author of the *Philosophical Letters*, in which he developed an original philosophy of history. Only one of the *Letters* was published during his lifetime (in 1836); this contained a sharply critical view of Russian history, as a result of which he was officially declared insane. To this day, no complete edition of the *Philosophical Letters* has ever been published in Russia.

CHALIAPIN, FEDOR (1873–1938). Celebrated singer; emigrated and died abroad.

CHERNYSHEVSKY, NIKOLAY (1828–1889). A revolutionary democratic publicist who greatly influenced the Russian intelligentsia in the 1860s and 1870s. He was exiled to Siberia.

CHICHIKOV, PAVEL. Main character in Gogol's *Dead Souls* (1842), representing a grotesque type of Russian scoundrel.

CHUKOVSKAYA, LIDIA. Writer and literary critic who has written several brilliant essays expressing dissident views, for which she was expelled from the Union of Soviet Writers.

CUSTINE, MARQUIS ASTOLF DE (1790–1857). French traveler who visited Russia in the reign of Nicholas I and wrote *La Russie en 1839,* a major study of the nature and character of traditional Russian despotism. An English-language edition, entitled simply *Russia,* was published in London in 1854.

DANIEL, YULY (b. 1925). A prose-writer, poet, and translator. For publishing some stories abroad he was sentenced to five years in "strict regime" corrective labor camps. It was his arrest and that of Andrey Sinyavsky (q.v.) which triggered the fight for human rights in the USSR.

DEGAYEV, SERGEY (1857–1920). A member of Narodnaya Volya, and its virtual leader after the assassination of Alexander II (q.v.), he was at the same time an agent of the secret police and betrayed many members of the organization. He was eventually found out by his fellow-conspirators and at their behest murdered Sudeykin, his chief in the police hierarchy.

DELONE, VADIM (b. 1947). A poet, sentenced to three years in corrective labor camps for taking part in a demonstration against the Soviet invasion of Czechoslovakia on August 25, 1968; afterwards forced to emigrate.

DERZHIMORDA. A character in Gogol's comedy *The Inspector General* (1836): the police chief who is noted for his coarseness and brutality toward the public, on the one hand, and his servile submissiveness to his superiors, on the other.

DOBROLYUBOV, NIKOLAY (1836–1861). Literary critic and publicist of socialist and democratic views, who had immense influence on Russian intellectuals of the 1860s and later generations.

DREMLYUGA, VLADIMIR (b. 1940). Fighter for human rights in the USSR; took part in the demonstration of August 25, 1968, against the Soviet invasion of Czechoslovakia, and was sentenced to three years in corrective labor camps. At the end of this term he was sentenced to another three years. Later forced to emigrate to the U.S.

DUDINTSEV, VLADIMIR (b. 1918). Novelist, whose *Not By Bread Alone* (1956) was the first work of Soviet literature to take a critical view of the Stalin period. The book was officially condemned, but was received with enthusiasm by the public.

DUNAYEVSKY, ISAAK (1900–1955). Composer of many songs of an optimistic and patriotic character, which played an important part in popularizing the official Soviet outlook.

EHRENBURG, ILYA (1891–1967). A writer of fiction and essays who combined Soviet conformism with attachment to the traditions of Russian and Western culture.

ELIZABETH (YELIZAVETA PETROVNA), EMPRESS (1709–1761). Daughter of Peter the Great; succeeded to the throne in 1741 through a conspiracy which ousted the infant Ivan VI.

ETKIND, YEFIM (b. 1918). Literary critic, writer on the theory of translation and on French literature. Member of the civil-rights movement, for which he was persecuted and forced to emigrate.

FAINBERG, VIKTOR (b. 1931). Art critic and member of the civil-rights movement; took part in demonstration against the Soviet invasion of Czechoslovakia, and was imprisoned in a psychiatric hospital. Subsequently forced to emigrate to Britain.

FEDOTOV, GEORGY (1886–1951). Religious philosopher, historian of Russian culture, and publicist. His main interest was in the specific character of Russian history, and he developed the idea of Christian socialism. His literary activity took place in emigration.

FRANK, SEMEN (1877–1950). Religious philosopher, a disciple of Vladimir Solovyov (q.v.) and contributor to *Landmarks* (1909). Forced to emigrate.

GABAY, ILYA (1935–1973). Poet and member of the civil-rights movement. Served three years in corrective labor camps for slandering the Soviet system. Under pressure of incessant persecution he committed suicide by jumping off his apartment balcony.

GALICH, ALEKSANDR (b. 1919). Dramatist and writer of screenplays. Beginning in the early sixties he wrote highly popular songs and verses expressing dissident views and feelings. Expelled from the Soviet Writers' Union in 1971, he was subsequently forced to emigrate.

GERSHENZON, MIKHAIL (1869–1925). Historian of Russian literature and social thought; editor of Chaadayev and Kireyevsky (qq.v.); editor of and contributor to *Landmarks* (1909).

GINZBURG, ALEKSANDR (b. 1926). Member of the human-rights movement in the USSR; published a "White Book" on the case of Sinyavsky and Daniel (qq.v.)., and was sentenced for this to five years' imprisonment. Rearrested in 1976 for operating a fund to aid political prisoners in Soviet jails and the prisoners' families.

GONCHAROV, IVAN (1812–1891). Novelist, author of *Oblomov* (1859), the hero of which is a proverbial epitome of the Russian traits of passivity and indolence.

GORBANYEVSKAYA, NATALYA (b. 1936). Poetess and member of the human-rights movement, one of the organizers of the *Chronicle of Current Events*. Took part in the demonstration against the Soviet invasion of Czechoslovakia, and wrote a book on the subject, translated as *Red Square at Noon* (1972). Confined several times in prison psychiatric hospitals. Has emigrated to the West, and now lives in Paris.

GRIBOYEDOV, ALEKSANDR (1794–1829). Poet and diplomat, author of the classic comedy *The Misfortune of Being Clever.*

GRIGORENKO, MAJOR-GENERAL PETR (b. 1907). Member of the human-rights movement; commanded a division at the front in World War II. Reduced to the ranks as a punishment for his civil-rights activities. Twice confined in psychiatric hospitals.

GUAGNINI, ALESSANDRO (1538–1614). A native of Verona, in the service of King Stephen Batory of Poland; author of *Sarmatiae Europeae descriptio* and other works.

GUMILYOV, NIKOLAY (1886–1921). Poet, leader of the Acmeist group. He was shot by the Bolsheviks, and his poetry was officially suppressed, although it now has a wide circulation in *samizdat.*

HERZEN, ALEXANDR (1812–1870). Writer and publicist, founder of Russian "Westernism" and organizer of émigré political journalism.

IONA (JONAH) (d. 1461). Metropolitan of Moscow 1448–61. Under his rule the Russian Orthodox Church became virtually independent of the Greek.

IVAN IV (IVAN THE TERRIBLE) (1530–1584). Notorious for his cruelty, he destroyed the remnants of the Russian feudal gentry and established the autocratic Tsardom.

IVAN VI (1740–1764). Emperor for a year in infancy; deposed in 1741 by Elizabeth (q.v.). Imprisoned in the Schlüsselburg fortress, and eventually put to death there.

IVANOV, VYACHESLAV (1866–1949). Poet, dramatist, and theoretician of Russian Symbolism; aspired to interfuse art with everyday life. Died in emigration.

IVANOV-RAZUMNIK (pseudonym of R. V. Ivanov) (1878–1945). Literary historian, publicist, and sociologist, author of a two-volume *History of Russian Social Thought* (1906); theoretician of populism *(narodnichestvo)* in its later phase.

IZGOYEV, A. (pseudonym of Aleksandr Landa). A liberal-democratic publicist and contributor to *Landmarks* (1909). Died in emigration.

IZVESTIYA (Bulletin) of the Councils of Workers' Deputies. Newspaper published since 1917. Since the Bolshevik seizure of power, it has been considered the official organ of the Soviet government.

KARAMZIN, NIKOLAY (1766–1826). A writer of sentimental fiction and also an eminent historian who did much to form the Russian literary language. He wrote a *History of the Russian State* in twelve volumes, and was close to Alexander I (q.v.).

KGB (Committee of State Security). Formed under Khrushchev out of the Ministry of State Security (MGB), in order to place that dangerous organization under firm government control. Under Brezhnev, however, the KGB, to which the secret police are subordinate, once again has acquired the status of a many-branched organization free of any public control.

KHLESTAKOV, IVAN. Main character in Gogol's comedy *The Inspector General* (1836), an empty fellow who continuously lies and himself believes his own fabrications.

KHOMYAKOV, ALEKSEY (1804–1860). Religious philosopher, poet, publicist, and the chief Slavophile ideologist of the 1830s and 1840s. His social views were based on idealization of the Russian peasant commune *(mir* or *obshchina)* and on "collectiveness" *(sobornost'),* the unforced unity of members of the Orthodox church.

KIM, YULY (b. 1936). Poet and member of the civil-rights movement. His verses, many of them satirical, are widely circulated on tape.

KIREYEVSKY, IVAN (1806–1856). A philosopher and pioneer of Slavophilism, he criticized Western rationalism and developed a theory of the integrality of man's spiritual faculties, seeking the realization of his ideal in the Russian popular tradition.

KISTYAKOVSKY, BOGDAN (1868–1920). A lawyer and sociologist, member of the Kadet party (constitutional democrats). Studied the philosophical foundations of law from the point of view of the Baden school of neo-Kantianism. Contributor to *Landmarks* (1909).

KLYUCHEVSKY, VASILY (1841–1911). Member of the Kadet party; wrote an influential *Course of Russian History* in several volumes (1904–11).

KOROLENKO, VLADIMIR (1853–1921). Writer, publicist, and political activist, popular for his literary qualities and for his writings and speeches in defense of human rights. Protested against the Bolshevik terror after 1917.

KORZHAVIN, NAUM (pseudonym of Naum Mandel) (b. 1925). A poet who under Stalin's rule was sentenced to three years of exile in 1947. He later joined the Writers' Union, but besides officially printed work some of his verses appeared in *samizdat.* Emigrated to the U.S. in 1974.

KOSTERIN, ALEKSEY (1904–1970). A writer and party member, he spent seventeen years in camps and exile under Stalin and afterwards joined the civil-rights movement. Expelled from the party in 1968, he died soon after.

KOVALYOV, SERGEY (b. 1932). A biologist and specialist in cell physiology, author of over seventy scientific works. Member of the Action Group for the Defense of the Rights of Man, and of the Moscow section of Amnesty International. Arrested in December 1974, and sentenced a year later at Vilnius to seven years in "strict regime" camps and five years' exile thereafter.

KRASIN, VIKTOR (b. 1929). Economist. Arrested under Stalin while still a student; he later joined the civil-rights movement and was again arrested and exiled. In 1973 he and Petr Yakir (q.v.) were put on trial together, and pleaded guilty; while under interrogation they gave much evidence against other members of the movement, and the case was made much of by Soviet radio, press, and television. As a reward for his false confessions Krasin was soon released, and he emigrated to the U.S.

KRIZANIC, JURAJ (Yury) (c. 1618–1683). Croatian nationalist and writer, who lived in Russia and advocated pan-Slavic unity. He was exiled to Siberia.

KURBSKY, ALEKSEY (1528–1583). Russian nobleman, at one time close to Ivan IV (q.v.). Learning that the Tsar intended to take action against him, he fled to Lithuania, thus becoming one of the first Russian political émigrés. Noted for the recriminatory correspondence which ensued between him and the Tsar.

KUZNETSOV, ANATOLY (b. 1929). Writer who in the 1960s was representative of the younger generation in Soviet literature. He was a member of the Communist Party and occupied a high post in the Union of Soviet Writers. However, in 1969, while on a visit to England, he requested political asylum and came forth with revelations of how Soviet writers are subjected to the power of the secret police.

LAVROV, PETR (1823–1900). Philosopher, sociologist, and an important theorist of populism. He sought to establish a materialistic interpretation of morality, and his theory of the party as an underground organization was taken over by Lenin.

LEC, JERZY (1909–1966). Polish writer, whose *Disheveled Thoughts* (1957), a book of aphorisms expressing disillusionment with communism, was translated into Russian and widely circulated in *samizdat*.

LERMONTOV, MIKHAIL (1814–1841). A poet of the first rank, who expressed the feelings of disappointment and confusion that pervaded Russian society after the accession of Nicholas I.

LESKOV, NIKOLAY (1831–1895). A novelist whose work is characterized by religious humanism.

LITERATURNAYA GAZETA (Literary Gazette). Organ of the administration of the Union of Writers of the USSR, founded in 1929. Since 1947, the height of Stalin's persecution of the intelligentsia, *Literaturna-*

*ya Gazeta* has been transformed into a "social-political" newspaper for the purpose of making charges inspired by the party leadership against individuals in culture and the arts as though in the name of an independent public. In 1962 A. B. Chakovsky, who often performs assignments for the secret police, became editor-in-chief of *Literaturnaya Gazeta.*

LITVINOV, PAVEL (b. 1940). Member of the human-rights movement, celebrated for his appeal to world opinion (jointly with Larisa Bogoraz, q.v.) in connection with the trial of Galanskov, Ginzburg (q.v.), and others. He published a record of this trial and also of Bukovsky's (q.v.). For taking part in the demonstration on August 25, 1968, against the Soviet invasion of Czechoslovakia, he was sentenced to five years' exile. Compelled to emigrate to the U.S. in 1974.

LUNACHARSKY, ANATOLY (1875–1933). Writer and Bolshevik politician. People's Commissar (Minister) of Enlightenment from 1917 to 1929.

LYAPKIN-TYAPKIN, AMMOS. Character from Gogol's comedy *The Inspector General* (1836), a bribe-taking judge.

MANDELSHTAM, OSIP (1891–1938). Poet who introduced lexical and semantic reforms into the Russian poetic language. In the Soviet period he openly fought for his spiritual independence, in consequence of which already in the 1920s his poetry was no longer published. He was exiled in the 1930's, and later arrested, and he died in a concentration camp, apparently from hunger.

MAYAKOVSKY, VLADIMIR (1893–1930). Poet, leader of the Russian Futurists. Stalin called him "the best, the most talented poet of the Soviet era." Mayakovsky committed suicide.

MEREZHKOVSKY, DMITRY (1865–1941). Poet, essayist, publicist, and theoretician of Russian Symbolism. Sought to reconcile the Revolution with a new religion. Died in emigration.

MEYERHOLD, VSEVOLOD (1874–1938). Theatre director, founder of a new aesthetic of the theatre. In the late 1930's Meyerhold's theatre was closed on government orders and, as its director, he was arrested. He perished in prison under unknown circumstances; he was apparently shot.

MIKHAILOVSKY, NIKOLAY (1842–1904). Sociologist, publicist, literary critic, and leading ideologist of populism.

MILYUKOV, PAVEL (1859–1941). Politician and historian, leader of the Kadet party, author of *Notes on the History of Russian Culture* and other works. Died in emigration.

NAUMOV, VLADIMIR (b. 1927). Film director and collaborator with Aleksandr Allov (q.v. for their joint productions).

NELIDOV, DMITRY. Pseudonymous author of "Ideocratic Consciousness and Personality."

NICHOLAS I, EMPEROR (1796–1855). Succeeded Alexander I (q.v.) in 1825. His reign began with the cruel suppression of the Decembrist revolt and was marked by the intensification of bureaucracy and police oppression.

NICHOLAS II, EMPEROR (1868–1918). The last Tsar, he reigned from 1894 to 1917 and was shot by the Bolsheviks in 1918 together with his wife and children.

NIKON (1605–1681). Patriarch of Moscow. The revision of the Church Slavonic translations of Greek religious texts that took place during his reign led to the schism of the "Old Believers."

NOVGORODTSEV, PAVEL (1863–1924). A jurist and philosopher, whose views evolved from the idea of "natural law" to an Absolute conceived in religious terms. Died in emigration.

NOVIKOV, NIKOLAY (1744–1818). Freemason, journalist, and publisher.

PASTERNAK, BORIS (1890–1960). A distinguished poet, and author of the novel *Doctor Zhivago,* reflecting the spiritual experiences of the intelligentsia after 1917.

PAUL I, EMPEROR (1754–1801). Succeeded his mother Catherine II (q.v.) in 1796. An extreme reactionary, he maintained a strict policy of censorship, forbidding private presses and the importation of foreign books. He was murdered by conspirators including his son, who succeeded him as Alexander I (q.v.).

PETER I, EMPEROR (Peter the Great) (1672–1725). Ascended the throne in 1682, and carried out many reforms designed to overcome Russia's backwardness in relation to Western Europe.

PETER III, EMPEROR (1728–1762). An admirer of Prussia, he reigned from 1761 to 1762, but was overthrown by a conspiracy in which his wife, the future Catherine II (q.v.) took part. Peter was arrested and killed.

PHILOTHEUS. Political writer in the first half of the sixteenth century, a monk at the Eleazar Monastery at Pskov. He launched the idea of Moscow as "the third Rome," which became the state doctrine of Imperial Russia.

PISAREV, DMITRY (1840–1868). Popular publicist who had a great influence on the younger generation of the Russian intelligentsia in the 1860's. From a position of extreme positivism, Pisarev rejected all moral and aesthetic values that were not tied to "utility."

PLATONOV, ANDREY (1899–1951). Writer noted for the incisiveness of his style and the vividness and force of his imagery. Those works of Platonov which, beginning in the 1930's, expressed an extremely pessimistic perception of Soviet life have still not been published in the Soviet Union.

POGODIN, MIKHAIL (1800–1875). Historian and publicist, an advocate of "official populism."

POMERANTS, GRIGORY (b. 1918). Philosopher and publicist. Spent many years in concentration camps under Stalin. One of the ablest *samizdat* writers, defending ideals of humanism and toleration. A collection of his essays, *Neopublikovannoye* (Unpublished), was recently published in the West, in Russian.

POTEMKIN, GRIGORY (1739–1791). A favorite of Catherine II (q.v.), and an important political and military figure during her reign.

PRAVDA. Newspaper, the official organ of the Communist Party of the Soviet Union. Published since 1912.

PUGACHEV, YEMELYAN (ca. 1742–1775). Leader of the principal peasant revolt in Russian history, 1773–75.

PYPIN, ALEKSANDR (1833–1904). Liberal historian, first cousin to Chernyshevsky (q.v.).

RADISHCHEV, ALEKSANDR (1749–1802). Writer and publicist, representing the radical viewpoint of the later Enlightenment. Exiled to Siberia for publishing *A Journey from Petersburg to Moscow* (1790).

RAZIN, STEPAN ("Stenka") (executed in 1671). Leader of an important peasant revolt, 1667–71.

SADOMSKAYA, NATALYA (b. 1927). Anthropologist and fighter for human rights, the present author's wife. Emigrated to the U.S. in 1974.

SAKHAROV, ANDREY (b. 1921). Physicist, Nobel Prize winner, and fighter for human rights in the USSR.

SALTYKOV-SHCHEDRIN (real name Mikhail Saltykov; wrote under the pseudonym N. Shchedrin) (1826–1889). Satirical writer of democratic views.

SHAFAREVICH, IGOR (b. 1923). Mathematician, corresponding member of the Soviet Academy of Sciences, honorary member of the American Academy of Sciences, holder of Lenin Prize and of a mathematical prize from the Göttingen Academy of Sciences. Religious writer and fighter for human rights in the USSR.

SHESTOV, LEV (pseudonym of Lev Shvartsman) (1866–1938). Religious philosopher, critic of rationalism, one of the chief representatives of Russian existentialism. Died in emigration.

SHULGIN, VASILY (1878–19?). Tsarist politician and publisher of the Russian nationalist newspaper *Kievlyanin*. Returned to the Soviet Union late in life, having come to regard Soviet policy as fulfilling Tsarist aims.

SHVARTS, YEVGENY (1896–1958). Dramatist and film scenarist; devised a genre of theatrical fable well adapted to keen sociopolitical satire.

SINYAVSKY, ANDREY (pseudonym Abram Tertz) (b. 1923). Writer, critic, and literary historian. Sentenced in 1965 to seven years' imprisonment in "strict regime" camps for publishing his works abroad. Later compelled to emigrate; now a professor at the Sorbonne.

SKVOZNIK-DMUKHANOVSKY, ANTON. Character from Gogol's comedy *The Inspector General,* the governor of the town. In the description of the author, he makes "the transition from fear to joy, from baseness to arrogance, rather quickly."

SOBAKEVICH, MIKHAIL. Character from Gogol's *Dead Souls* (1842), a crude, intellectually limited type of landowner-serfholder.

SOLOVYOV, SERGEY (1820-1879). Author of the monumental *History of Russia from the Earliest Times;* father of Vladimir Solovyov (q.v.).

SOLOVYOV, VLADIMIR (1853-1900). Religious philosopher, exponent of a theory that world unity should be embodied in a worldwide theocratic state. Exercised a strong influence on the development of Russian philosophy. His later writings were eschatological and pessimistic in character.

STRUVE, PETR (1870-1944). Philosopher, economist, publicist, and politician, a leader of the Kadet party. Originally a fervent Marxist, he came to support the idea of the Russian state. Died in emigration.

SUKHOVO-KOBYLIN, ALEKSANDR (1817-1903). Dramatist, author of the satirical trilogy *Krechinsky's Wedding, The Affair,* and *The Death of Tarelkin.*

SUPERFIN, GABRIEL (b. 1943). Translator, literary historian, and fighter for human rights. Sentenced to five years' imprisonment in 1974.

SVETLOV, MIKHAIL (1903-1964). Poet, member of Writers' Union; well known as a Moscow wit.

TARASENKOV, ANATOLY (1909-1965). A literary critic who made a career of persecuting the chief poets of his time. He nevertheless valued their works, as is shown by the unique collection of editions that he accumulated.

TELEGIN, SEMEN. Pseudonymous author of the article "What Are We to Do?"

TOLSTOY, ALEKSEY KONSTANTINOVICH (1817-1875). Poet and writer of fiction, a distant cousin of the great novelist. Wrote some popular satirical verses on Russia and its history.

TROPARYOVO. Name of an ancient village near Moscow which in the 1960's was transformed into a new district inhabited mostly by the intelligentsia.

TUKHACHEVSKY, MIKHAIL (1893-1937). Marshal of the Soviet Union and Civil War hero, executed on a false charge in 1937.

TVARDOVSKY, ALEKSANDR (1910–1971). A poet, and a faithful adherent of the regime in Stalin's day. Later he became a critic of Stalinism and edited the liberal journal *Novy Mir,* which published the best works of Soviet literature until he was removed from the editorship shortly before his death.

VERETENNIKOV, A. (apparently a pseudonym). The author of the article "Molva i spory" ("Rumor and Quarrels"), which circulated in *samizdat.*

VOLOSHIN, MAKSIMILIAN (1871–1938). Symbolist poet. After the Revolution he wrote a cycle of poems on Russian history, emphasizing the tragic link between past and present.

YAKIR, IONA (1896–1937). Marshal of the Soviet Union, executed on a false charge in 1937.

YAKIR, PETR (b. 1923). Historian, son of Iona Yakir. Subjected to police measures at the age of fourteen, he later became an active member of the human-rights movement. Put on trial with Viktor Krasin (q.v.) in 1973.

YERMILOV, VLADIMIR (1904–1965). Literary critic, editor of *Literaturnaya Gazeta* from 1946 to 1950, the darkest years of Stalinist repression in the arts and sciences.

YESENIN-VOLPIN, ALEKSANDR (b. 1924). Mathematician, poet, and philosopher who developed the legal premises for the struggle for human rights in the USSR. His well-known book, *A Leaf of Spring* (New York: Frederick A. Praeger, 1961), was the first dissident work openly published in the West. In 1972 he emigrated to the U.S.

# Index

Boris Shragin was born in 1926 in Viazma, U.S.S.R. He was a research fellow at the Institute of History of the Arts in Moscow, and a teacher at the Surikov Art Institute and elsewhere. He received his Ph.D. in philosophy from the Plekhanov Institute of Economics in 1966. Mr. Shragin has published more than forty articles and essays on aesthetics, modern art, and cultural history. He became active in the dissident movement in 1965, and various essays of his since then have appeared in *samizdat* publications. Since emigrating from the Soviet Union in 1974, he has taught courses in Russian culture and social thought at Boston College and Amherst College in Massachusetts, and at Queens College and Hunter College in New York. During 1976 he was a senior fellow in Russian studies at Columbia University. His articles have appeared in magazines in Italy and in the *New York Review of Books*. He has co-edited *The Political, Social and Religious Thought of Russian Samizdat* (1977) with M. Meerson-Aksyonov, and the English edition of *Landmarks* (1977) with Albert Todd. He lives with his wife in New York City.

A NOTE ON THE TYPE

The text of this book was set on the Linotron in a face called
Times Roman, designed by Stanley Morison for *The Times*
(London) and first introduced by that newspaper in 1932.

Among typographers and designers of the twentieth century,
Stanley Morison has been a strong forming influence, as typo-
graphical advisor to the English Monotype Corporation, as a
director of two distinguished English publishing houses and
as a writer of sensibility, erudition and keen practical sense.

Composed, printed and bound by The Book Press, Inc.
Brattleboro, Vermont.

Typography and binding design by Camilla Filancia